A Beginning Teacher's Portfolio Handbook

Documenting and Reflecting on Your Professional Growth and Abilities

Bill R. Foster, Jr.
University of Missouri, St. Louis

Michael L. Walker
Educational Development Project

Kim Hyunsook Song
University of Missouri, St. Louis

PEARSON

Merrill
Prentice Hall

Upper Saddle River, New Jersey
Columbus, Ohio

Library of Congress Cataloging-in-Publication Data

Foster, Bill R.

 A beginning teaching portfolio handbook : documenting and reflecting on your professional growth and abilities / Bill R. Foster, Michael L. Walker, Kim Hyunsook Song.

  p. cm.

 Includes bibliographical references and index.

 ISBN 0-13-094750-4

 1. Portfolios in education. 2. Teachers–Training of.   I. Walker, Michael L. II. Song, Kim Hyunsook. III. Title.

LB1029.P67F67 2007

370'.71–dc22   2005036200

Vice President and Executive Publisher: Jeffery W. Johnston
Publisher: Kevin M. Davis
Editorial Assistant: Sarah N. Kenoyer
Production Editor: Mary Harlan
Production Coordination: Thistle Hill Publishing Services, LLC
Design Coordinator: Diane C. Lorenzo
Cover Designer: Jeff Vanik
Cover Image: Corbis
Production Manager: Laura Messerly
Director of Marketing: David Gesell
Marketing Manager: Autumn Purdy
Marketing Coordinator: Brian Mounts

This book was set in Garamond by Laserwords Private Limited. It was printed and bound by Bind-Rite Graphics. The cover was printed by Phoenix Color Corp.

Pearson Prentice Hall™ is a trademark of Pearson Education, Inc.
Pearson® is a registered trademark of Pearson plc
Prentice Hall® is a registered trademark of Pearson Education, Inc.
Merrill® is a registered trademark of Pearson Education, Inc.

Pearson Education Ltd.   Pearson Education Australia Pty. Limited
Pearson Education Singapore Pte. Ltd.   Pearson Education North Asia Ltd.
Pearson Education Canada, Ltd.   Pearson Educación de Mexico, S.A. de C.V.
Pearson Education–Japan   Pearson Education Malaysia Pte. Ltd.

10 9 8 7 6 5 4 3 2 1
ISBN: 0-13-094750-4

PREFACE

A Beginning Teaching Portfolio Handbook is designed to help preservice teachers understand the meaning and intent of the Interstate New Teacher Assessment and Support Consortium (INTASC) principles. Specifically, it teaches these candidates how to select powerful artifacts of their teaching and how to construct meaningful reflective statements in the context of powerful professional portfolios. The book represents the convergence of three authors' experiences in preparing educators and teaching critical thinking to college students. Before coming to educator preparation, Bill Foster and Mike Walker taught rhetoric and composition; central to their teaching of composition was training college students to analyze and marshal evidence. Within the field of educator preparation, these authors have facilitated the statewide implementation of candidate portfolios, advised colleges and universities in the design of portfolio assessment systems, taught educator preparation faculties how to score and respond to candidate portfolios, and taught preservice candidates how to construct standards-based portfolios. Kim Song, also a teacher educator, has specialized in the development of electronic portfolios.

A Beginning Teaching Portfolio Handbook is based on the INTASC principles—the most widely recognized and used set of national standards for classroom educators. In the mid-1990s, states, learned societies, and colleges and universities throughout the United States began adopting or adapting these principles of effective teaching or ones similar to them. Whether an institution or its state education agency has simply adopted the INTASC principles or has developed its own definition of quality teaching, it has likely grounded its philosophy in the same basic thinking that forms the core of the INTASC principles. Thus, the book is applicable to educator preparation in every state.

Consistent with the conception of a handbook, *A Beginning Teaching Portfolio Handbook* approaches each INTASC principle for teachers with three goals:

1. To define and explain the principle for candidates
2. To provide candidates with multiple models and critiqued examples for discussion
3. To provide candidates with feedback tools (rubrics) to assist them in evaluating and improving their performance

Throughout, *A Beginning Teaching Portfolio Handbook* engages candidates in rigorous questioning, discovery, and self-assessment.

Meeting the challenges of the INTASC principles requires candidates to demonstrate that they are reflective, problem-solving, and problem-posing professionals. Unfortunately, for many candidates, reflection is synonymous with description. Because analytic reflection is such an essential critical-thinking skill, *A Beginning Teaching Portfolio Handbook* devotes one full chapter and part of every other chapter to specific instruction that will improve candidates' principle-based analyses. However, as important as analytic reflection is to every candidate's success, a professional portfolio is primarily a means of evaluating a candidate's knowledge and skills relative to each of the principles. So, while the handbook presents reflection as an analytic skill within which description is distinguished from analysis and unsupported assertion is distinguished from evidence, it does so within the context of the demand of each principle. Finally, in an effort to help candidates see themselves in the book, the authors have drawn examples from all grades and from many areas of the curriculum.

If candidates are to become proficient in analytic reflection and in thinking deeply about the implications of the INTASC principles for their teaching and their students' learning, they need criteria against which to evaluate their work. *A Beginning Teaching Portfolio Handbook* provides rubrics both for analytic reflection and for each INTASC principle. These rubrics not only assist candidates in self-assessing their progress but also provide candidates and their instructors a common language with which to talk about performance.

Whereas the INTASC principles have provided a definition of quality teaching, their publication in the early 1990s preceded the explosion of technology (particularly computer-based technologies) in pK–12 education. Therefore, *A Beginning Teaching Portfolio Handbook* goes beyond INTASC to base a chapter on the widely recognized and used International Society for Technology in Education (ISTE) National Educational Technology Standards for Teachers (NETS•T). Most institutions will have already added a technology in teaching and learning standard to their program curricula.

In recognition of the learning trajectories of becoming teachers, the authors have designed *A Beginning Teaching Portfolio Handbook* for use throughout a candidate's preparation curriculum. The book could be used first in an introduction to teaching a course in which candidates are first presented with the idea of a standards-based portfolio. Then, as candidates proceed through their preparation course work and clinical experiences, they can revisit specific chapters. Methods faculty might, for example, revisit chapters focused on subject-matter knowledge (Principle 1), instructional strategies (Principle 4), curriculum development (Principle 7), and assessment (Principle 8); educational psychology faculty might revisit chapters focused on human growth, development, and learning (Principle 2) and diversity (Principle 3); foundations faculty might revisit chapters focused on collaboration (Principle 10) and professionalism (Principle 9); and internship supervisors might use the book to guide an intern's formative and summative analyses of his or her classroom performance. *A Beginning Teaching Portfolio Handbook* will be as useful for graduate students pursuing teaching credentials as it will be for undergraduates. If used in conjunction with other standards sets by subject or level-specific learned societies (NAEYC, NCTE, NCTM, CEC, etc.), which are themselves increasingly based on the INTASC principles, *A Beginning Teaching Portfolio Handbook* will help these candidates not only understand their learned society's expectations but also compile their evidence of readiness to enter the profession. Appendices and URLs for all national educator standards are provided on the Companion Website at **www.prenhall.com/foster.**

A Beginning Teaching Portfolio Handbook concludes with guidelines for transforming one's certification portfolio into a job-search portfolio and then into a career professional portfolio, thereby extending the book's usefulness beyond the candidate's preparation program and into the professional educator's career.

DISCOVER THE COMPANION WEBSITE ACCOMPANYING THIS BOOK

Technology is a constantly growing and changing aspect of our field that is creating a need for content and resources. To address this emerging need, Prentice Hall has developed an online learning environment for students and professors alike—Companion Websites—to support our textbooks. In creating a Companion Website, our goal is to build on and enhance what the textbook already offers. For this reason, the content for each user-friendly website is organized by chapter and provides the professor and student with a variety of meaningful resources. Common Companion Website features for students include:

- **Chapter Objectives**—outline key concepts from the text.
- **Interactive Self-quizzes**—complete with hints and automatic grading that provides immediate feedback for students. After students submit their answers for the interactive self-quizzes, the Companion Website **Results Reporter** computes a percentage grade, provides a graphic representation of how many questions were answered correctly and incorrectly, and gives a question-by-question analysis of the quiz. Students are given the option to send their quiz to up to four email addresses (professor, teaching assistant, study partner, etc.).
- **Essay Questions**—allow students to respond to themes and objectives of each chapter by applying what they have learned to real classroom situations.
- **Web Destinations**—links to www sites that relate to chapter content.

To take advantage of the many available resources, please visit the Companion Website for *A Beginning Teaching Portfolio Handbook: Documenting and Reflecting on Your Professional Growth and Abilities* at

www.prenhall.com/foster

ACKNOWLEDGMENTS

We gratefully acknowledge the Education Division of Missouri Baptist University (St. Louis, Missouri) and the College of Education of the University of Missouri, St. Louis, for granting us permission to use candidate reflections from their file portfolios. We are also appreciative of the opportunities afforded us by educator preparation programs and state departments of education in Missouri, South Dakota, and New York; it has been through the opportunities to work with education professionals and their students that we have developed and tested many of the ideas about portfolios, reflective analysis, standards, and rubrics that appear in this book.

We also thank the following reviewers for their comments: Carol J. Christine, Arizona State University; Christine Givner, California State University, Los Angeles; Sue Grossman, Eastern Michigan University; Dennis M. Holt, University of North Florida; Hari Koirala, Eastern Connecticut State University; Natalie B. Milman, George Washington University; Ann Potts, Virginia Tech; and Shelli Whitworth, University of South Florida.

We are also grateful to Kevin Davis, Assistant Vice President and Publisher at Merrill/Prentice Hall, for giving us the opportunity to create this text. We also wish to thank Mary Harlan, Associate Managing Editor at Merrill/Prentice Hall, and Amanda Hosey Dugan, Senior Project Editor at Thistle Hill Publishing Services, for their kind assistance and hard work in preparing the manuscript for publication. We would also like to offer special thanks to Susan Merten for her thoughtful suggestions and guidance, without which this text would still be in our heads rather than in print. Finally, Bill Foster would like to sincerely thank his wife and partner, Kathy Kuper, for her unfailing confidence, love, friendship, and support.

Teacher Preparation Classroom

Your Class. Their Careers. Our Future. Will your students be prepared?

We invite you to explore our new, innovative and engaging website and all that it has to offer you, your course, and tomorrow's educators! Organized around the major courses pre-service teachers take, the Teacher Preparation site provides media, student/teacher artifacts, strategies, research articles, and other resources to equip your students with the quality tools needed to excel in their courses and prepare them for their first classroom.

This ultimate on-line education resource is available at no cost, when packaged with a Merrill text, and will provide you and your students access to:

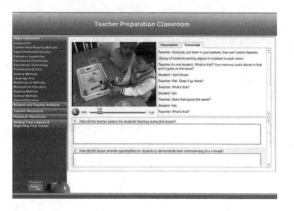

Online Video Library

More than 150 video clips—each tied to a course topic and framed by learning goals and Praxis-type questions—capture real teachers and students working in real classrooms, as well as in-depth interviews with both students and educators.

Student and Teacher Artifacts.

More than 200 student and teacher classroom artifacts—each tied to a course topic and framed by learning goals and application questions—provide a wealth of materials and experiences to help make your study to become a professional teacher more concrete and hands-on.

Research Articles

Over 500 articles from ASCD's renowned journal *Educational Leadership*. The site also includes *Research Navigator*, a searchable database of additional educational journals.

Teaching Strategies

Over 500 strategies and lesson plans for you to use when you become a practicing professional.

Licensure and Career Tools

Resources devoted to helping you pass your licensure exam; learn standards, law, and public policies; plan a teaching portfolio; and succeed in your first year of teaching.

How to ORDER *Teacher Prep* for you and your students:

For students to receive a *Teacher Prep* Access Code with this text, instructors **must** provide a special value pack ISBN number on their textbook order form. To receive this special ISBN, please email: Merrill.marketing@pearsoned.com and provide the following information:

- Name and Affiliation
- Author/Title/Edition of Merrill text

Upon ordering *Teacher Prep* for their students, instructors will be given a lifetime *Teacher Prep* Access Code.

BRIEF CONTENTS

CONTENTS

CHAPTER 5

IMPLEMENTING INTASC PRINCIPLE 2 IN YOUR PORTFOLIO   61

CHAPTER 6

IMPLEMENTING INTASC PRINCIPLE 3 IN YOUR PORTFOLIO   75

CHAPTER 7

IMPLEMENTING INTASC PRINCIPLE 4 IN YOUR PORTFOLIO   87

Note: Every effort has been made to provide accurate and current Internet information in this book. However, the Internet and information posted on it are constantly changing,

What You Need to Know About Portfolios and Portfolio Assessment

In ways that no other assessment can, portfolios prove a connection to the contexts and personal histories that characterize real teaching and make it possible to document the unfolding of both teaching and learning over time.

Lee Shulman

Jason, a student teacher, found out in his methods course that he had to submit a "teaching portfolio" in order to gain his teaching certificate, but he has no idea what a teaching portfolio is! He has a B.A. degree already and is ready to complete his teacher education program. That he is upset about yet another hoop to jump through is an understatement. He doesn't know anything about developing a teaching portfolio. "I came to the university to become a teacher, not waste my time on this portfolio stuff. What is a portfolio, anyway, and what are they good for? Busywork! That's all they are. I've passed all my courses; I have good grades. What more proof do they need that I deserve my license to teach?"

QUESTIONS TO CONSIDER

- What is a portfolio?
- What would it take to prove that you are ready to assume your professional role in the classroom?
- What do test scores, grade-point average (GPA), and class grades tell about your ability to teach?
- What do you need to know and be able to do as a professional educator?

Portfolios are not new. For centuries, artists and artisans have collected examples of their work for presentation or advertising. What is comparatively new, however, is the increasing use of portfolios in education. Two ideas in education have converged to shape the teacher education portfolio required by many states, districts, and teacher education programs. The first idea—teachers as reflective professionals—identifies a particular characteristic of professionals that distinguishes them from practitioners: Professionals take responsibility for analyzing and refining their own performance using a variety of sources of evidence. The second idea—teacher accountability—represents a response to the public's concern that simply possessing a college degree or having passed a test of teacher knowledge is not sufficient evidence of an individual's readiness to teach children; today, people want assurance that their children's teachers can actually teach.

Teacher education portfolios, with their twofold expectation (demonstrations that the educator can actually teach plus the educator's analyses of those demonstrations), are well suited to achieve both of these goals. This chapter orients you to portfolios in general and to an Interstate New Teacher Assessment and Support Consortium (INTASC) principle–based teacher education portfolio in particular.

WHY IS EVERYONE TALKING ABOUT PORTFOLIOS?

Are you a good teacher? How do you know? How will someone else know? While your transcript, your scores on state or national teacher's examinations, and even your letters of recommendation provide glimpses into the likelihood of you being a good teacher, they will not answer the *big* question being asked by school administrators, your education faculty, or your state's licensing agency: What do you know, and what are you able to do in the classroom?

The first response to why everyone is talking about portfolios is *accountability*. States, university faculty, and school district administrators want assurance that you will be a good teacher. Portfolios, better than any other form of assessment currently available, provide a comprehensive and holistic perspective on your readiness to assume your professional responsibilities in the classroom.

Would you like to be a better teacher? Most would agree all professionals can improve their practice, but how will you figure out what areas of your teaching need improvement? By waiting for someone else to point them out to you? Or by taking responsibility for your own professional growth and development? This introduces the second reason why everyone is talking about portfolios: Portfolios require *reflection* on and *analysis* of your knowledge and skills, today and potentially for the rest of your career.

You will devote years to preparing yourself for the classroom. Over that time, you will take content courses, education courses, and have practiced your skills in many classrooms; each of these experiences adds a piece to your storehouse of knowledge about teaching. At each step along the way, you assess yourself and others will assess you. Can you now put together everything you have learned about a subject matter, about individuals, about groups of children, about adolescents, about instructional strategies, about motivation strategies, about assessment, about communication, and so on? Here, then, is a third reason why everyone is talking about portfolios. Portfolios offer an *assessment* opportunity unlike any single test or clinical evaluation. Like the most comprehensive final exam you can imagine, your portfolio provides you the opportunity to put together in your own mind all of the theories and strategies you have studied and practiced.

WHAT ARE THE INTASC PRINCIPLES AND WHAT DO THEY HAVE TO DO WITH YOU AND YOUR PORTFOLIO?

Like any academic assessment, portfolios are designed to assess students' progress toward identified learning goals. In the case of you and your teaching portfolio, those learning goals are likely to have been identified for you—directly or indirectly—by the **Interstate New Teacher Assessment and Support Consortium (INTASC)** (see appendix A: INTASC Principles).

Origin and Adoption of the INTASC Principles

In the mid-1990s, INTASC, a group of professional educators representing the interests of all 50 states, published 10 principles (or standards) expressing what every teacher should know and be able to do. According to the authors of the principles, "these standards represent a common core of teaching knowledge and skills that will help all students acquire an education appropriate for the 21st century."[1]

Since their original publication, the INTASC principles have been adopted (or at least adapted) by most states for use in the initial certification and licensure process. At the national level, the National Council for the Accreditation of Teacher Education (NCATE) and its affiliated specialty professional associations (the National Council of Teachers of Mathematics, the Council for Exceptional Children, etc.) have similarly integrated the INTASC principles into their expectations for granting national recognition or accreditation to colleges and universities engaged in preparing teachers (see appendix C: Web Sites for Learned Societies and pK–12 Standards, or our Web site, www.prenhall.com/foster). Because your college or university has state approval to prepare teachers and perhaps also your NCATE accreditation, your faculty have likely based their expectations for what you must demonstrate in your portfolio on the INTASC principles.

Applicability of the INTASC principles doesn't stop there, however. Not only have your state and your faculty likely built their expectations for you on these 10 principles, but so too have the publishers of the exit tests required by many states. According to the authors of the principles, "This effort took another step toward creating a coherent approach to educating and licensing teachers based upon shared views among the states and within the profession of what constitutes professional teaching."[2]

So, what does this emerging consensus of what constitutes professional teaching mean for you and your portfolio? Primarily, it means that wherever you go in the nation, you are likely to find these principles being used, at least generally, to describe what you, as a beginning teacher, must know and be able to do. Just as you wouldn't expect to do well on a midterm or final examination without knowing what the professor expected you to know, you should not expect to do well on your portfolio without understanding what the INTASC principles require of you.

WHAT IS AN INTASC-BASED PROFESSIONAL TEACHING PORTFOLIO?

An INTASC-based professional teaching portfolio is a *purposeful, organized, self-reflective* collection of evidence produced by a beginning teacher to demonstrate professional growth and achieved competence on the constellation of teaching knowledge and skills described in the principles.

Teaching portfolios are commonly misunderstood to be merely folders or resource notebooks laden with lesson plans, teaching resources, and tips of the trade. The adjectives

---

[1]Model Standards for Beginning Teacher Licensing and Development: A Resource for State Dialogue. (1992) www.ccsso.org/intascst.html.

[2]Model Standards for Beginning Teacher Licensing and Development: A Resource for State Dialogue. (1992). www.ccsso.org/intascst.html.

modifying "collection of evidence" in the previous definition will help you distinguish the INTASC-based professional teaching portfolio from the folder or resource notebook:

■ *Purposeful*. Over the course of your preparation to teach, you will accumulate many items that represent valuable learning experiences for you. Although your resource notebook (or your filing cabinet) is a valuable tool for you, it does not represent a conscious effort to prove your competence to anyone; rather it is a potentially useful storehouse of ideas from which you will choose when you have a purpose. The professional's portfolio is, therefore, distinguished from the resource notebook in that its purpose is to support your assertion that you are ready to move on. Having the INTASC principles clearly in mind will help you transform your folder or resource notebook into a professional's *purposeful* teaching portfolio. Chapters 4 through 15 of this book will help you understand what the principles expect of you and, therefore, what you must demonstrate in your portfolio.

■ *Organized*. Organization is a valued characteristic in any professional. Without organization, you do not have a portfolio. But not just any organization will do. Remembering that your purpose is to demonstrate to yourself and some external audience that you have the knowledge and skills to move on requires a particular organization, one that clearly reveals your understanding of the principles by which you will be evaluated. Chapter 2 will help you implement an efficient process to do the following:
  • Systematically collect and categorize evidence of your emerging knowledge and abilities
  • Purposefully select and reflect on those evidences most illustrative of your knowledge and abilities
  • Present your portfolio in ways that reveal you to be an organized teacher

■ *Self-reflective*. In the language of INTASC Principle 9, *"The teacher is a reflective practitioner who continually evaluates the effects of his/her choices and actions on others (students, parents, and other professionals in the learning community) and who actively seeks out opportunities to grow professionally."* Your portfolio must reveal you to be the kind of educational professional who not only analyzes, critiques, and evaluates the impact of your actions, but who also identifies areas in which you still need to grow. Thus, your professional teaching portfolio is a carefully assembled document created to reveal, relate, describe, analyze, and interpret your competence and growth in your chosen profession. Each assertion of competence you make in your portfolio is then supported via an *artifact* and a *reflection*.

Chapter 3 will guide you through the challenging task of analyzing and interpreting your evidence and, finally, communicating what you know, what you are able to do, and that you are ready to take on the responsibilities of the classroom teacher.

WHAT ARE ARTIFACTS, WHERE DO THEY COME FROM, AND WHAT IS REFLECTION?

Before going on, we should define the two most important elements of your portfolio: artifacts and reflections. Portfolios contain two kinds of evidence:

Artifacts, sometimes called supporting documentation, are *demonstrations* of what you know about teaching and learning.

Reflections are *explanations* of what you were thinking when you created the artifact, what impact the artifact had on your learning or your pK–12 students' learning, and what you would do the same and differently the next time. Reflections (rather than artifacts) will reveal you to be a reflective practitioner. Chapter 3 is devoted to helping you understand reflection as a way of thinking and explaining how you should write a reflection.

WHAT KINDS OF ARTIFACTS MIGHT BE FOUND IN A TEACHING PORTFOLIO?

Although each INTASC principle calls for particular kinds of artifacts, it is important to understand two things about artifacts:

1. All of your experiences—both at the university and during nonteaching opportunities—represent at least the potential to produce an artifact.
2. Without interpretation, artifacts mean very little. Each requires explication, analysis, and interpretation if we are to know what they mean and what they demonstrate about the professional who produced them.

The following list shows the wide range of possibilities you will accumulate as potential artifacts:

- Anecdotal records
- Article summaries or critiques
- Assessments created or taken
- Awards and certificates
- Bulletin board ideas
- Case studies
- Classroom management plans
- Community resources documents
- Communications between the teacher and community (e.g., press releases)
- Communications between the teacher and home (newsletters, videotape of parent conference, etc.)
- Computer programs
- Cooperative learning plans
- Curriculum plans
- Essays from college courses
- Evaluations
- Field-trip plans
- Goal statements
- Individualized education plans (IEP)
- Interviews with students and teachers
- Interdisciplinary lessons
- Journal entries
- Learning centers
- Lesson plans
- Letters to parents
- Management strategies
- Media competencies
- Meetings and workshop logs
- Observation reports
- Peer critiques
- Philosophy of teaching and learning
- Pictures and photographs
- Portfolio (pK–12 student)
- Position papers
- Problem-solving logs
- Professional memberships
- Professional development plans
- Professional readings list
- Projects
- References
- Research papers
- Rules and procedures
- Schedules
- Seating arrangement diagrams
- Self-assessment instruments
- Simulated clinical experiences
- Student contracts
- Subscriptions to professional journals
- Teacher-made curriculum and instruction materials
- Testing modification examples
- Tests you took in your college coursework
- Theme studies
- Transcripts
- Unit plans
- Videotapes of your teaching and critiques
- Volunteer experience descriptions
- Work experience descriptions

FOR WHAT PURPOSES IS THE TEACHING PORTFOLIO USED?

You have learned the importance of students' understanding and valuing learning goals. You, too, need to understand how you and others will use your portfolio. Portfolios are such rich documents that they lend themselves to many uses. A variety of people, including yourself, are likely to use your portfolio (or adaptations of it) for a variety of purposes:

- *You*. Just as artists compile portfolios of their work to study and improve their talents, teachers collect examples of their work to study and improve their performance in the classroom. Through the act of reflection, your portfolio offers you the opportunity to critique your work and to evaluate the effectiveness of lessons or interpersonal interactions with students or peers. Through the portfolio actions of collection, selection, reflection, and projection, you will come to take responsibility for your learning, thereby experiencing directly something you will try to instill in your own students.

- *Your college/university faculty*. As an education tool, portfolios offer both a means of authentic assessment in evaluating your effectiveness as a beginning teacher and a means of providing you with feedback to help you improve your teaching and level of professionalism. At one or more times during your preparation, your faculty will use your portfolio to monitor and assess your progress. Through feedback, then, faculty members will help you continue your journey toward assuming your professional responsibilities in the classroom.

- *Your state's licensing agency*. Because certification by your state gives you the legal license to affect a great many lives over a long period of time, states take issuing you that license very seriously. For this reason, many states require you to pass a portfolio review prior to receiving your license, frequently in addition to requiring the more traditional assessment measures of standardized tests, grade-point averages, background checks, and observations of your performance in the classroom.

- *A school administrator*. Just as your faculty and your state's licensing agency have come to see portfolios as powerful indicators of your effectiveness in the classroom, school administrators are increasingly incorporating portfolio review into the hiring process. Simply reviewing your transcript and verifying that you have a license to teach is frequently insufficient to answer the question: Is this a person I want to hire to teach in my school? Although the portfolio you prepare for an interview with a school administrator will not be the same portfolio you prepare for your faculty or your state's licensing agency, it will nonetheless document the depth of your understanding about what will be expected of you as a professional. Chapter 15 will help you transform your licensure portfolio into a job-search portfolio. However, maintaining a portfolio will not likely end with getting your first teaching position. All across the country, school districts are incorporating portfolio reviews into the teacher evaluation process. In short, the portfolio you are beginning today will evolve with you over a lifetime of teaching.

- *The National Board of Professional Teachers (NBPT)*. Many states are pressing for more teachers to become national board certified. Much like the Bar Association and professional medical boards, teachers have a professional standards board. Teachers with a minimum of three years experience may apply to the board, submit a teaching portfolio, and sit for an exam to gain board certification. This certification is a great honor and a testament to the teacher's professional expertise and ability. Many states and individual school districts are rewarding nationally certified teachers with increased salaries, bonuses, and enhanced status within the schools. If in the future you are interested in becoming nationally certified, you must have a portfolio of artifacts to document your professional abilities and dispositions. It is better to start now developing a habit of collecting and organizing documentation of your best practice in order get a head start on this worthwhile pursuit.

WHAT ARE THE STRENGTHS AND WEAKNESSES OF PORTFOLIOS?

No means of assessment is perfect or sufficient for all situations; however, educators across the country are recognizing that the strengths of portfolio assessment outweigh the challenges portfolios present.

STRENGTHS OF PORTFOLIO ASSESSMENT

1. Portfolios are well suited to reveal your depth of understanding.
2. Portfolios can be used to evaluate both products (such as lesson plans) and processes (i.e., what was going on in your mind when you created the lesson plan).
3. Portfolios can reveal your growth from novice teacher to competent teacher— and even to expert teacher.
4. Portfolios present a holistic view of your achievement, not just your GPA or the results of a final exam or a standardized test.
5. Portfolios help candidates and professionals develop analytic skills necessary for lifelong learning.
6. Portfolios can reveal your ability to synthesize large and diverse bodies of knowledge from many different courses and learning experiences; in other words, they are well suited to reveal your ability to "put it all together."

In short, portfolios enable a multidimensional form of evaluation not readily available through other means of assessment.

CHALLENGES PRESENTED BY PORTFOLIO ASSESSMENT

Despite their great potential, portfolios do not meet every assessment need. Fortunately, you can address each of the challenges potentially presented by portfolio assessment.

1. Portfolios are not well suited to reveal breadth of understanding. Therefore, you need to include more traditional measures (like test scores and transcripts) in your portfolio to augment depth.
2. Portfolios are thought by some to present management problems. Therefore, you need to prevent your portfolio from getting bulky by carefully *selecting* only the most informative artifacts and by clearly interpreting how the artifacts demonstrate your understanding of the principles.
3. Some believe that portfolio assessment is overly subjective. To counteract this challenge, you must keep your focus on the principles and the rubrics you will find in each chapter.

For those who value good teaching, portfolios, particularly when used with other forms of assessment, offer a means to promote better teaching and to document teaching achievement.

WHAT ARE THE DIFFERENT KINDS OF PORTFOLIOS?

Although there are as many kinds of portfolios as there are purposes for portfolios, all of them can be summarized in the following two descriptions:

- A *showcase portfolio* compiles your best work: your best lesson plan, your best case study, your best chemistry project. As the name implies, it is designed to show you at your best; it does not, however, reveal how you got there or that you are aware of what you still need to learn.
- A *growth-over-time portfolio* reveals your growth in knowledge and ability over the course of your preparation to teach. Every teacher acknowledges that the first lesson he or she taught was less than successful. Growth-over-time portfolios demonstrate how you have improved on those early efforts.

Form Follows Function

Although these descriptions generally describe any portfolio, the specific form your portfolio takes within those general descriptions will change as the function for your portfolio changes. From the moment you start collecting evidence of your knowledge and skills, you are compiling your *working portfolio,* an ever-expanding record of your experiences in preparing yourself to teach. Periodically, you will be asked to select from your working portfolio evidences of your understanding and abilities at a particular moment in time; this narrowed selection for a particular purpose and audience is a *presentation portfolio* and represents a subset of your working portfolio used to document publicly your knowledge and skills at transition points in your program of study.

Near the end of your preparation program, you will compile an *initial certification (or licensure) portfolio* as a summative assessment of your readiness to enter the profession; this portfolio will require you to demonstrate your ability to put together everything you have learned about teaching.

After completing your preparation program, you will likely transform your initial certification portfolio into a *job search (or interview) portfolio,* a carefully refined subset of your initial certification portfolio tailored to reveal your qualifications for a specific teaching position.

Once you are employed by a school district, you will likely be asked to compile a *professional growth portfolio* as part of your school district's annual teacher evaluation process.

After a few years in the classroom, we hope you will once again transform your portfolio, this time into a *National Board Certification portfolio,* a document required by the National Board for Professional Teaching Standards as part of its assessment process for recognizing excellence in the classroom. *Which kind of portfolio you produce depends on the purpose for which it will be used.*

As you can see, each variation in function requires you to understand your purpose at that moment in time. Whereas the purpose of a working portfolio is to collect all kinds of evidence that might be useful, the purpose of a presentation portfolio is to reveal required knowledge and skill at a particular moment in time. This book is intended to assist you in developing a *summative, initial certification portfolio,* which will be used to determine your readiness to enter the teaching profession. For that purpose, we recommend you present a combination of both your best work *and* comparative examples from multiple points in time to demonstrate your ability to take responsibility for your own growth.

WHAT SHOULD YOU LOOK FOR WHEN YOU READ THE INTASC PRINCIPLES?

Since shared understanding of the principals represents the first step in meeting the challenge of perceived subjectivity, let's start by getting to know the 10 INTASC principles. Although you will study each principle in its own chapter, here let's focus on what all of the principles have in common and what those commonalities mean for you and your portfolio. Four clues will help you understand what the principles require of you and your portfolio.

Clue 1

You will find the first important clue to understanding what is expected of you and your portfolio in the pattern of language used in the principles. Read the following 10 statements about what a beginning teacher needs to know and be able to do, paying particular attention to the italicized words.

1. The teacher *understands* the central concepts, tools of inquiry, and structures of the discipline(s) he or she teaches and *can create learning experiences* that make these aspects of subject matter meaningful for students.
2. The teacher *understands* how children learn and develop and *can provide learning opportunities* that support their intellectual, social, and personal development.
3. The teacher *understands* how students differ in their approaches to learning and *creates instructional opportunities* that arc adapted to diverse learners.
4. The teacher *understands and uses* a variety of instructional strategies to encourage students to develop their critical thinking, problem solving, and performance skills.
5. The teacher *uses an understanding* of individual and group motivation and behavior *to create a learning environment* that encourages positive social interaction, active engagement in learning, and self-motivation.
6. The teacher *uses knowledge* of effective verbal, nonverbal, and media communication techniques *to foster* active inquiry, collaboration, and supportive interaction in the classroom.
7. The teacher *plans instruction based on knowledge* of subject matter, students, the community, and curriculum goals.
8. The teacher *understands and uses* formal and informal assessment strategies to evaluate and ensure the continuous intellectual, social, and physical development of the learner.

What pattern did you discover? Despite some differences in word choice, all eight statements require you to *understand* a knowledge base (subject matter; growth, development, and learning; differences in learning; instructional strategies; etc.) and *apply* your knowledge base purposefully to the classroom (i.e., to create [or provide] learning experiences [or opportunities]; to encourage critical thinking; to foster active inquiry; to evaluate and ensure development; etc.). Now read statements 9 and 10. In what ways do they reveal the same pattern?

9. The teacher is a reflective practitioner who *continually evaluates* the effects of his or her choices and actions on others (students, parents, and other professionals in the learning community) and who *actively seeks out* opportunities to grow professionally.

10. The teacher *fosters relationships* with school colleagues, parents, and agencies in the larger community to support each student's learning and well-being.

Both statements express themselves solely in terms of an action (or application) you will need to demonstrate (e.g., evaluates, seeks out, fosters). Is there a knowledge base that you must understand in order to fulfill the action of the statement? Certainly there is. What do you need to understand if you are to evaluate your choices and actions continually? What do you need to understand if you are to seek out growth opportunities? What do you need to understand about collaboration and student support systems if you are to demonstrate your ability to foster relationships with colleagues, parents, and agencies in the larger community to support each student's learning and well-being?

WHAT THEN CAN YOU GENERALIZE TO ALL PRINCIPLES?

Your portfolio must reveal that you possess the knowledge base specific to each principle and that you can apply that knowledge base to real classrooms. Let's zero in on each requirement: understand and apply.

What Does It Mean to Demonstrate *Understanding*?

Minimally, demonstrating your understanding requires that you communicate your comprehension of the knowledge and skills required by each principle. Demonstrating and communicating comprehension implies your ability to put the knowledge base into your own words and to provide examples of it. Frequently the best way to provide examples is to apply the knowledge base to a teaching and learning experience and then to explain in your own words how the experience illustrates the knowledge base you are expected to understand.

What Does Your Audience Expect to See About Your Understanding?

To assess your understanding, those evaluating your portfolio will expect to see evidence of your ability to use appropriately the vocabulary of professional educators. So, for example, they will be sensitive to your ability to distinguish a classroom management plan from a discipline plan or your ability to distinguish an instructional strategy from an instructional activity. They will also expect to see specific evidence that you comprehend the variety of educational theories you have studied, that you comprehend the steps that you must take to implement particular instructional or management strategies, that you know when to select one strategy over another, and that you know how to evaluate the impact of your actions on your own learning and on the learning of your pK–12 students. As you can see, demonstrating understanding involves the full range of cognition—from recognition all the way through synthesis and evaluation.

What Does It Mean to Demonstrate Your Ability to *Apply*?

Although the idea of *apply* is self-evident, it is important for you to demonstrate that you have applied (done) a thing rather than just that you are *able* to apply it. Whereas demonstrating understanding might involve *application* in hypothetical situations, demonstrating that you can create meaningful learning experiences for pK–12 students implies you have actually done so with pK–12 students versus just having thought about it or having done so with your college peers in a microteaching assignment. Thus, the farther you get into your preparation program, the more instances you will accumulate of your ability to apply those skills in classroom situations. Conversely, you will accumulate many demonstrations of your understanding early in your program of study.

WHAT APPLICATION DOES YOUR AUDIENCE EXPECT TO SEE?

Demonstrations of *understanding* and ability to *apply* converge in the reflections you will write about your artifacts. Suppose you choose to include in your portfolio a reading lesson you taught to a third grader. Standing alone, the lesson plan tells us nothing about why you constructed the lesson as you did or what impact the lesson had on the student's reading skills. However, in reflecting on the lesson, you would explain what you understand about reading (Principles 1 and 2), how you selected which reading skill to teach to this particular student (Principles 1, 3, and 8), why you selected a particular instructional strategy over another (Principles 1, 3, 4), how you assessed the impact of the lesson (Principle 8), and what you learned about your teaching from the experience (Principle 9). As you can see, the reflections you will write about your artifacts demonstrate that you do indeed understand and are able to apply these practices consciously.

WHAT ARE *INDICATORS*, AND HOW SHOULD YOU USE THEM?

Clue 2

The first clue involved understanding the two-part structure of each principle. The second clue involves narrowing your focus to the three categories of *indicators* used to clarify each principle:

- *Knowledge indicators* describe what you must know and what you must know how to do.
- *Disposition indicators* describe beliefs or values found to be important to successful teaching and learning.
- *Performance indicators* translate knowledge and beliefs or values into observable actions.

As the label *indicator* implies, these statements are examples of what any given principle should suggest to you. You should *not* assume them to be synonymous with the principle. Similarly, you should not assume that the sum of the indicators completely equals the principle. Again, they are just examples to help you understand the scope of a principle. Since the indicators do not represent an exhaustive list, you must avoid treating them as a checklist.

Clue 3

The specific verbs used in the indicators direct you to the kind of performance, action, or behavior the principle is seeking. Some verbs will indicate something of which you should be aware or something you should appreciate; other verbs will suggest more comprehension-related explanations (e.g., "The teacher understands measurement theory and assessment-related issues, such as validity, reliability, bias, and scoring concerns."). In other words, studying the indicator sentences will help you reveal not only the kind of knowledge you must demonstrate (e.g., declarative, procedural, or conditional knowledge) but frequently also the level of thinking about that knowledge you are expected to demonstrate (e.g., recognize versus analyze versus evaluate).

How Can Rubrics Further Refine Your Understanding of the Principles?

Clue 4

While the first three clues were found in the principles themselves, this final clue takes you outside of the principles to the rubrics. Having the rubrics in hand prior to submitting your presentation portfolio for evaluation is like having the answer key to a test before you take it. The rubrics included in this book are designed to highlight the most important elements of reflection in general (chapter 3) and of each principle (chapters 4 through 15). Studying these rubrics in advance of compiling your artifacts and writing your reflections will guide you in what to select and what to write. Comparing what you have selected and what you have written to the levels of performance described in the rubrics will not only help you assess the degree to which you have addressed the most important requirements of each principle but will also help you identify elements you might have overlooked.

How Can You Possibly Demonstrate Competence Relevant to All the Principle's Indicators?

You cannot. More important, you should not. Please keep the following in mind:

1. Foremost, you are being evaluated on your understanding of the principle—not on your demonstration of each and every indicator. The indicators are important, but they are only important because they help to refine your understanding of what a principle expects of you.
2. As you saw in the definition of *purposeful* at the beginning of this chapter and as you will learn more about in chapter 2, you must be highly selective in choosing artifacts that are most illustrative of what you know and what you know to do. You should not expect to have an artifact for each and every indicator in your portfolio; in fact, you might not end up with separate artifacts for each and every principle.
3. Finally, look to the rubric to help you assess the degree to which you addressed everything important about a principle. Remember that portfolios provide a holistic assessment and are better at revealing depth than they are at revealing breadth.

A Word About Electronic Portfolios

Most of the same collection, selection, reflection, and organizational issues work for electronic portfolios. However, electronic portfolios differ from traditional portfolios in that information is collected, digitized, saved, managed, and stored electronically in the form of pictures, text, graphics, sound, and video. Electronic portfolios can be a solution to the problem of creating, managing, and storing teaching portfolios. Multimedia artifacts, for example, are not easily incorporated into paper portfolios, thereby limiting the candidate's use of technology-oriented artifacts. Electronically created portfolios are more than static words on a page; they can include graphic images, photographs, larger documents (e.g., a 50-page unit plan), active links to teaching resources on the Internet, and audio/video recordings. This enhanced medium offers additional and dynamic ways to showcase your progress and achievement.

Electronic portfolios can be used to (a) prepare lesson plans and class newsletters; (b) record scores, run statistics, and calculate grades; (c) orient lesson-specific instructional resources or materials; and (d) create interactive links to the exam textbook that publishers provide through the Internet. After a portfolio's template has been created, preservice teachers are able to (a) copy narratives from a data file into the template, (b) drag pictures from other documents to the template page, and (c) insert audio and video recordings. Electronic portfolios are easily edited, cross-referenced, and inexpensively duplicated for faculty or employers. Numerous software packages, including desktop software, make it easy for candidates to develop these portfolio templates (Microsoft Word, Netscape Composer, Microsoft PowerPoint, Front Page, TaskStream, FolioTek, Open Source Portfolio, and so forth). In addition, candidates can easily tailor and streamline their portfolios to showcase their work for potential employers as well as for teacher licensure officers. Finally, electronic portfolios offer the following capabilities that may recommend them over the traditional paper portfolio:

1. Since most documents are created with a computer anyway, transferring them into an electronic portfolio is as easy as saving them to a different folder on your computer.
2. Hypertext links allow simple, direct connections between standards, reflections, and portfolio artifacts.
3. An electronic portfolio can develop, reinforce, and showcase multimedia technology skills.
4. Electronic portfolios can be easier to manage, especially in terms of storage, presentation, and duplication.
5. Electronic portfolios make candidate works replayable, portable, examinable, reviewable, and widely distributable.

You will find a more detailed discussion of electronic portfolio development in chapter 16.

SUMMARY

Teachers don't just train for a job; they prepare for a *profession*, and a profession is much different than a technical position. The professional is recognized as having a greater impact on the lives of others and, therefore, holds a more significant place in the community. Your portfolio is a reflection of the kind of professional you are or will be. Its appearance, correctness, organization, understanding of the INTASC principles, reflective quality, and choice of artifacts all point to the level of professionalism you possess.

How do you see yourself? How do you want others to see you? If you want to present a picture of the type of emerging professional the community desires and expects, you must care for every detail of the reflective self-portrait you are creating. The results are well worth the effort.

DISCUSSION QUESTIONS

1. Why are colleges, universities, state departments of education, and other agencies asking certification candidates to create portfolios of their teaching?
2. What are the INTASC principles? How are they organized? How do they provide a useful way to organize a portfolio?
3. How do knowledge, performances, and dispositions differ?
4. What different functions may a teaching portfolio serve?
5. How will portfolios differ based on differing audiences and purposes?
6. What is the relationship between artifacts and reflection? What purpose does each serve in the portfolio?
7. What is *understanding*? How might it differ from knowledge? How can you demonstrate understanding?

Getting Started on Your Portfolio

The reason most people never reach their goals is that they don't define them or ever seriously consider them as believable or achievable. Winners can tell you where they are going, what they plan to do along the way, and who will be sharing the adventure with them.

Denis Watley

Ayla is befuddled by all the paper in front of her. "Where do I start? I have so many papers, lessons, pictures, test scores, transcripts, evaluations, journals. And they are all over the place. And I know there are plenty of things I have lost or that are in some drawer or notebook or box or—oh my!—the trunk of my car! What am I going to do?"

QUESTIONS TO CONSIDER

- How do I get started putting my portfolio together?
- How much does it take to prove I know how to teach?
- How do I organize all this information?

In chapter 1 you explored what portfolios are. They are thoughtfully assembled documents that your faculty, your state education agency, and, most important, you use to evaluate your readiness to progress in your preparation or to transition into the profession. Because compiling such a document is a large and frequently long-term project, this chapter breaks the process into four manageable steps to make the work more efficient, more conscious, and more clearly illustrative of what you know and are able to do.

FOUR STEPS IN CREATING A PORTFOLIO

1. *Collecting, categorizing, and annotating* potential evidences of your understanding and ability

2. *Selecting* the best evidences of your understanding and abilities
3. *Reflecting* on your selections
4. *Presenting* your portfolio for external review

STEP 1: COLLECTING, CATEGORIZING, AND ANNOTATING YOUR EVIDENCE

The first step in the portfolio process really has three components:

- Collecting your evidence
- Categorizing your evidence
- Annotating your evidence

Collecting evidence is really very simple. You must first get yourself into the habit of assessing everything you do—in your course work, in your extracurricular activities, in your clinical experiences, in your service learning experiences, and so on—for its potential use in your portfolio. Too often, preservice educators do not save their tests, essays, projects, journals, and clinical evaluations, only to realize later they have little evidence from which to construct a portfolio.

Categorizing helps transform a collector's box of memorabilia into a professional's demonstration of knowledge and skills. Having a rich collection is one thing; having a collection within which you can find something specific is a very different thing. A collection without some consciously applied organizational scheme might be compared to an unorganized hard drive on your computer; you know the file for which you are searching is somewhere, but you must open every file to find the one you want.

Those who begin early to organize their potential artifacts according to a reasonable plan will make their lives easier, especially if they devise an organization scheme from the start of their training.

You will be well served by employing a simple classification scheme based on the INTASC principles (or those principles proscribed by your state or your teacher training institution). Let's be practical here:

1. Purchase a divided accordion folder, an orange crate with hanging folders, or some other container that allows you to sort its contents.
2. Label each section with a principle.
3. Organize a set of folders on your computer's hard drive (or at least part of your hard drive) or on your diskettes to correspond to your physical container. *Tip:* More than one student has discovered along the portfolio path that he or she has lost computer files. *Solution: Back up your computer files often.*
4. As you begin to collect artifacts from your course work, field experiences, and other sources, sort them into the slot of the principle for which the artifact best illustrates your competence or development. *Tip:* When an artifact might demonstrate more than one principle or when you are not yet sure which principle an artifact best illustrates, either include the artifact in more than one place or, better yet, include a reference to it in more than one slot (e.g., "See also Principle 3").

Your real and virtual containers need at least enough slots to deal with all the standards or principles you are having to document. If you are using the INTASC principles, you will need one slot for each of the 10 principles and an eleventh for demonstrations of your technology competence. Many states and many more universities are adding technology competencies to what they expect to see demonstrated in candidates' portfolios.

Therefore, you should start collecting evidence today to demonstrate your understanding of the following:

1. The theory and practice of technological operations
2. Concepts, tools, and software
3. Your ability to use technology to create meaningful learning opportunities for all students

You will find a complete discussion with examples of technology standards, artifacts, and reflections in chapter 14. The ISTE National Education Technology Standards for Teachers (NETS•T), developed by the International Society for Technology in Education (see appendix D: International Society for Technology in Education [ISTE] National Educational Technology Standards for Teachers [NETS•T]) will help guide your collection efforts with regard to technology.

While portfolio beginners may use the principles alone as their organizational scheme, more advanced candidates will want to refine their organizations. Several alternatives (among many others) might be useful:

1. Using the indicators within each principle
2. Organizing within principles by types of artifact
3. Organizing based on a different set of professional standards or dispositions (e.g., NAEYC, NCTM, NCTE, etc.)
4. Basing your scheme on major themes (e.g., Teacher as Researcher, Teacher as Motivator, etc.)
5. Building your portfolio around major questions raised by potential reviewers (such as "How do you accommodate differences among learners in your teaching?" "What learning and developmental frameworks support your teaching practice?" "How do you ensure effective communication within your classroom?")

Of course, many organizational structures for portfolios are possible, most of which deal with the same issues and domains though sometimes using different language or varying their emphasis on different elements or issues (see appendix B: Alignment of INTASC Principles, Charlotte Danielson's Domains, and the NBPTS Core Proposition and Criteria).

Using the Indicators within Each Principle

The indicators for the INTASC principles (knowledge, dispositions, and performance) may give you even finer categories for sorting your selection of artifacts within a given principle. Principle 2, for instance, includes the following indicators:

Knowledge

- The teacher understands how learning occurs—how students construct knowledge, acquire skills, and develop habits of mind—and knows how to use instructional strategies that promote student learning.
- The teacher understands that students' physical, social, emotional, moral, and cognitive development influences learning and knows how to address these factors when making instructional decisions.
- The teacher is aware of expected developmental progressions and ranges of individual variation within each domain (physical, social, emotional, moral, and

cognitive), can identify levels of readiness in learning, and understands how development in any one domain may affect performance in others.

Dispositions

- The teacher appreciates individual variation within each area of development, shows respect for the diverse talents of all learners, and is committed to help them develop self-confidence and competence.
- The teacher is disposed to use students' strengths as a basis for growth and their errors as an opportunity for learning.

Performances

- The teacher assesses individual and group performance in order to design instruction that meets learners' current needs in each domain (cognitive, social, emotional, moral, and physical) and that leads to the next level of development.
- The teacher stimulates student reflection on prior knowledge and links new ideas to already familiar ideas, making connections to students' experiences; providing opportunities for active engagement, manipulation, and testing of ideas and materials; and encouraging students to assume responsibility for shaping their learning tasks.
- The teacher accesses students' thinking and experiences as a basis for instructional activities by, for example, encouraging discussion, listening and responding to group interaction, and eliciting samples of student thinking orally and in writing.

From these lists, you might develop a checklist for artifacts documenting Principle 2 in your folder (Figure 2.1).

Realistically, you will likely fill out several such forms for any given artifact, especially if you are using it to document more than one principle. Therefore, you may want to save this checklist for when you are making your final choices for artifacts to include in your portfolio.

FIGURE 2.1

Principle 2
Expectations Chart

Expectations Presented by Principle 2
Teaching strategies based on how learning occurs—how students construct knowledge, acquire skills, and develop habits of mind
Applying knowledge of student physical, social, emotional, moral, and cognitive development
Recognizing developmental progressions and ranges of individual variation within each domain
Respecting and using the diverse talents of all learners
Using students' strengths as a basis for growth and their errors as an opportunity for learning
Supporting student reflection on prior knowledge
Providing opportunities for active engagement, manipulation, and testing of ideas and materials, and encouraging student responsibility learning
Accessing students' thinking and experiences as a basis for instructional activities

Organizing Within Principles by Types of Artifact

Alternatively, you might subdivide each principle into several categories based on the form of artifact being gathered:

- Lesson plans
- Instructional materials
- Assessments
- Reflections and journal entries
- Evaluations
- pK–12 student work
- Other materials (e.g., philosophy, college course work, essays, action research projects)

In either of these alternatives, you are beginning to make finer distinctions in your analysis of the artifacts you are gathering. *Annotating your evidences* will help you avoid the dilemma of not remembering the details of early entries into your collection folder. Attaching a brief annotation to each artifact as you place it in your collection will save you plenty of time and headaches later on.

What should go into your annotation?

- When the artifact was created (e.g., "Fall 2001")
- For what class or learning experience it was created (e.g., a practicum for "Teaching Science in the Elementary School")
- What assignment led to the creation of the artifact (***Tip:*** Attach to the artifact a copy of the assignment and scoring guide, if appropriate.)
- If the artifact involved a classroom observation or other clinical experience, what grade and subject area you were observing. (***Reminder:*** When you actually incorporate these kinds of artifacts into your portfolio, you *must* change the names of teachers hosting you in their classrooms, of students in those classrooms, and even the school's name to protect the privacy of those people referenced within your portfolio artifacts. This is a professional, ethical behavior intended to protect the children with whom you interact. Learn your college or university's policies regarding the use of any visual or audio image of a pK–12 student, as well as the school district's policies, and apply them carefully.)
- A reflection on (a) what it reveals about your ability to create meaningful learning experiences for students, (b) what strengths or weaknesses it reveals about your knowledge and abilities, and (c) what you learned from doing it that will impact your teaching in the future and your professional development.

Figure 2.2 gives you an idea of how to capture this information for future reference. This student chose to focus the reflection and checklist on Principle 4 (instructional strategies) (Figure 2.3). Remembering that you should try to use fewer artifacts to demonstrate more principles, which other principles might the student have chosen to emphasize?

STEP 2: SELECTING THE BEST EVIDENCES OF YOUR UNDERSTANDING AND ABILITIES

Most portfolios are read among a larger grouping of portfolios, frequently competing with many other end-of-the-semester activities. Inevitably, readers will feel pressure to finish with some speed; consequently, they will likely feel some impatience with portfolios that make them work too hard to get at the important information. Therefore, you need to give focused attention to the richness of your artifacts. Not only must your

FIGURE 2.2

Sample Collection
Cover Sheet

Sample Collection Cover Sheet

When created: Fall 2001

Class created for: Student Teaching—10th grade Chemistry Erehwon High School

Assignment: The curriculum called for teaching about the periodic table. This assignment was both a learning activity and an assessment.

The assignment asks students to create a Web page about an element commonly viewed as a component of pollution and therefore dangerous to human life and the environment. I introduced the attached Web page project by outlining for the students my expectations for the content and quality of the Web pages. I also taught them how to use the software that we would be using (Netscape Communicator Page Composer).

The assignment shows how I use authentic instruction and assessment in the classroom and how I can use technology for learning purposes other than just for teaching (i.e., a fancy substitute for a blackboard). It also reveals my ability to relate learning to meaningful, real-life issues and to the students' abilities, interests, and experiences. It shows how I can develop and communicate my expectations for student work and how I can creatively address the requirements of the district curriculum and state standards. It reveals some weaknesses, however. I did not consider the differing ability levels in the class with regard to computers and the Internet. Also, I failed to think about how this lesson would need to be adapted for the three special-needs students in the class. It taught me to find out more about what my students know about what I am asking them to do and to scaffold better those students who might need a little more help with the . . .

FIGURE 2.3

Principle Expectations
Checklist

Expectations Presented by Principle 4

Evaluates how to achieve learning goals by choosing alternative teaching strategies and materials to achieve different instructional purposes and to meet student needs (e.g., developmental stages, prior knowledge, learning styles, and interests).

Uses multiple teaching and learning strategies to engage students in active learning opportunities that promote the development of critical thinking, problem solving, and performance capabilities and that help students assume responsibility for identifying and using learning resources.

Monitors and adjusts strategies in response to learner feedback.

Varies his or her role in the instructional process (e.g., instructor, facilitator, coach, audience) in relation to the content and purposes of instruction and the needs of students.

Develops a variety of clear, accurate presentations and representations of concepts, using alternative explanations that help students to understand and present diverse perspectives to encourage critical thinking.

---

portfolio create a complete picture of what you know and can do, but it must also do so quickly. Believe it or not, reviewers may spend as little as 15 minutes with your portfolio, making a decision about your preparation before they get beyond the first two or three reflections or artifacts. The overstuffed three-ring binders many preservice teachers submit reveal their difficulty in making purposeful selections.

Identifying Selection Criteria Aligned to the Principles Being Illustrated

Chapters 4 through 15 will help to deepen your understanding of the INTASC principles, their language, and their intent. *When choosing artifacts, you must select evidence showing your possession of a professional knowledge base in the area identified within the principle, as well as evidence of application and synthesis of that professional knowledge.*

Two overarching issues should guide your selection:

1. The extent to which an artifact demonstrates your knowledge and abilities
2. The extent to which an artifact can demonstrate multiple principles

Since you are tying your artifacts and reflections to the principles being used to judge your preparation, you should use the requirements of the principles as a measure for selecting your artifacts. By reading the principle carefully, you can develop criteria for choosing your artifacts. For example, returning to our hypothetical organization scheme for Principle 2, we find a ready set of criteria for evaluating a potential artifact for that principle (see Figure 2.1). The overarching question is this:

> To what degree does the artifact offer evidence that you understand how children learn and develop, and can provide learning opportunities that support their intellectual, social and personal development?

Will any one piece of evidence need to or even be likely to exhibit all of these issues? No. If selected for your portfolio, it would, however, need to offer evidence of your competence in some combination of these issues.

Getting Extended Use from Fewer Artifacts

Before making your final selections, you should submit your possibilities to the second overarching criterion: the extent to which an artifact can demonstrate multiple principles. One of the biggest criticisms of portfolios comes not from the quality of the contents but from the magnitude of their girth and weight. Reviewers simply have trouble muscling the huge notebooks around.

Even if you are compiling an electronic portfolio, you must carefully consider how many artifacts you must present to convince your reviewer you possess the knowledge and skills a principle requires. A smaller, more thoughtfully selected array of artifacts is, in itself, impressive to reviewers because it presents a picture of a more thoughtful educator.

You should be selective when choosing artifacts, opting for documents rich enough to illustrate more than one principle. For example, your portfolio will, obviously, contain lesson plans. The less-than-thoughtful student might include many lesson plans, one (or more) for each of several principles. The thoughtful student, who imposes the criterion that each artifact should demonstrate more than one principle, would select one or two lesson plans or, better yet, a unit plan rich enough to illustrate more than one principle. One well-chosen unit might illustrate knowledge of the discipline, ability to adapt lessons for diverse learners, a variety of instructional strategies, and a range of assessment types and uses, as well as a number of other principles. The web diagram shown in Figure 2.4 illustrates how many principles might be demonstrated through a carefully developed and selected unit plan. You may also want to use the table shown in Figure 2.5 to categorize your artifacts as you put them into your filing system.

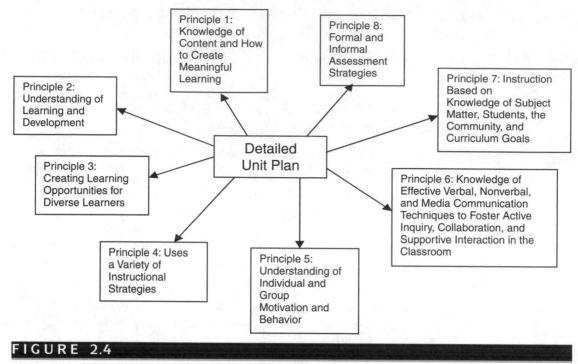

FIGURE 2.4

Using a Single Rich Artifact to Document Multiple Standards

Artifact	Principle or Standard										
	1	2	3	4	5	6	7	8	9	10	ISTE
Unit Plan	x	x	x	x	x	x	x	x			x
Math Lesson	x	x	x	x	x	x	x	x		x	x
Transcript	x	x	x		x						x
Content Exit Test Scores	x										
Pedagogy Exit Test Scores		x	x	x	x	x	x	x		x	
Agency Interview			x						x	x	
Tutoring Journal	x	x	x	x	x		x	x			

FIGURE 2.5

Example Artifact Categorization Table

STEP 3: REFLECTING ON YOUR SELECTIONS

Reflection is such an important component of your portfolio that two chapters are devoted to it: chapter 3 guides you in developing and critiquing all of your reflections, and chapter 12 (Principle 9) identifies specific knowledge, dispositions, and performances indicative of the reflective professional. Remember these points:

1. Every artifact requires a reflection.
2. Every reflection must include broadly two components: contextual information (the information you are encouraged to include in your annotations) and an analysis of what the artifact reveals about your teaching and learning.

Reflections Separated From or Included with the Artifacts

Portfolio developers have at least two big options for how they connect their reflections to their artifacts:

Option 1. Writing a reflection for each artifact. This option has the advantage of directly connecting your reflection to a particular artifact. In this way, portfolio readers are likely to see the artifact and its reflection as a package. The disadvantage is that this option tends to lead to having to file several copies of each artifact under different principles.

Option 2. Collecting all of the reflections together (usually at the beginning of the portfolio) and including the artifacts as appendices to the portfolio. This option has the advantage of focusing your reflection and your reviewers' attention on what you understand about the principle; in other words, the reflections you write under this option focus on the principles and use the artifacts as evidence to support your assertion that you understand the principle. Within the reflection, you would refer (e.g., by number of the artifact) to the artifacts that best illustrate competence relative to the principle being addressed. In electronic portfolios (e.g., CD-ROM or Web-based portfolios), these references may appear as hyperlinks to take a reviewer directly to the artifact from the reflection. Artifacts are then organized and numbered in a separate section in the back of the notebook or in separate locations on the Web or CD-ROM. This type of organization helps eliminate the need for multiple copies of each artifact within the portfolio. It also eliminates the need for complicated cross-referencing. Moreover, it allows reviewers to read the reflections and then go to the artifacts to validate points or to explore issues that arise as they are reading the reflection. In a way, this allows reviewers to better manage their time and effort. The disadvantage of this option is that it might lead you to lose sight of your artifacts, thereby communicating to your reviewers that you cannot substantiate your assertions.

If your faculty has not already decided this question for you, you should consider which structure better demonstrates your understanding of the principles.

STEP 4: PRESENTING YOUR PORTFOLIO FOR EXTERNAL REVIEW

For many candidates, packaging a portfolio for final evaluation means decorating it; for others, it means making sure that the typing is clean. The former is nice (although not required by the principles); the latter is essential to a professional presentation.

Professionalism is a key element of your preparedness. Your portfolio must demonstrate your professionalism in appearance, in content, and in final editing and proofreading.

Take time to have a friend or faculty member review your work for clarity, coherence, and correctness of language and punctuation. Make sure your words say what you intend and do so in clear and concise ways. Many good academic sources and grammar/style handbooks are available to help you polish your portfolio's written presentation. Disorganized or unorganized presentations, like unedited and ungrammatical writing, create an impression in the mind of a reviewer that negatively colors her or his judgments.

Your goal is to make reviewing your portfolio as effortless as is reasonably possible. If you can do this, you will automatically improve your portfolio's reception.

STRATEGIES FOR PRESENTING YOURSELF AS AN ORGANIZED AND THOUGHTFUL EDUCATOR

There are a number of ways to organize your portfolio materials once you begin the selection and reflection process. You need to choose one you believe will best order your materials for the person or persons reviewing your portfolio for a grade, for a certification recommendation, or possibly for a job.

1. *Organizing by the Principles*—By far the best way to organize your portfolio is by principle (versus, for example, organizing the entire portfolio around teacher-developed products such as lesson plans or assessments). A principle-based organization ensures that your portfolio reviewer will see a direct connection between the artifacts you present and the principles they are intended to demonstrate. In your tabbed notebook (or on your CD-ROM or within your Web site), then, you would label each section of the portfolio by principle.

    Unless your institution specifies another format, we strongly suggest that you use this organization for your portfolio. In this organization, then, the reflection for each principle is contained within the tab for that principle. In that tab, your reflection will appear with references to the artifacts (identified by where they may be found in the appendices of your portfolio).

2. *Creating a Table of Contents to Guide the Reviewer*—A detailed table of contents is a must for any portfolio. By identifying all the documents in the table, you give reviewers a road map to the pieces for which they may be looking. After each document, simply place in parentheses the principle(s) the artifact is intended to document. Compare the tables of contents in Figures 2.6 and 2.7. You will note that Figure 2.6 gives the reviewer a greater opportunity to connect principles with reflections and reflections with artifacts. Thus, it would be easy for reviewers to identify one principle of particular importance and then to look down the list of artifacts to see which serve as documentation for that principle.

    By contrast, the table of contents in Figure 2.7 presents a list of artifacts unrelated to specific principles or even to reflective essays. This organization is fine for a different kind of portfolio (e.g., a job-search portfolio; see chapter 15: Converting Your Certification Portfolio into a Job-Search Portfolio, Professional Development Portfolio, or National Board Portfolio). Reviewers at the end of your program, however, might look at the list and guess which reflection and artifact might correspond to any given principle, but it would be just a guess and more likely a waste of the reviewers' time.

FIGURE 2.6

Example Teaching
Portfolio Table of
Contents

Table of Contents

Artifact A: Transcript (Principle 1)
Artifact B: PRAXIS Scores (Principle I)
Artifact C: History Research Project (Principle I)
Artifact D: Westward Expansion Unit Plan (Principles 1, 2, 3, 4, 5, 6, 7, 8)
Artifact E: Examples of Student Work and Learning From Westward
Expansion Unit (Principles 1, 2, 3, 4, 5, 7, 8)
Artifact F: Journal Entries
    1. Principles 1 and 2
    2. Principles 5 and 7
    3. Principles 9 and 10
Artifact G: Newsletters (Principles 6, 9, and 10)
Artifact H: Conference Notes (Principles 6, 9, and 10)
Artifact I: Professional Development Plan and Actions (Principle 9)
    I. Reflections
    2. Artifacts

FIGURE 2.7

Table of Contents for a
Job-Search Portfolio

Table of Contents

1. Reflections

2. Artifacts

(a) Autobiography
(b) Philosophy of Education
(c) Transcripts and PRAXIS Scores
(d) Letters of Recommendation
(e) Student Teaching Evaluations
(f) Lesson Plans
(g) Tests
(h) Journal Entries
(i) Newsletters and Notes to Parents
(j) Professional Development Certificates
(k) Class Projects and Essays
(l) Student Teaching Evaluations
(m) Pictures and Bulletin Boards
(n) Discipline Plan
(o) Field Experience Time Sheets and Notes
(p) Thank You Notes From Students and Teachers
(q) IEP Conference Notes
(r) Videotape

3. *Cross-Referencing*   If you are successful in selecting artifacts rich enough to document competence in more than one principle, then you will have to develop an easy system of cross-referencing to help your reviewer follow your path of evidence.

One way of guiding your reader to the appropriate artifacts is to make good use of your reflection page. At the top of the page, reserve a spot to list the artifacts you will be referencing and their location in the portfolio. You might repeat these references within the reflective statement, too, with parenthetical notes (if needed) identifying the artifact and pointing the reader to the artifact's location. Then the reviewer can locate the important pieces and refer to them while reading the statement or later in the review process. Figure 2.8 is an excerpt of a cover page using this technique.

Another approach to cross-referencing your portfolio is to use color coding to guide the reviewer from principle to artifact. This is a simple process. First, decide which element will be color coded: the principles or the artifacts. Next assign a color to each element. For example, if you want reviewers to base the bulk of their efforts on the reflections, using the artifacts as validation of your assertions, then you might assign each artifact a different color. Within the reflection, then, you would place a colored dot next to the first mention of the artifact or type the name of the artifact in the color matching the artifact.

You might, however, want the reviewer to spend more time among the artifacts, especially if your selection of artifacts is rich and supports more than one

---

FIGURE 2.8

Example Cover Page
with Reflection

Principle 3: The teacher understands how students differ in their approaches to learning and creates instructional opportunities that are adapted to diverse learners.

Artifact D: Journal Entries

Artifact I: Letter from Dean of Students at Balboa High School

Artifact J: Unit Plan for Study of Gas Laws

Artifact M: Performance Based Assessment in Biology

As partial fulfillment of the requirements for Sec Ed 386, Teaching Reading in the Secondary School Content Areas, I did 10 weeks of tutoring at Crosston Middle School during the winter semester of 1999. **Artifact D** includes a series of journal entries from this time, and **Artifact I** is a letter written by the school's dean of students on my behalf, which mentions my tutoring and its success. I had three students who were all struggling in a seventh grade life science class. Once a week, I took the three to the library for individualized instruction. I worked closely with the classroom teacher, and each week I covered the same material she was covering in the classroom with my three students. In the beginning I reviewed their tests and homework, as well as interviewed them, to determine the nature of their difficulties and needs. I also talked to the teacher and read the IEP of one of the students. Each had different areas of need, but they all had two common needs: individualized attention on reading comprehension and study skills (e.g., note taking and test taking).

During some of the sessions, I helped my students as they were reviewing the day's reading assignments, writing reports in the computer lab, and studying for tests. One of the main things I worked with them on was how to read a science textbook. Textbooks are notoriously hard to read, but . . .

principle. In that case, you would assign a color code to each principle. On the first page of each artifact or on the tab identifying the artifact, you would place colored dots corresponding to the principle that the artifact documents. In this way, again, you are giving the reviewer visual cues to illustrate the relationship between principles and artifact, but you are also graphically illustrating how well you have chosen your artifacts (i.e., that your artifacts are rich enough to illustrate multiple principles).

In either case, color-coding provides reviewers with visual cues to lead them to either artifacts or reflections. Packets of colored dots are available at most office supply stores. Of course, if you are developing an electronic portfolio, color coding might be replaced by hyperlinks or bookmarks within the text of a reflection.

OTHER WAYS OF ORGANIZING YOUR PORTFOLIO

While we are suggesting an INTASC-based portfolio, there are a number of ways to organize your portfolio. Institutions, states, or agencies have different expectations for their beginning teacher portfolios. It is important that you give these reviewers what they are looking for. It may be a set of specific categories you are expected to fulfill. It may be a set of specific questions you must answer via your artifacts and reflections. It may be a wholly different set of standards against which you are being judged (e.g., the standards of national specialty professional associations [SPAs]), organizations that represent different content areas or grade levels (see appendix C: Web Sites for Learned Societies and pK–12 Standards or the Companion Website at www.prenhall.com/foster). Groups such as the National Association for the Education of Young Children (NAEYC), the National Council for the Social Studies (NCSS), the National Council for Teachers of Mathematics (NCTM), and the National Council for Teachers of English (NCTE) have each developed standard sets outlining what teachers (and their students) ought to know and be able to do. While these standards are increasingly being revised to reflect the structure and perspective of the INTASC standards, they do so from many perspectives. A beginning early childhood teacher may have a different set of expectations than would a beginning secondary history teacher. Depending on the expectations of those who will be judging your portfolio, you will want to organize your portfolio in a way that specifically addresses their expectations.

SUMMARY

Creating a reviewer-friendly portfolio is not a difficult task if you go about it in an organized and thoughtful way. Take time to get to know the expectations established by IN-TASC, ISTE, or whatever standards or principles against which you are to be evaluated. Once you clearly understand what you need to prove about your knowledge and abilities, go about *collecting, selecting, reflecting upon,* and *presenting* your artifacts in ways that will paint a rich picture of you as a teacher. It is a professional thing to do, and establishing this practice will help you become a better educator even after leaving the comfort of your college or university for the real world.

DISCUSSION QUESTIONS

1. What are the four main activities in preparing a beginning teacher portfolio? What does each require a teacher to do?
2. Why is reflection so important to a professional portfolio?
3. What is a portfolio artifact, and what purpose does it serve?
4. What are several categories of artifacts you will find useful in a teaching portfolio?
5. What criteria might you use to select artifacts?
6. What are several alternative ways of organizing a beginning teacher portfolio?
7. Who is the audience for your portfolio, and what will that audience want to see in your portfolio?

Reflective Analysis and Your Portfolio

The ability to pose questions to understand ourselves and our world is at the heart of what it means to be human.

Harpaz and Lefstein

"Reflect, reflect, reflect. These professors sound like broken records!" ranted Kathy, as she flung herself into the chair beside several of her classmates. "What's the big deal about reflection? I haven't even gotten into the classroom, and they are harping on me in every class to reflect on this and reflect on that. Case studies, tutoring experiences, teacher observations. Heck, I don't even know what I am looking at, let alone how to reflect on it. I wish somebody would explain it to me"

"I don't know," said Kateri. "I think I am beginning to get an idea. I mean, I took all these notes while observing my teacher and her class the other day, and I couldn't make any sense out of them. So I sorted them out into different columns; you know, teacher behaviors, student behaviors, communication lines, 'ah ha's', and the like. Then I started seeing a pattern. I was amazed! The teacher didn't ask yes or no questions at all, and she made a point of not calling on the same person twice in a row. She repeated the student's response in different words and then put it to the class to evaluate the correctness or completeness of the answer. Wow! She really had the class involved, and yet all she did was ask questions and repeat responses. I like that idea. I also noticed how she got students to bring in their own experiences and then got them to relate what they were studying to their own lives and what they already know. And it worked! Made me finally understand what Professor Kilner was saying the other day about constructing knowledge. Seems to me that is what this reflection business is all about. It's a way of seeing and understanding what you see."

QUESTIONS FOR CONSIDERATION

■ What does it mean to reflect?
■ Why is reflection an essential behavior for professionals, especially professional educators?
■ What are the characteristics of reflection?
■ How is reflection related to problem solving?
■ What are "reflection in action" and "reflection on action"?
■ Why do professionals reflect? What should you reflect?
■ Why is reflection an important part of a professional portfolio?

WHAT IS REFLECTION, AND WHY IS IT IMPORTANT?

The teacher is capable of reflection leading to self-knowledge, the metacognitive awareness that distinguishes craftsman from architect, bookkeeper from auditor. A professional is capable not only of practicing and understanding his or her craft, but of communicating the reasons for professional decisions and actions to others.[1]

A debate has gone on for many years about whether teachers are truly professionals or merely technicians, about whether teaching requires more than just a textbook, a teacher's edition, and a few teaching tricks to create meaningful learning for students. The balance has most recently shifted in favor of the view of teachers as professionals, especially highlighting at least one essential behavior that separates the professional from the technician: *reflective action*. Reflective action means examining experience, actions, and decisions, to understand their reasoning, their impact, and how they might be refined for greater success.

Reflection, then, is a skill that every professional educator should apply to all areas of educational practice. From curriculum development to instructional strategies to assessment of student performance to professional relationships and interactions, all aspects of the professional life are open to and require ongoing reflection. As your students grapple with new knowledge and skills, and as you seek to facilitate their learning experiences, you must continually evaluate both the processes you employ and the results of those efforts, always with an eye toward identifying problem areas and seeking ways of challenging and overcoming them. In essence then, reflection is problem solving and inquiry in their highest forms.

REFLECTION IN ACTION AND REFLECTION ON ACTION

Many problems confronted by educators in the course of a day require nearly instantaneous analysis and response; this kind of reflection is referred to as *reflection in action*. Indeed some have observed that a teacher makes more decisions (i.e., responds to more problems) in a day than any other professional with the exception of an air-traffic controller. Why do one teacher's decisions seem consistently right on target while another's decisions seem to create more problems than they solve? The answer is fairly obvious: knowledge, experience, and a disposition to look for patterns among problems. But how

---

[1]Shulman, L.S. (1983). Autonomy and obligation: The remote control of teaching. In L. S. Shulman & G. Sykes (Eds.), *Handbook of teaching and policy*. New York: Longman.

did one educator come by the knowledge and experience and the other did not? Although snap decisions might appear unconscious (or reflex), if we examine them more closely, we might find that the problem solver has observed something, compared that observation to his or her storehouse of knowledge and experiences, and selected (seemingly unconsciously) a response to correct the problem.

The ineffective educator tends to see every classroom problem as independent of all other problems, reacting to situations only as they arise. Once taken, the action is left unanalyzed. Conversely, the effective educator sees classroom problems as interconnected with other problems. This educator *re-views* the action to figure out what happened, what might have precipitated the problem, the degree to which the action taken worked, what other problems the action may have precipitated, and what might be done the next time a similar problem occurs. This after-the-fact analysis (referred to as *reflection on action*) determines our ability to improve our response the next time the problem arises. Your portfolio represents an opportunity to turn back time, allowing yourself the luxury of analyzing your actions and looking for those patterns that will increase your effectiveness in the classroom.

HOW IS REFLECTION LIKE INQUIRY?

Certainly many problems arise quickly and must be dealt with equally quickly, but many other problems afford the luxury of thoughtfulness, time, and a more conscious application of a problem-solving process. These situations frequently derive from a moment of "what-if" thinking: "What if I did this?" or "What would happen if I substituted this for that?" For example, if direct instruction and worksheets are the typical practice in a school but do not meet the needs of students with different ways of learning, then the reflective professional will investigate and employ alternative methods to better meet students' needs.

Reflection is a skill, and like any other skill you learn it through study, practice, and feedback. That which takes so long and requires so much conscious effort at first, with practice, becomes second nature or routine. In general, *good reflection, like good inquiry, begins with good observation and assessment.*

What must educators observe to determine how well they are doing? How can educators find out if students are learning? Observing is more than just "seeing." It is focusing on the important behaviors and interpreting those behaviors to determine their significance. It also involves viewing problems from multiple perspectives: the educator's, the student's, the principal's, the community's. It is looking beneath the surface of the problem to identify the multiple causes of the problem and to anticipate the multiple consequences of any proposed action.

WHAT IS THE ROLE OF QUESTIONING IN REFLECTION?

But let's step back in the process. Although reflection naturally begins when the teacher observes something in the classroom, analysis—the action of reflection—begins best when the teacher transforms this observation into questions:

- How are my students doing? Are they achieving to their potential?
- Where are they experiencing difficulties? In what areas are they meeting or not meeting my expectations?
- What areas of my own teaching seem most/least effective to me? Why do these appear effective/ineffective?

- How do I manage my classroom? Why do I manage it in this way?
- Who directs the learning in my classroom?
- Who does most of the work in my classroom, me or my students?
- What kinds of questions do I ask my students? Who poses the questions that guide class discussion? Do these questions close discussion or do they generate open discourse? What is the flow of conversation in my classroom? Is it unidirectional? Is it multidirectional? Am I always the locus of conversation?
- To what degree are the learning experiences in my classroom inquiry or problem based?
- To what degree are the learning experiences open-ended, student directed, or student initiated?

The result of such questioning is further observation, investigation, and reflection.

Asking a series of "Why?" questions is an effective way of getting at root causes, with each successive question getting at another layer of causality.[2] To illustrate this process of question posing, suppose a teacher notices that her or his students score poorly on assessments requiring critical thinking and problem solving. The teacher should ask the question "Why?" There are several possible answers:

- Maybe students lack basic skills.
- Maybe students are not engaged by the task.
- Maybe students lack experience with critical thinking/problem solving.
- Maybe students lack the intelligence to think critically or to solve open-ended problems.

If each of these "maybe"s becomes a further exploration to eliminate it as a possibility or to validate its likelihood, then the teacher can explore a second round of "Why" questions to delve deeper into the potential cause. For example: Why do the students lack experience in critical thinking? Possible answer: Because their teachers—present and past—have not engaged them in critical thinking and have not taught them how to think critically.

"Why?" Possible answer: Because their teachers do not know how to build lessons and activities that teach not only content but also require and reinforce critical thinking.

"Why?" Possible answer: Because the teachers themselves were not taught to think critically and have not seen it modeled in their own learning experiences.

"So what can be done?" Probable solution: Seek information, examples, and training on how to engage students in meaningful critical thinking and on how to reinforce those skills every day.

Armed with new information and skills, the teacher begins to implement new strategies to help students succeed in tasks requiring critical thinking and problem solving. When viewed from this perspective, reflection is not just a requirement to pass one's portfolio review or even to demonstrate one's understanding of the INTASC principles. Rather, and much more important, reflection is a tool that effective teachers employ to improve their students' learning.

Once an intervention has been identified, other questions must come into play: "How can I create learning opportunities to address this need among my students? How do I know that this intervention has a chance of working? What evidence is there in the literature or in my experience or that of others to support the use of this intervention?"

---

[2]Haigh, N. (1999). Teaching about reflection and ways of being reflective. University of Waikato, New Zealand, www.cce.auckland.ac.nz/herdsa98/HTML/Workshop/Haigh.HTM.

In other words, the professional educator must base practice on the dual foundations of solid theory and proven practice. But the process does not end with implementation of a new strategy. Later, one must necessarily assess the results by asking further questions: "How will I know whether or not my intervention has yielded the intended impact on student learning and achievement?" Of course, this leads to the issue of assessment of student learning, itself a source of data (observation) in support of good reflection—one that you will study in chapter 11 (Principle 8).

REFLECTION MUST BE GROUNDED IN RESEARCH

Let's pause for a moment to consider this professional obligation to ground your actions in research and knowledge of best practice. On one level, your portfolio, like a final examination, is a backward-looking assessment of what you have learned about teaching and learning; consequently, to fulfill the expectations of your audience, you must demonstrate your understanding of contemporary theories of curriculum, learning, development, instruction, and classroom management, among others. For some beginning teachers, educational theory is just so much irrelevant stuff they were forced to study in college; once they enter the classroom, they intentionally leave it behind, choosing to operate on experience or intuition alone. Unfortunately, the portfolios of these educators tend to fail the backward-looking assessment because they fail to reveal an understanding of, much less a professional appreciation for, research and best practice.

On another and more important level, your portfolio is a forward-looking assessment of your disposition to test theory against the reality of your particular classroom situation, thereby not only applying theory to practice but also contributing to the knowledge base available to all future educators. Those with a disposition to apply theory to particular situations "find inevitably that nothing quite fits the [theory]."[3] Here is where reflective practice comes into play. The reflective educator wants to know why the theory didn't explain her or his particular situation. Such educators open themselves to the possibility of inquiry and in the process become contributors to the knowledge of best practice. This educator has met both the backward- and the forward-looking expectations and in the process met her or his responsibility as a developing reflective professional.

WHAT ARE THE CHARACTERISTICS OF EFFECTIVE REFLECTION STATEMENTS?

The heart of any portfolio resides in the reflective statements that interpret and give context to the artifacts housed within the portfolio. These reflective essays help the reviewer put the artifacts into perspective and allow the teacher to interpret their meaning for the reviewer. When the threads of this investigative process are woven together, they reveal a picture of effective reflection statements.

- *Effective reflections establish a context for artifacts and overtly declare which principles are being demonstrated.*   Effective reflections not only make clear the who, what, when, and where context of a teaching episode, but they also make clear what principle is being demonstrated through the use of the artifact.
- *Effective reflections display good observational skills: they are honest, accurate, supported by relevant details, and nonjudgmental.*   Observing your own behavior and making

---

[3]Shulman, L. (1997). Professing the liberal arts. In R. Orrill (Exec. Ed.), *Democracy and Education*. New York: College Entrance Examination Board, p. 158.

honest, accurate, and informed judgments is difficult, but that is exactly what must occur. You must gather the right information and data from assessments, from observations and conversations, and from other relevant sources, presenting these data objectively for the reviewer.

■ *Effective reflections ground practices, observations, and interpretations in appropriate and specific theory.*   Analytic reflection not only leads to better understanding of your actions and their effects, but it also demonstrates your ability and disposition to link theory and practice. Most of the 10 INTASC principles and the NETS•T technology standards are founded on a research base; your reflection statements must demonstrate your understanding of that research and how you have applied it to your professional practices.

■ *Effective reflections uncover and interpret underlying issues, causes, and effects within what has been observed.*   Not only must you accurately describe what happened in the teaching and learning event, but you must also dig beneath the surface observations to uncover possible explanations for what happened.

■ *Effective reflections project from observations and analyses conclusions about practice, plans of action for future instructional activities, or plans for ongoing professional development and self-learning.*   Reflection is incomplete if it does not lead to decision making or action. The decision may be to continue using a particularly successful practice, or it may be to seek additional professional training in order to understand better how to motivate students. More likely it will be to employ a particular intervention in the future to address what was discovered in the process of reflection. Effective reflection statements lead into the next stage of action.

HOW DO I WRITE A GOOD ANALYTIC REFLECTION?

The nuts and bolts of writing an analytic reflection are really quite simple. You might approach it as you would an essay for a composition class. Like any good essay, your reflection statements should have a beginning, middle, and end. Let's look at each part and explore what it should contain.

THE BEGINNING

Every essay has an introduction and a thesis statement. In most portfolio reflections, the thesis statement acts as both. Remember that the reflection is intended to explain two things:

1. The relevance of the artifact(s) to the principle you are documenting
2. The significance of the artifact(s) as evidence of your development as a professional educator, both overall and in reference to a particular principle

The opening statement should, then, identify the principle being documented and the artifacts being used to address that principle. These sentences should be short, direct, declarative statements. For example, the following statement was written by an elementary education candidate regarding the artifacts selected to document having met INTASC Principle 2 (*The teacher understands how children learn and develop, and can provide learning opportunities that support their intellectual, social, and personal development*):

> To demonstrate my understanding of how children learn and develop and my ability to create learning opportunities that support their intellectual, social, and personal development, I have included two artifacts: teacher evaluations from my student teaching and reading assessments with lessons from my Analysis and Correction of Reading Problems course.

Stepping back from the opening sentence, you might note several important points. First, it identifies and repeats language from the principle being documented. Second, it identifies each artifact being offered in support of the teacher's assertion of "understanding." Third, the teacher includes a mix of artifacts, intended to document theoretical knowledge and the pedagogical application of that knowledge.

Now let's analyze the opening paragraph. Does this teacher's opening sentence establish a thesis? Not overtly; however, behind the descriptive nature of the sentence ("I have included . . .") is an implied argument: "I understand *how children learn and develop and can provide learning opportunities that support their intellectual, social, and personal development* and the two artifacts I have included are my evidence for that assertion." Formally asserting your understanding of the principle is usually not necessary, so long as you clearly identify which principle you are demonstrating and inventory your evidence, as this author has done. The opening does, however, establish an expectation in the reader's mind: the reader will expect to see in the two artifacts evidence of the teacher's knowledge of learning and development theory and ***evidence*** of the teacher's disposition and ability to apply that knowledge in ways that support student growth in three areas (intellectual, social, and personal development). This "thesis," then, effectively becomes a checklist the reader (and you) can use to evaluate the proof of your knowledge and understanding.

THE MIDDLE

Having read the previous opening statement, a reader naturally expects the remainder of the reflection to explore how each of these artifacts does indeed offer evidence of the teacher's knowledge and ability to apply that knowledge in his or her teaching. Since the opening statement acts as a promise of what is to follow, the reader has already developed an expectation for what will be discussed and in what order. The reader will expect the following from the body of the reflection statement:

1. Some discussion (it may be distributed throughout the reflection) of a variety of the theories of how students learn and develop as they relate to the grade level being taught, including specific references to theories and theorists. (See chapter 5 for a complete discussion of the requirements of Principle 2.)
2. A description, including a context, and an analysis of each artifact, establishing for the reader its relevance to the specific issues raised by the principle and what it reveals about the teacher's understanding of the principle. This expectation offers the opportunity for the teacher to demonstrate the ability to integrate theory into practice and to demonstrate awareness of the interconnections among educational decisions.
3. A discussion of the major issues relevant to learning and development that must be taken into consideration when designing and implementing instruction. Here again is an opportunity for the teacher to integrate theory into practice, as well as to demonstrate awareness of the interconnectedness of educational decisions and the ability to see interconnections among practices.
4. An argument for how the artifacts reveal the teacher's ability to make the learning meaningful for students.
5. A discussion of the outcomes of the teacher's implementation of the learning activities.

Let's see to what degree the teacher's next section delivers on the promises established by the opening paragraph.

The student teaching evaluations I have included as Artifact E were written by my university supervisor and my cooperating teacher at Erehwon School. These evaluations were part of the ongoing oversight of my student teaching and occurred over the course of my 12-week placement in Mrs. Butler's third-grade classroom at Erehwon School.

Within these evaluations is evidence, based on the knowledge and experience of seasoned teachers, that I understand the theories addressing the issues of how students learn and develop, that I build on what students already know, and that I encourage students to be responsible. The reviewer will note that both my supervisor and my cooperating teacher consistently circled "G" (the highest score possible) in the area of "understands how students learn and develop and applies this understanding to creating a rich learning environment."

Many theorists have explored the development and learning issues of elementary-aged children. Of the many I have studied, I have always believed that the constructivist paradigm ought to be the guiding principle governing the management of the elementary classroom. As Brooks and Brooks (*Case for the Constructivist Classroom*) advocate, I worked very hard to develop a classroom environment and learning opportunities that allowed students to uncover their own theories about the world and then, through active exploration and diverse experiences, refine their understanding and create new knowledge in the context of their exploration. Moreover, recognizing that all students do not learn best in the same way, I have taken liberally from Howard Gardner's theory of multiple intelligences and Vygotsky's theories of language acquisition to develop learning activities, cooperative challenges, and study stations that allow for multiple approaches to learning and that reinforce my students' strengths and strengthen their weak areas of intelligence.

One good example appears within the March 12 evaluation. During the lesson I was teaching that day, I developed a series of learning stations, each matching one of the eight intelligences identified by Gardner. Each station dealt with issues and content related to multiplication and division but in the context of different intelligences. One station had students using counting cubes to model multiplication as a series of repeated addition problems. Another station had students reading word problems requiring multiplication, performing the tasks, and then writing their own problems. A third station asked students to create posters teaching next year's students how to understand the principles of multiplication and division. Other stations had students collaborating to develop products, reading and creating stories, and using their bodies as a means of understanding multiplication and addition. Interestingly, the stations ran themselves, and I was there as a resource for students needing added attention or input. The result was a very satisfying morning of learning about math and reinforcing other skills (reading, writing, interpersonal communication, and science) and intelligences.

Not surprising, my students did well in their classroom work and were consistently motivated to complete their assigned tasks and get involved in classroom discussions and other activities. It is interesting how a well-structured, varied, and engaging activity can promote active learning and eliminate issues of discipline and attention at the same time. It seems like the opportunity to use different intelligences and the quick-moving progression between stations and challenges were key elements in the students' engagement and success. The experience reinforced in my mind the connection between instruction and classroom management. Using pre- and posttests as a guide, as well as informal observation checklists, I determined that every one of the 25 students in my class increased his or her knowledge and ability in all areas of the district curriculum for which I was responsible. Of course, some students did better than others, but I was able to use the test information to individualize instruction for those who lagged in their learning, and even these students made significant gains over the course of the 12 weeks of my placement.

For these reasons and others (see additional comments on the evaluations), both my supervisor and my cooperating teacher also consistently ranked me as "G" in the following areas:

- Consistently factors student's cognitive, social, and emotional development in planning
- Consistently uses students' prior knowledge as a factor in planning and teaching
- Effectively develops individual and cooperative learning activities that engage students in learning and promotes self-motivation
- Consistently motivates and clearly expects students to perform to the best of their abilities

Before going on to the author's next artifact, let's consider the degree to which the teacher has addressed the expectations set by the opening paragraph.

1. *Does the section discuss how children learn and develop and how the artifact identified reveals understanding and application as is required by Principle 2?* To a great degree, yes it does, and on several levels. First it establishes the authority of the authors of the artifact ("seasoned teachers") and the conclusions these "authorities" came to in evaluating the preservice teacher's performance in the classroom. It offers at least some references to pertinent theories and theorists, as well as specific actions that arose out of those theories. Moreover, it offers further evidence from the artifact, including focusing the reader's attention on four or five relevant categories within the evaluations. This is enough to establish that the preservice teacher is conscious of the theories informing his or her instructional decision making and that his or her actions are to some extent effective in the classroom—at least in the eyes of those evaluating his or her performance.

2. *Does the section describe (including a context) and analyze the artifact, establishing for the reader its relevance to the principle, the issues identified as needing demonstration in the principle, and what it reveals about the beginning teacher's understanding of the subject matter? Does the author exercise the opportunity to integrate theory into practice? Does the author exercise the opportunity to demonstrate awareness of the interconnections among his or her practices?* Certainly the artifact is described, including what it is, where and by whom it was completed, and in what context (student teaching in a third-grade classroom at Erehwon School). Does it establish the relevance of the artifact to demonstrating the author's understanding of learning and development? It certainly begins to because the theories and theorists mentioned are important in elementary education and appear to have informed the actions of the preservice teacher, as described. More could have been said about why the preservice teacher believed these theories were the most fruitful for his or her work within the third-grade classroom and in a more detailed way what these theories have to say about learning and development. The student's efforts to direct the reader to a specific example of the application of theoretical knowledge is also useful and supports the assertions made in the opening paragraph. Moreover, the author reveals an inclination to see interconnections between the way he or she set up and ran the activity and the students' being on task and motivated.

3. *Does the author exercise the opportunity to integrate theory into practice and to demonstrate awareness of the interconnections among his or her practices?* The author's ability

to integrate theory into practice is apparent in his or her references to personal theories of the world, learning in the context of exploration, learning stations, and cooperative learning. The teacher underscores this ability by referencing appropriate issues within the evaluations. In addition, the use of assessment data to evaluate student progress supports the theory-practice connection at yet another level. At the same time, the author reveals his or her integration of learning theory into classroom practice by overtly connecting those theories back to the behaviors exhibited by the students. In other words, the author proclaims awareness of the interconnections rather than depending on the reader to see them.

4. *Does the section present an argument for how the artifact reveals the teacher's ability to make meaningful learning opportunities for students?* To some extent it does because the example of the learning stations and the use of assessment data begin to support the conclusion that this preservice teacher is able to create meaningful learning opportunities. Moreover, the references to his or her findings from the pre- and posttesting yield some evidence that the writer is conscious of the need to individualize instruction and is inclined to use data to do so. This, again, is evidence of translating theory into practice.

5. *Does the section discuss the outcomes of the teacher's implementation of the learning activities?* The author corroborates the importance of connecting present learning to what the students already know and the value of using both formal and informal assessment to evaluate student learning and to individualize instruction. Of course, we only have the preservice teacher's assertion of these findings. We will likely expect to see other evidence here and in other places in the portfolio to further corroborate these assertions.

You are encouraged to subject the next section to the same examination, asking yourself the following questions:

1. To what degree does the section satisfy the reader's expectations for a context, an explication of knowledge base and decision making, an analysis and interpretation of impact, an acknowledgment of the teacher's awareness of the interconnections among his or her practices and students' performance, and a projection of what will happen the next time?

2. What advice would I give the author to improve the reflective statement?

Artifact F consists of an assessment I did on a student in reading, including tests and lessons I developed as part of my action plan for addressing the student's needs. The project was completed for my Analysis and Correction of Reading Problems class, which I completed in the fall of 2001. I was assigned a young girl who had trouble with her reading and comprehension. This artifact includes an attitude and interest survey, a writing sample, a miscue analysis summary, an analytic reading inventory (ARI), and three lessons. I developed the lessons based on my findings from the various assessment instruments I used to determine the student's needs.

This set of artifacts shows that I understand how students learn and the theories behind this. Moreover, the set shows that I plan lessons according to students' existing knowledge. Before beginning this assignment, I did some research into reading assessment and how it could be used to help students learn. I felt that I had to get a sense for how elementary-aged students' minds work and how they learn to deal with texts. Based on my findings, I decided to test my student using miscue analysis, a writing sample, and an ARI because I knew that people learn to read and show what they have learned in observable kinds of ways. For example, I studied theories on how one can identify a child's reading level by examining a writing sample since writing is often a reflection of a reader's level of ability in comprehending text. Based on this theory, I had my student write a short paragraph about what she likes to do in her free time. Based on this writing sample, I determined that she was at the transitional level in her spelling and sentence structure. Based on these findings, I developed an intervention plan for working with her. This plan consisted of three lessons designed to help her become more successful in areas where she was struggling. From the interest surveys, I knew her likes and dislikes, and from the ARI and miscue analysis, I knew her strengths and weaknesses. Clearly she struggled with phonics, and she liked books from Marc Brown's "Arthur" series. The lessons dealt specifically with the phonics she had trouble with, using the "Arthur" stories as a primary set of texts.

These assessments and lessons went very well. I learned how to find out what students are struggling with in reading and writing, and I learned how to successfully help a student deal with those problems. The student responded well to the experience by working hard and seeming to enjoy the time and activities we shared. Specifically, the student exhibited a noted improvement in reading accuracy and comprehension in her classroom work. Also, her scores on tests that required considerable reading increased by more than 20 percentage points. Her teacher, moreover, reported greater confidence in the student and more engagement in classroom discussion. I learned a lot from the experience as well. I learned about the application of various forms of reading assessment and the theories that support their use. I also learned that it is most effective to plan lessons around what your students know and what you know they are struggling with. Further, it is important to assess students often to find out where they are individually in learning relevant to the curriculum and district/state standards.

In conclusion, I plan to continue to explore ways to use the constructvist theories and multiple intelligences in my classrooms. And I will continue to gather more information on how others have gone about doing this in their own classrooms because I think I can still learn a lot from other teachers. My goal now is to transfer this knowledge into other content areas, such as math and social studies, since these are not so well explored by theorists in terms of misconceptions and mistakes. However, I can easily see how a teacher can tap students' prior knowledge, experiences, and learning to build meaningful learning activities in these and other areas. I will continue to try to discover my students' interests and abilities as a way of making my teaching fit each student's needs better.

THE ENDING

After presenting and analyzing the artifacts, the author next needs to *project* from these artifacts their significance relevant to the present and the future. In other words, you should not only reiterate for the reader that these artifacts do, indeed, reveal some level of understanding and some ability to teach in meaningful ways, but you should also reflect on gaps you still have in your knowledge and your ability to create meaningful learning experiences for learners. This will likely include thinking about what sorts of changes might be implemented in future efforts, as well as what continued learning and refinement of practice you will need to engage in to address the gaps in your knowledge and practice.

Go back to the author's reflection statement. Do you find an ending? Yes, you do. It is accomplished in the final paragraph where the author expresses the desire to continue and refine the successful practices, the need to get more information from various sources, and finally the intention of transferring the knowledge of student assessment to other content areas in the elementary curriculum.

Does the reflection statement need a concluding paragraph? Maybe not a formal one; however, reflection statements are still obligated to address the other ideas described earlier:

1. Gaps you still have in your theoretical knowledge or in your ability to make content/learning meaningful for students
2. Potential changes you would make in your practice based on what you learned from the experience of creating (and teaching, if appropriate) the artifact
3. Some indication of how you will address those gaps in your knowledge or changes in practice

Does this reflection statement provide this information to the reader? Again, yes, to a limited degree, it does. While the final statement does not address how the preservice teacher will address the gaps he or she sees in knowledge of assessment in other content areas, it does express a need to explore this transfer of knowledge and the practices of others in the profession. It also outlines a couple of areas in which the writer might be searching relevant to other content areas: "since these are not so well explored by theorists in terms of misconceptions and mistakes."

HOW CAN I ASSESS THE QUALITY OF MY REFLECTIVE STATEMENTS?

Knowing what to write in a reflection is only half the challenge. If you are to develop your own internal sense of quality, you need benchmarks, or a scoring guide, against which to evaluate your performance. Figure 3.1 presents a generic two-point scoring guide that can help you evaluate the quality of your reflections. When used in conjunction with the scoring guides you will find in each of the *Principle* chapters, you can not only evaluate the overall quality of your reflection statements but also know what to revise to make them more effective.

Let's return to the example reflection statement, this time applying the generic reflection rubric. To facilitate your assessment of the strengths and weaknesses of the example, we've broken up the rubric according to the characteristics of effective reflection statements you saw earlier in this chapter. Reread the reflection statement, and compare it to the descriptions for "Good Reflection" and "Weak Reflection," looking for evidence to support your assessment.

CHARACTERISTIC 1: CONTEXT

Relevant to this characteristic, the reflection would score in the Good Reflection column. Specifically, the author makes explicit and overt use of the language used by the principle prior to introducing the artifacts. One might like to see more exploration of the principle itself, but the remaining reflection reveals a clear understanding of the principle. For each artifact the author gives a detailed description of where the artifact was created, by whom, and for what purpose. There is no question then about the context surrounding the creation of the artifacts.

CHARACTERISTIC 2: DETAILED AND OBJECTIVE OBSERVATION

The contents of the reflection clearly display good observational skills, defined as "accurate, supported by relevant details, and nonjudgmental." The reflection describes in some

Criteria	Good Reflection	Weak Reflection
Identification of context and awareness of professional standards of practice	Provides a context for the artifact(s) used, including overt identification and explication of the principle to which the reflection and artifacts relate	Provides only the date and course from which the artifact came but little else by way of context for the artifact(s) used; implies rather than clearly identifying the principle to which the reflection and artifacts relate
Observation and description of artifact (experience or document)	Clearly describes the teaching episode (either simulated or real), learning experience, or other artifact being offered as evidence, including nonjudgmental details regarding when and where the event occurred, what the teacher did (i.e., self or other), what the students did, what the assessment data and teacher observation indicate were the results of the teaching episode or experience, and how those involved reacted	Describes a teaching episode (either simulated or real), learning experience, or other artifact being offered as evidence, including nonjudgmental detail regarding what the teacher did and what the students did, although tending either to omit outcomes or reactions or to substitute an emotive assessment (e.g., "students liked the activity") for description of outcomes or reactions
Application of theories or principles of effective practice (Note: The substance of this criterion will vary with the principle being demonstrated.)	Associates the details of the teaching episode with relevant and appropriate theories or clearly demonstrates theoretical knowledge by applying theory appropriately, thus indicating comprehension of those theories cited	May or may not associate the details of the teaching episode with theories of practice, but in doing so reveals either misunderstanding of the theories cited or such a narrow understanding that a reviewer might question depth of understanding
Identification, analysis, and interpretation of causes and effects	Explains (perhaps by applying appropriate and relevant teaching theory or concepts) the events of the teaching episode and what resulted from it; analysis may focus principally (or even exclusively) on the classroom teacher's perspective	Analyzes the events of and results from the teaching episode, but the analysis reveals overgeneralization, misrepresentation, or misunderstanding of the teaching concept(s) applied
Projection from observations toward problem solving and lifelong learning	Predicts and justifies what he or she would do the next time based on the evidence; acknowledges professional development needs without necessarily identifying the means for addressing those needs	Does not reveal an inclination to revise practice in light of the evidence; alternatively, may revise a practice in ways that are superficial or inconsistent with good practice or theory; does not acknowledge professional development needs

FIGURE 3.1

Reflective Writing Rubric

detail what the teacher did to prepare for the teaching episode, what the students were doing during the instruction, and how the participants reacted. This information was supported by specific examples from the lesson. Based on the information given in the reflection, one can create a fairly clear and accurate picture of the situation surrounding the artifact and its creation. It is supported by relevant details.

CHARACTERISTIC 3: LINKING THEORY WITH PRACTICE

There can be little doubt the reflection "consciously and thoughtfully interpret[s] observations and ground[s] practices, observations, and interpretations in appropriate and specific theory (e.g., developmental, learning, motivation, assessment, communication, etc.), as well as in the principles by which the profession is evaluated." Statements such as "recognizing that all students do not learn best in the same way, I have taken liberally from Howard Gardner's theory of Multiple Intelligences and Vygotsky's theories of language acquisition to develop learning activities, cooperative challenges, and study stations that allow for multiple approaches to learning and that reinforce my students' strengths and strengthen their weak areas of intelligence" clearly indicate that the author has considered relevant theorists. This reveals some knowledge of theories and an ability to relate pedagogical decisions to theories. Even though the reflection on the second artifact does not cite specific theorists, the writer clearly has a theoretical foundation for the decisions he or she makes:

> Before beginning this assignment, I did some research into reading assessment and how it could be used to help students learn. I felt that I had to get a sense for how elementary-aged students' minds work and how they learn to deal with texts. Based on my findings, I decided to test my student using miscue analysis, a writing sample, and an ARI because I knew that people learn to read and show what they have learned in observable kinds of ways.

One might like to see specific references to theorists, but the mention of miscue analysis and the ARI clearly rest on some theoretical background developed and utilized within the teaching episode.

CHARACTERISTIC 4: INTERPRETATION OF CAUSES AND EFFECTS

The reflection offers several instances of analysis of causes and effects. For the first artifact (the learning stations), the author gives specific descriptions of the activities in the teaching episode and explores the resulting student behaviors: "Interestingly, the stations ran themselves, and I was there as a resource for students needing added attention or input. The result was a very satisfying morning of learning about math and reinforcing other skills (reading, writing, interpersonal communication, and science) and intelligences." The writer continues to explore other effects including motivation and engagement in learning. The author offers the same sort of cause-and-effect analysis for the second artifact (reading assessment and lessons). Here the author describes the actions taken and the results on the student's reading ability. Moreover, the author discusses the impact of these activities on the student's performance in subjects other than reading. Both artifact analyses work together to satisfy this rubric area and the following (interconnections).

CHARACTERISTIC 5: SELF-ASSESSMENT AND PROFESSIONAL PLANNING

Here again, the author would be scored in the Good Reflection column because of the final paragraph. It clearly indicates the inclination to discover and fill in specific gaps in knowledge/understanding (e.g., miscues in other content areas) and to examine, evaluate, and refine practice based on reflection (e.g., discovery of student prior knowledge and interests and the use of multiple intelligences).

We think you will agree this preservice teacher's reflection substantially meets all of the requirements of a good reflection set forth in the rubric. Now a portfolio reviewer could with some confidence turn to the artifacts given and validate the assertions made in the reflection.

SUMMARY

The ultimate goal of professional preparation is student learning and achievement—yours and the students you will affect in the years to come. Through focused and disciplined reflection, you and your colleagues can continually grow as professionals and continually provide greater opportunities for your students' learning and success.

The following questions will help you to think about your portfolio reflections:

1. What do I understand about the principle upon which I am reflecting? What do I know from theory, course work, and experience about the principle and its expectations of me and my portfolio?
2. How does my artifact (or how does each artifact) reveal my understanding and knowledge?
3. What impact did it have on me, my students, their motivation, behavior, and so on? What evidence do I have for that impact? How did I collect the evidence?
4. If I were to do it again, what would I do or not do? Why? What am I going to do to increase the likelihood of being more effective next time?

DISCUSSION QUESTIONS

1. What is reflection, and why is it an important characteristic of professionals?
2. What is the difference between reflection in action and reflection on action?
3. In what ways is reflection similar to problem solving?
4. How does reflection differ from observation or description? How do descriptive reflection and analytic reflection differ?
5. What are the characteristics of good reflections?

Implementing INTASC Principle 1 in Your Portfolio

That which distinguishes the man who knows from the ignorant man is an ability to teach.

Aristotle

Ella was confused and frustrated. "How can my portfolio show I understand social studies—in all its forms?" she sighs. She looked at the stack of possible artifacts: her transcript, the letter notifying her of making the dean's list for high GPA, and her exit content test scores. She asked herself, will these be enough? When she looked at Principle 1, however, she saw that these documents can speak to only a few of the expectations it sets. Ella thought, what are "central concepts," "tools of inquiry," and "structures of the disciplines," anyway? And how will I show that I can get students to understand these things? Then, a light came on in Ella's mind: "What about that project I did in the senior seminar, making use of primary sources to evaluate the work of different historians over time? That should show I know history and how it works. And what about that paleontology unit I taught in my internship? The students really ate it up, and it covered archaeology, geology, paleontology, anthropology, and lots more. Now all I have to do is find them!"

QUESTIONS TO CONSIDER

- Why must I know my discipline(s) so thoroughly to be an effective teacher?
- What are the central concepts, tools of inquiry, and structures of the discipline(s) I will be teaching?
- Why is it important to connect the content of my discipline(s) to that of other disciplines?
- Why should I encourage students to see, question, and interpret ideas within the discipline and the world from diverse perspectives?
- Why do I need to discover and employ different representations and explanations of disciplinary concepts that capture key ideas?
- What is the value of linking disciplinary concepts to students' prior understandings and experience?

Should your portfolio merely document that you have achieved high grades in your subject-area course work, or that you have achieved high scores on standardized tests of your subject-matter knowledge? No. You need to do more than point to other people's measures of your knowledge. Transcripts, test scores, and letters of recommendation represent third-party testimony of what you understand; they do *not* document your understanding of the generalizations and concepts around which you will help your students organize their knowledge. So even though you will likely want to include transcripts and test scores in your portfolio, you are still obligated to demonstrate your understanding—*not* just point to your transcript or test scores as self-evident documentation of your understanding. Ultimately, those who review your portfolio are looking for evidence that you can integrate what you know about your subject area with how you teach it to students.

UNDERSTANDING PRINCIPLE 1

Principle 1: The teacher understands the central concepts, tools of inquiry, and structures of the discipline(s) he or she teaches and can create learning experiences that make these aspects of subject matter meaningful for students.

Principle 1 raises two expectations for understanding:

1. Demonstration of your *understanding* of (a) the *central concepts* of your discipline(s), (b) the *tools of inquiry* of your discipline(s), and (c) the *structures of your discipline(s)*
2. Demonstration of your *ability to create learning experiences* that make these aspects of subject matter meaningful to students

Many people are surprised to find out that the term *discipline* refers to *how* the facts, principles, theories, and skills of a content area are put into practice. Therefore, the *discipline* of science, or mathematics, or history is less a description of the knowledge contained within it than it is a description of how people who practice the discipline use their knowledge and skills to make sense of the world around them. Principle 1 anticipates *both* senses of the word: what is to be learned (central concepts) and how it is practiced and structured (tools of inquiry and structures of the discipline). Your reflection on this principle and your choice of artifacts must reveal your understanding of both aspects of your discipline(s).

If you are a candidate for a single-subject, K–12 certificate (such as art, music, or physical education), for a middle school certificate, or for a secondary certificate, your choice of discipline and your challenge is fairly straightforward. You have prepared yourself to teach one or possibly two subject areas; therefore, you need to demonstrate understanding of at most two subject areas.

If you are a candidate for elementary certification, however, you have multiple subject areas about which you need to demonstrate understanding. Early childhood education candidates are similarly responsible for the whole curriculum. Special education offers yet another twist on the challenge; although you have prepared yourself to teach students with particular disabilities, you still must demonstrate your understanding of the central concepts of the entire curriculum.

Central concepts are the major elements or issues that make up the discipline. In physics, for example, we have principles and properties of matter, motions and forces, and transfer and transformations of energy. In English, we have literature and its various genres, linguistics (syntax, semantics, and grammar), and rhetoric/composition (audience analysis, purposes, and organizational principles). Fortunately, most state education agencies and national associations for teachers have identified those most important concepts. For example, the National Science Teachers Association (NSTA, www.nsta.org) and the National Science Content Standards (www.nap.edu/readingroom/books/nses/html) identify both the major

"Performance Standards the Lesson Is Based on—In Communication Arts, students will acquire a solid foundation, which includes knowledge of and proficiency in reading and evaluating fiction, poetry, and drama." *Elementary Language Arts Lesson*

concepts within each of the disciplines of science (e.g., properties of matter in the physical sciences or organisms and environment in the life sciences) and the major concepts that unify all scientific effort (e.g., system, order, and organization; or change, constancy, and measurement). Therefore, it will help you enormously to investigate how the professional association for your subject area (e.g., ACEI, NSTA, NCTM, NCTE, etc.) has described these major concepts (see appendix C for the URLs of many of these associations), as well as what your state's education agency has identified as being most important for each subject area at particular grade levels. If you do not already know the URL for your state's education agency, you can either conduct a Web search to find it or visit www.ccsso.org for links to each of the 50 state agencies.

Tools of inquiry are those instruments, methodologies, heuristics, and so on that people who practice a discipline use to make sense of the world from their disciplinary perspective. The National Science Content Standards[1] identify the following as a definition of inquiry—one that with minor adjustment could be applied to any subject area:

- Ask questions.
- Plan and conduct investigations.
- Employ equipment and tools to gather data and extend the senses.
- Use data to construct a reasonable explanation.
- Communicate investigations and explanations to others.

Inherent in this process are the mental and mechanical tools practitioners of a discipline use to conduct their inquiry. For example, historians use primary source documents or physical evidence (original documents, letters, diaries, cave paintings, government documents, tracts, archeological data, etc.) to inquire into the period and lives of the time they are studying. Mathematicians use formulas, shapes, graphs, tables, mathematical models, and calculus, among other tools, to help them inquire into and represent their topics of research. If you were a secondary or mid-level math teacher, you would need to demonstrate an understanding and ability to use these tools of the discipline(s) to inquire into relevant phenomena and to express your findings.

Structures of the discipline is somewhat easier to understand and is related to how one generally approaches the discipline to understand it. The phrase *structures of the discipline* has two components: The first refers to the "variety of ways in which the basic concepts and principles of the discipline are organized to incorporate its facts." The second refers to the "teacher's ability to explain why a particular aspect of the discipline is necessary to know, why it is worth knowing, and how it relates to other propositions, both within the discipline and without."[2]

Your exploration of central concepts will help you to document your understanding of how your subject area may be organized. However, the second issue challenges you to answer the question, "Why should my students know about or care about this content area?" Revealing your grasp of the relevance and importance of a discipline is essential to revealing your overall understanding of that discipline. This is a more complex issue and requires demonstrating your understanding of what role(s) a discipline plays in the world, the impact of the discipline on our everyday lives, and the instances of the work of that discipline visible in the world around us. For instance, how is mathematics used every day? Engineers use it to design and test new technologies. Financial institutions use it to calculate money and to predict economic trends and report financial data. How are art, music, literature, language, and history applied every day in ways that impact our lives?

"What about that project I did in the Senior Seminar, making use of primary sources to evaluate the work of different historians over time?"

---

[1]National Science Content Standards, www.nap.edu.
[2]Shulman, L. S. (1986). Those who understand: Knowledge growth in Teaching. *Educational Researcher* (15)2, 9.

"Each station dealt with issues and content related to multiplication and division but in the context of different intelligences. One station had students using counting cubes to model multiplication as a series of repeated addition problems. Another station had students reading word problems requiring multiplication, performing the tasks, and then writing their own problems. A third station asked students to create posters teaching next year's students how to understand the principles of multiplication and division. Other stations had students collaborating to develop products, reading and creating stories, and using their bodies as a means of understanding multiplication and addition."
Reflection on an Elementary Mathematics Lesson

The ability to answer these questions and use that knowledge to give subject matter learning a place in our students' lives is essential to making content meaningful and learnable.

The ***ability to create meaningful learning experiences*** challenges you to demonstrate that you know how to teach your subject to students. It is important to remember that the emphasis in Principle 1 is *not* on your knowledge of development (Principle 2) or instructional strategies (Principle 4); rather the emphasis is on *the subject matter itself*. You will want to demonstrate some of the following in your choice of artifacts and your reflections upon them:

- Your ability to connect one subject area to another in meaningful rather than superficial ways (e.g., connect mathematics to science or history)
- Your ability to engage your students in the construction of new knowledge through questioning
- Your ability to present your subject area from multiple perspectives, as well as your ability to present your subject using powerful analogies, illustrations, examples, explanations, and demonstrations
- Your ability to place your subject area in a variety of real-world contexts
- Your ability to evaluate the variety of materials you are likely to use in teaching a subject area

Finally, you must also reveal your "understanding of what makes the learning of specific topics easy or difficult: the conceptions and preconceptions that students of different ages and backgrounds bring with them to the learning of those most frequently taught topics and lessons."[3] Again, by carefully selecting artifacts and thoughtfully discussing them, you can reveal to your portfolio reviewers that you are not only inclined to think this way about your students' understanding, but that you have prepared yourself to anticipate where your students might have trouble with a specific concept.

One final note: Despite the challenge presented by Principle 1, you must resist the temptation merely to present transcripts or test scores or even letters of recommendation as self-evident documentation of your possession of subject matter knowledge and your ability to teach it to others. While these documents may be useful as supporting evidence of what you know about and are able to do with subject matter knowledge, they will not by themselves convince reviewers of your portfolio that you can integrate what you know about your subject area with how you teach it to students.

WHAT ARE THE IMPLICATIONS OF THIS KNOWLEDGE BASE FOR MY PORTFOLIO?

The preservice teacher ought to have a clear sense of how the discipline he or she is preparing to teach is most logically and usefully structured for the purposes of teaching, learning, and understanding.

You need to be able to demonstrate that not only do you *understand* the discipline, but also that you can create learning experiences that make these aspects of the subject matter meaningful for students—that is, help students reach that same understanding (knowledge and ability to apply). Moreover, this principle expects teachers to be able to draw on the prior knowledge and experience of their students as a means of creating meaningful learning. Finally, teachers need to demonstrate the ability and inclination to make connections between their primary discipline and other disciplines.

---

[3]Shulman, 9.

For more specific details about what the standard requires, look closely at the knowledge, skills, and dispositions presented with Principle 1.

Knowledge

- The teacher understands major concepts, assumptions, debates, processes of inquiry, and ways of knowing that are central to the discipline(s) she or he teaches.
- The teacher understands how students' conceptual frameworks and their misconceptions for an area of knowledge can influence their learning.
- The teacher can relate his or her disciplinary knowledge to other subject areas.

Dispositions

- The teacher realizes that subject matter knowledge is not a fixed body of facts but is complex and ever-evolving. She or he seeks to keep abreast of new ideas and understandings in the field.
- The teacher appreciates multiple perspectives and conveys to learners how knowledge is developed from the vantage point of the knower.
- The teacher has enthusiasm for the discipline(s) she or he teaches and sees connections to everyday life.
- The teacher is committed to continuous learning and engages in professional discourse about subject matter knowledge and children's learning of the discipline.

Performances

- The teacher effectively uses multiple representations and explanations of disciplinary concepts that capture key ideas and link them to students' prior understandings.
- The teacher can represent and use differing viewpoints, theories, ways of knowing, and methods of inquiry in his or her teaching of subject matter concepts.
- The teacher can evaluate teaching resources and curriculum materials for their comprehensiveness, accuracy, and usefulness for representing particular ideas and concepts.
- The teacher engages students in generating knowledge and testing hypotheses according to the methods of inquiry and standards of evidence used in the discipline.
- The teacher develops and uses curricula that encourage students to see, question, and interpret ideas from diverse perspectives.
- The teacher can create interdisciplinary learning experiences that allow students to integrate knowledge, skills, and methods of inquiry from several subject areas.

From these statements from Principle 1, we can pull out the following general issues, themes, or strands that need to be exhibited via your portfolio's reflection and artifacts:

- Understanding and practicing the discipline well enough to draw out of it the most important issues and skills for students to understand and be able to apply
- Viewing knowledge as an interconnected range of developing ideas that are informed and refined in the real world, as well as in the context of other disciplines
- Developing curricula and instructional activities that encourage students to see, question, and interpret ideas within the discipline and the world from diverse perspectives
- Using multiple representations and explanations of disciplinary concepts that capture key ideas and link them to students' prior understandings

ARTIFACT SELECTION

When selecting artifacts to reveal your understanding of and ability to teach your discipline(s), you should keep the following questions in mind:

1. Which documents reveal my depth of knowledge and understanding of the central concepts, tools of inquiry, and structures of the discipline?
2. Which artifacts reveal my ability to engage students actively in the knowledge and skills associated with the discipline?
3. What evidence reveals my understanding and use of the interconnections between my discipline and other disciplines to make learning meaningful for my students?
4. What artifacts reveal my ability to challenge my students to wrestle with multiple representations of knowledge within the discipline and to actively engage in thinking within the discipline?

Consider these two additional thoughts on possible artifacts:

■ No artifact should be left to stand on its own. As you saw in chapters 2 and 3, you are responsible for explaining what each artifact shows about your understanding and your abilities. Do not expect your portfolio's reviewers to interpret for you.

■ Understanding subject matter is not isolated to Principle 1. As your portfolio emerges, consider ways you can demonstrate and reinforce your Principle 1 understanding in the artifacts and reflections for other principles.

TYPES OF ARTIFACTS

For this principle, you have at least six categories of artifacts from which to select and on which to reflect:

■ *Lesson plans and unit plans*, especially those clearly revealing uses of the tools of inquiry relevant to your discipline(s), as well as development issues, student experience/knowledge levels, and attention to the potential misconceptions among your students

■ *Assessments* that ask your students not only to present remembered information but also show your expectation that students demonstrate their understanding and ability to apply that information in different situations

■ *Evaluations from cooperating teacher and student teaching supervisor* revealing your grasp of the content knowledge and, more important, your ability to present the subject matter in appropriate and effective ways for your students

■ *Documents from your own course work* including papers, tests, projects, and other assignments that reveal your deep and pedagogical understanding of your discipline(s)

■ *Journal entries* especially those that capture your reflections on other's teaching and reflections on your own teaching and learning

■ *Philosophy of education* revealing how you think about the subject you teach and how your attitude toward teaching and learning are mirrored in your classroom practice

■ (potentially) *Transcripts, test scores, and citations of achievement or honors*, though less valuable, may help document your basic grasp of the content area and your having taken courses (e.g., a letter notifying you that you had made the dean's list)

Transcripts are the least revealing of all the evidence you might present because they only document that you took a specific course and received a grade; the fact that the grade might be quite high still doesn't tell anyone much about what you know and are able to do as a result of the course. Similarly, test scores (like the subject area specialty tests required by many states) and citations of achievement are really no more telling than your transcripts. While such evidence may document exposure or even success, it does little to reveal your understanding and internalization of the subject matter you will be teaching to students.

Evidence from your teacher-preparation *and* subject matter course work is considerably more valuable for showing your understanding and application of disciplinary content. A research project you completed for a chemistry or history course could reveal your ability to think and act like a scientist or an historian. A project in which you studied elementary students' misconceptions of number or force could reveal your understanding of what you will look for in your own students' understanding. An annotated bibliography evaluating current curriculum resources in your discipline could reveal your understanding of how to evaluate resources for content accuracy and comprehensiveness. Even a test or quiz on which you did not score well could, when analyzed in an accompanying reflection, reveal how much you have come to understand about how people learn your subject matter.

However revealing artifacts from your own course work might be, remember that you not only need to demonstrate *what* you know about your discipline and *how* your discipline is practiced, but also that you know how to teach it to students. For that reason, you will want to include carefully selected instructional plans, videotapes, or other demonstrations showing the following:

- ■ Your use of inquiry appropriate to the discipline
- ■ Your design of active learning strategies that (a) involved students in the learning process, (b) built on what they already know and can do, or (c) helped students correct a misunderstanding or deepen their understanding
- ■ Your ability to integrate knowledge in one discipline with the central concepts of another discipline
- ■ Your ability to analyze student work samples

EXAMPLE ARTIFACT

Look at the following example artifact. How well does it address the expectations expressed in Principle 1?

ARTIFACT: LESSON 2–*CORDUROY*

Title of Lesson: Using *Corduroy* to build comprehension skills

Subject Area Involved: Communication arts

Performance Standards the Lesson Is Based On: State standard in communication arts; students will acquire a solid foundation, which includes knowledge of and proficiency in reading and evaluating fiction, poetry, and drama.

Materials/Resources Needed for the Lesson: The book *Corduroy*, a game called Tie It Together, sentence strips, brown paper bag, paper outline of a bear, an overhead projector

Anticipatory Set: We will begin the lesson by playing Tie It Together, a game that I made up to build student's comprehension skills. Students will determine the main idea when presented with a list of five words that have a common theme. Students will use the interpretive and synthesis level of thinking when attempting to integrate the meanings of the words and to synthesize them in relation to main ideas. Students will work together in groups to discover the main ideas. The first group to determine the common theme wins that round. The themes will be centered on the plot, characters, and ideas in the book *Corduroy*.

Goal: Students will develop and build their ability to construct meaning from interaction with text.

Objective: Given the book *Corduroy*, the game Tie it Together, and sentence strips, the student will place sentence strips in the correct order with 80% accuracy demonstrating the comprehension skill of *sequence* of events.

Communicate the Goals and Objectives: I will explain to students how important it is to understand what we read. I will explain that being able to decipher the main idea in a story line is helpful in building comprehension skills. I will also explain that we will be paying careful attention to the sequence of events in the story. By paying careful attention to the order of events, we are better able not only to predict what will happen next but also to understand the story line.

Teacher Model Explanation: I will use the directed listening, thinking activity (DLTA) instructional strategy for the book *Corduroy* to promote comprehension skills and higher order thinking. I will read the book *Corduroy* to the students, stopping at various preselected points in the text to ask questions designed to promote active thinking and learning. I will again emphasize the importance of paying attention to the order in which things occur.

Teacher-Generated Focus Questions:

1. What do you think this story will be about? (I will show the front cover only and will record students' predictions. This question is designed to build the skill of predicting outcomes.)

2. Do you think someone will come along and take him home? Followed up by, who? (I will ask this after reading the first paragraph. This is another question designed to predict outcomes.)

3. Why did Lisa and her mother walk away? (This is a factual-level question designed to elicit simple recall of information read.)

4. Why do you think that Corduroy felt sad when Lisa and her mother walked away? (I will ask this question after page 4. This question is an interpretive-level question that requires determining cause and effect and involves integrating text-based information and making inferences based on that information.)

5. Do you think Corduroy has ever seen a palace? Why or why not? (I will ask this question after page 11. This is an applicative level question that requires the student to reach beyond what is written in the text and formulate an answer based on text and personal knowledge.)

6. Why was Corduroy hiding under the covers? (I will ask this after page 18. This is an inferential question.)

7. How do you think Corduroy felt when he opened his eyes in the morning and saw Lisa standing there with a smile? (I will ask this after page 22. This is a transactive-level question, which requires the reader to imagine how Corduroy felt. The reader is required to use text, personal knowledge, and his or her own value system to answer the question.)

8. How would you feel if you were Corduroy and someone came in and selected you out of all the animals to take home and make you his very own? (This is a transactive-level question, which requires the reader to go beyond what is written in the text and empathize with the character in the story.)

Student-Generated Focus Questions: I will encourage the students to think of questions that they have based on their prior experiences and what they would guess the story may be about.

Primary Activity: Sentence strips based on the story *Corduroy*. I will provide sentence strips for the students to use in establishing sequence of events. Students will place strips in the order in which they believe the events took place. Students will be encouraged to think back over the story and begin with the first event, followed by subsequent events. Students will not be able to use the text at this time. This is a comprehension skill designed to build the student's ability to remember the order in which story events took place. Once the student feels she has successfully completed the task, she will read the story according to the sentence strips and determine if the sentence-strip story matches the original text.

Subsequent Activity: Students will be given their own sentence strips to place in the correct order. Students will place these on a brown paper bag that will become a Corduroy puppet. The title and author of the book along with the sentence strips will be placed on the back of the bag. Students will be encouraged to read the strips to make sure they make sense. Students will also be encouraged to share the story with their parents at home. Retelling is another instructional strategy that can be used to build reading comprehension skills. Students will use the bear outline to make Corduroy on the front of the bag. Students will be encouraged to use their puppet to tell the story of Corduroy.

Provision/Adaptation/Modification for Diverse Student Population: If needed, I will modify the lesson based on the needs of the student population. My students seem to have trouble with reading comprehension. For these students, I may have to help them focus on the sequence of events by pulling out main events and asking if it came before or after that event.

Closure: I will give the students a final round of the game Tie It Together. I will provide the students with these clues and and then ask them for the common theme: listening, sequencing, determining main ideas, predicting, and identifying with the character. I will give the students several opportunities to provide the correct response. The correct response is reading comprehension. I will reiterate the importance of these key skills in understanding and effectively transforming text into meaningful information.

Evaluating Student Achievement: Students will complete with 80% accuracy the correct order of the sentence strips, demonstrating their ability to establish the sequence of events.

Evaluating Teacher Effectiveness: I will consider the lesson effective if students are actively engaged in learning and demonstrate an intellectual curiosity in what is being taught as well as if I perceive that students are building comprehension skills, as demonstrated by their successful completion of the lesson's guided and independent activities.

Here we have a good artifact for an elementary teacher who must demonstrate content area knowledge in a number of areas. As one artifact, she has chosen a language arts lesson demonstrating her knowledge of literacy and children's literature (knowledge). While it would not be sufficient on its own to demonstrate content knowledge, the choice of a literacy lesson is good since literacy is one of the more important areas of elementary education.

This artifact does a good job of demonstrating "ability to make these aspects meaningful for students," the application portion of the standard. The teacher draws an explicit connection between the lesson and her state's standards and its curricular focus, addressing the "central concept" of comprehension in literacy (knowledge and performance). The teacher, however, not only deals with comprehension but also embeds multiple opportunities for students to use and reinforce higher order thinking skills related to reading comprehension (disposition). Even the language the teacher uses to categorize her activities ("predicting," "inferential," "transactive") reinforces the impression that she knows the theoretical foundation of what she is doing and consciously applies it (knowledge).

In her activities, she clearly allows students to make multiple representations of their understanding on a number of cognitive levels and via different kinds of performances (performance). The activities engage her students in generating knowledge and testing hypotheses according to the methods of inquiry and standards of evidence used in the discipline (knowledge and disposition). Moreover she gives evidence of her ability to develop and use curricula that encourage students to see, question, and interpret ideas from diverse perspectives (disposition).

All in all, this is a powerful artifact, revealing to any reviewer a solid impression that this teacher knows about elementary literacy instruction, its theoretical foundations, and its practical applications.

WRITING A REFLECTION FOR PRINCIPLE 1

At this point, you have selected from among many possibilities what you believe to be strong artifacts of your own understanding of content and of your ability to make that content meaningful for your students. Now you need to compose your reflection statement explaining to someone else what it all means and how it reveals your understanding of the principle. Where should you start? First, you should revisit chapter 3 to refresh your understanding of the purpose, structure, and contents of a reflective statement:

1. Identification of context
2. Observation and description of artifact
3. Application of theories or principles of effective practice
4. Identification, analysis, and interpretation of causes and effect
5. Projection from observations toward problem solving and lifelong learning

After the first two activities on this list, you should find yourself citing/applying specific theories and theorists. Moreover, you ought to be using the language of the principle and its knowledge, skills, and dispositions.

Next you should ask yourself some questions to get your thoughts going. The following questions are constructed to apply to teaching artifacts as well as to artifacts of your own learning:

1. Why did I decide to teach (study) this content? What makes it so important? What concept, tool of inquiry, or structure of my discipline was I teaching (studying)? Did the lesson (project) help (me or) my students learn to perform like adults in the real world? Did my lesson (project) engage students (me) in doing real work (versus school work)? To what degree did it help resolve students' (my) misconceptions, preconceptions, or naive understandings? To what degree did it create cognitive dissonance?

2. How did I know whether the students (I) had the prerequisite knowledge and skills to be successful in the lesson (project)? In what ways did this lesson (project) build on students' (my) prior knowledge or address students' (my) preconceptions? What alternative representations did I use (or discover) in teaching (studying) this concept?

3. In what ways was the instructional strategy (tool of inquiry) I selected appropriate to the subject matter I was teaching (studying)? In what ways did my selected strategy promote critical thinking or problem solving in the students (me)? In what ways did my teaching (studying) reveal structure in my discipline?

4. What did I learn from teaching (studying) this concept? How will I teach (study) this concept the next time? Why? What evidence do I have to support my predictions of what I will do next time?

Combining responses to these sorts of questions with the more general guidance on analytic reflections that you encountered in chapter 3 will help you to demonstrate the depth of your understanding of the Principle.

Look at the following Principle 1 reflection by an elementary education candidate. As you read it, compare what the candidate writes to what you have learned about Principle 1 and the expectations it sets for your own portfolio.

REFLECTION ON PRINCIPLE 1

Command of subject matter is an area of extreme importance. Certification in elementary education requires a general knowledge base of all the core subjects. It also requires the ability to take the knowledge base that you have and create meaningful and powerful learning experiences for students. I feel well equipped to take on the task of providing these experiences as well as impressing upon students how this knowledge ties into the world at large. I have gained a general knowledge base from my core general education classes, such as advanced mathematics classes, biology, physical science, astronomy, foreign and United States history, art, music, psychology, sociology, and many business classes. I have consistently maintained a 4.0 GPA in all my education classes. I have passed the PRAXIS elementary education examination with a 199 out of a possible 200 points. My background, combined with my education, has given me the knowledge base I need to identify student needs and provide effective lesson plans that prepare students to be responsible citizens.

Since I cannot present my depth of understanding about all subject areas in this first part of my portfolio, I have chosen to focus here on parts of two subject areas: mathematics (specifically graphing) and reading comprehension. I have tried to discuss what I know about other subjects of the elementary school curriculum in other parts of my portfolio.

MATHEMATICS KNOWLEDGE

One of the important concepts for students in mathematics and the sciences to understand is that graphs symbolically represent data collected. Behind the idea of graphing is still another important concept for students: data can be sorted and grouped. Graphing is an important concept and skill in its own right, but its real importance is that it provides a tool for answering students' questions about data. When I was presented the opportunity to introduce a group of first graders to data collection and graphing, I worried that the ideas of data, graphing, and classifying would confuse them. In my Psychology of Teaching and Learning class, I learned about Piaget's studies of young children and how concrete youngsters tend to be in their thinking. I interpreted this finding as meaning that I needed to move students in small steps from the concrete to the symbolic when I introduced them to graphing. Please see artifact 1 for my lesson plan and my reflection on its impact and how I would modify it in the future.

When I interpreted the results of the graphing lesson, I found that because I used concrete examples of student's own choices, they were able to transfer their knowledge from the concrete to the symbolic. Students were engaged in the lesson because they made choices so the outcome of the survey was meaningful to them. I related it to real-world experiences by providing examples of graphs from newspapers, business reports, stock reports, and the principal's newsletter. Although students at this age cannot relate to most of these examples, they can see the value in learning the concept.

LANGUAGE ARTS KNOWLEDGE

Before talking about a lesson I taught, I want to talk about my philosophy of teaching and learning language arts. You will find more detail in the artifact itself.

Language arts entails providing a language-rich environment where I will provide meaningful instruction that students can use to extend their thinking and build their own knowledge. Language arts instruction includes reading, writing, listening, speaking, thinking, and reflecting. These need to be taught through authentic learning experiences so that students learn to apply their skills to real-world experiences.

Of this range of language arts skills, I am focusing in this reflection on just reading comprehension. Reading is the cornerstone of any language arts program. Reading touches every student in every subject area. It is crucial that from an early age and on, students are taught good word-analysis skills, good vocabulary skills, and good comprehension skills.

Based on what I have learned from my research into reading processes, I plan to read aloud to students in my classroom; modeling to children increases their reading comprehension, their vocabularies (both spoken and written), as well as their knowledge of print. I will also use quality literature in my instruction to create interest and build meaning for students. I believe it is important to provide meaningful activities that integrate reading, writing, listening, thinking, speaking, reflecting, and observing. Some of the ways I will develop a strong reading base with my students will be to teach mapping skills, decoding/encoding skills, word-analysis skills, sight-word strategies, phonics, context clues, and how to use the dictionary. I believe that daily-sustained silent reading is extremely important. Reading silently just 20 minutes each day can increase student's vocabulary by as much as 2,000 words annually.

In my Foundations of Literacy Instruction class, I learned the importance of teaching students to be strategic readers. Teaching students strategies to monitor their own reading comprehension is a valuable learning tool that they can use for a lifetime. Through the research project I did in this class and my field experiences in elementary school classrooms, I think I am developing a good understanding of how the reading process works and how to teach youngsters to be confident, competent, and strategic readers. I have included my research project as artifact 4. From my research, I have learned that successful readers do the following:

1. Clarify the purpose of reading to determine what strategy to use
2. Activate what they already know about the topic
3. Notice clues in the text to help them identify the main idea and distinguish main ideas from secondary ideas and details
4. Compare what they are reading to what they already know about the topic
5. Monitor their comprehension by paraphrasing, summarizing, self-questioning, and note taking
6. Draw inferences by interpreting, predicting, and generalizing to other situations

My reading comprehension lesson tries to teach students to use many of these characteristics of successful readers.

My lesson (see lesson 2 in my artifacts[4]) was designed to teach students strategies to actively monitor their own reading comprehension. I kept students engaged by activating prior knowledge, gaining students' interest, and offering activities designed to provide meaningful learning as well as real-world applications. The specific strategies that I taught were synthesizing the main idea, predicting outcomes, questioning, sequencing, and identifying with the main character. Students not only need to be taught reading comprehension strategies, but also when and why to use the strategies.

The strength of the lesson is that it is progressive and that it kept students' attention. It was progressive because it began by explaining concepts and providing practice and then allowed the students to apply the concepts. The lesson was engaging by requiring students to take an active part in learning. Students learned to apply specific reading comprehension strategies, such as practicing good listening skills, synthesizing the main idea, sequencing, and predicting. Questioning was designed to promote higher order thinking skills.

I began the lesson by informing students that we were going to be talking about reading comprehension. I went on to explain what reading comprehension is and some of the strategies that we use to improve reading comprehension. If I were to teach this lesson again, I would not introduce the lesson that way. Most students could not relate to the word *comprehension*, and even though I defined it, I think it was outside of a first grader's normal vocabulary. Another area that I would change involves the Tie It Together game. I designed the game to improve students' ability to synthesize the main idea. I gave students five words, and they were to find what the words have in common. Since many of my first-grade students were still emergent readers, I relearned the importance of providing students with visual clues to identify new words. My game did not make use of visual clues. If I were to teach the lesson again to first graders, I would adapt the game to include picture clues. Overall, the lesson went well, and the students were engaged in learning. In the following days and weeks, I noted that many of the students were using the strategies I had taught them to help them with reading in the classroom.

In the future, I will continue to grow as a professional. I plan to continue my education so that I may gain additional knowledge, which will benefit my students. I still need to develop my toolbox of strategies for engaging and supporting the development of emergent readers. In many ways, I still need to better understand the process developing readers go through to develop the ability to read. Also, I need to better understand how to incorporate and support reading in all the content areas so students will see the importance and usefulness of reading in their daily lives. I belong to a variety of professional organizations, such as the International Reading Association and the Association for Supervision and Curriculum Development, and I plan to remain actively involved in those organizations so that I am able to learn and share ideas with my colleagues. I have attended various educational conferences and plan to continue seeking out workshops and conferences that are designed to promote my ability to develop meaningful learning experiences for my students in reading, mathematics, and the other subject areas in the elementary school curriculum.

Now that you have studied the example reflection and artifact for Principle 1, let's analyze the example in detail. Specifically, we are going to analyze the example first in terms of its success as a reflection and then in terms of its success in meeting the expectations of Principle 1.

Go back to chapter 3 and locate the *generic reflection rubric.* Compare what the candidate writes to the descriptions of a "good" reflection and a "weak" reflection. We suggest

---

[4]Of the several artifacts identified in this reflection, Lesson 2—*Corduroy* is the only one reproduced here. The teacher uses this lesson to demonstrate other standards as well, such as Principle 6 (communication) and Principle 8 (assessment).

you identify words and phrases throughout the rubric that parallel your perceptions of the example's strengths and weaknesses. After developing your own sense of the example, compare your sense to the discussions that follows:

Contextual information and awareness of professional standards of practice. The first paragraph paraphrases the two major ideas of the principle: command of subject matter and ability to create meaningful learning for students. The paragraph goes on to provide third-party testimony (transcript, grade-point average, exit test score), which could be verified within artifacts. Finally, the opening paragraph acknowledges the scope of the principle and clarifies which parts of subject matter this reflection will address (graphing in mathematics and reading comprehension). Later, when introducing the reading section of the reflection, the teacher provides a specific explanation of his or her philosophy and background in reading instruction to establish some context for understanding the artifacts. More specific information about the artifacts is located (or referenced) in the body of the reflection.

Observation and description of artifact (experience or document). Between the reflection and the lesson plan, the author provides considerable information about the context of the teaching events. These details help us get into the mind of the teacher as well as understand what is going on in the artifacts described. Such detail is a hallmark of a good reflection.

Application of theories or principles of effective practice. We learn considerably more in this reflection about the candidate's understanding of reading than we do in the discussion of graphing in mathematics. Still, the teacher's inclination to apply theory is clearly revealed as she or he offers a rationale for the approach taken in the lessons. The reflection would be even stronger had the author made reference to specific theories or theorists on reading (versus more implied references in terms of the college course in which he or she studied the theories) and on mathematics; a reviewer is, however, likely to find convincing evidence here regarding the candidate's understanding of reading comprehension.

Identification, analysis, and interpretation of cause and effect. The author provides good information about how the lesson unfolded. Of particular interest is the analysis of the appropriateness of instructional choices for the age group being taught. Here the teacher reveals reflective ability as well as some application of theoretical knowledge. The reflection could be strengthened with more information about how the students actually performed, particularly since the lesson plan identifies specific criteria by which the teacher would determine the lesson's impact (i.e., "80% accuracy in sequencing sentence strips") versus the author's assertions that the lesson "went well."

Problem solving and lifelong learning. The reflection provides quite specific information about what would be changed the next time and why. The teacher even offers one specific area in which she or he needs professional growth:

> I still need to develop my toolbox of strategies for engaging and supporting the development of emergent readers. In many ways, I still need to better understand the process developing readers go through to develop the ability to read. Also, I need to better understand how to incorporate and support reading in all the content areas so students will see the importance and usefulness of reading in their daily lives.

This analysis clearly demonstrates the teacher's critical self-evaluation.

All in all, this reflection substantially meets the criteria for a good reflection. A reviewer would have no trouble believing this teacher's understanding of content and his or her ability to use that knowledge to create meaningful learning opportunities for students.

Now, let's apply the *Principle 1 rubric*. Read the example once again, this time comparing what the candidate writes to the descriptions under "Meets the Standard" and "Not Yet Meeting the Standard." It is important for you to remember we are trying to make *a holistic* determination about this candidate's apparent understanding of subject matter. Again, after drawing your own inferences, compare your opinions to those expressed in the following table.

Meets the Standard	*Not Yet Meeting the Standard*
• The candidate demonstrates strong knowledge of relevant central concepts and tools of inquiry as evidenced by performance in college content course work as well as in lesson preparation.	• The candidate demonstrates a basic command of the central concepts and tools of inquiry in the discipline(s).
• Artifacts demonstrate the candidate's ability to make connections to other disciplines and to student's prior knowledge and life experiences, even though instruction frequently appears only loosely connected to the real world.	• However, artifacts tend to emphasize knowledge acquired rather than conceptual understanding. The candidate's work may demonstrate flaws or gaps in disciplinary understanding.
• Although the candidate may assert knowledge of alternative ways the discipline may be organized and possibly even personal skills in the means by which evidence and argument are evaluated, instructional artifacts do not necessarily implement this knowledge.	• There is little or no evidence of the candidate's awareness of alternative organizations for the discipline or the means by which evidence and argument are evaluated.
• Instructional artifacts reveal a candidate with a competent repertoire of examples, explanations, and analogies, as well as a candidate able to engage students in generating knowledge and testing hypotheses in ways appropriate to the discipline.	• There is little or no evidence of teaching content in a meaningful context that connects to students' interests and lives or to connect subject matter within and across disciplines.
• The candidate demonstrates awareness of frequently held student preconceptions and misconceptions as well as an ability to implement strategies designed to affect misconceptions.	• Artifacts tend to reveal a candidate with a limited repertoire of examples, explanations, and analogies, as well as a candidate with little (to no) inclination in engaging students in generating their own knowledge or in testing their own hypotheses.
	• There is little or no evidence that the candidate is aware of frequently held preconceptions or misconceptions.

In both the reflection and the example artifact, the author identifies what he or she believes to be central concepts. In the case of reading comprehension, he or she reveals an appreciation for the structure of the discipline (i.e., where reading comprehension fits into reading in general and where reading fits into the overall discipline of literacy). Grades and test scores support the author's command of subject matter. This beginning teacher seems to be aware of the need to engage students through appeals to their interests and their prior knowledge. We see no overt evidence of a teacher able to make interdisciplinary connections; however, the lesson reveals a teacher aiming for conceptual understanding versus simple knowledge. The reading comprehension lesson especially is intended to teach students to predict, to test, and to evaluate. This reflection offers evidence of a competent repertoire—though limited—of strategies for teaching the content; still, a reviewer would want to look elsewhere in the portfolio (e.g., in the reflection for Principle 4, instructional strategies) before making a final determination.

The author does a solid job of describing and analyzing the strategies selected and recognizes how he or she needs to develop alternative means in recognition of students' development. We see a beginning teacher apparently more aware of his or her own misconceptions than we do one aware of students' misconceptions. Still, within the discussion of the concepts being taught, the teacher offers some implied understanding of the potential difficulties students might have engaging with the content and seems ready to apply that understanding when creating and refining her or his lessons.

Certainly, one would like to see in the reflection some more specific evidence that this teacher has studied and can apply the ways in which young learners misunderstand the sequencing of concepts. One cannot tell if this teacher has a disposition toward seeing knowledge as "ever-evolving" as is described in the dispositions for Principle 1. The teacher doesn't specifically reveal enthusiasm for either mathematics or reading comprehension although he or she is interested enough in the subjects to appreciate their value and the value of individual skills and concepts. Although the author does not overtly state his or her enthusiasm, one might infer, at least, a dedication to the subjects and certainly a dedication to his or her students' learning.

Based on the rubric, does this teacher meet the standard and demonstrate readiness to enter the classroom in terms of subject matter knowledge? Yes. The *preponderance of evidence* (as revealed by both the reflection rubric and the Principle 1 rubric) shows a beginner who possesses a command of his or her subject matter and some facility with teaching it to young children.

SUMMARY

Significant evidence exists to prove that deep content knowledge is essential to good teaching. It is not hard to understand, then, why content understanding is listed as the first principle of good teaching. Principle 1 demands that a teacher have a solid understanding of the content area(s) he or she is charged to teach. But knowledge is not enough; the ultimate proof is in the teaching, in what the teacher emphasizes in lessons, and in how he or she creates opportunities for students to learn. Your portfolio must demonstrate both your own knowledge and your ability to teach it to others.

Here are some questions your reflections and artifacts must answer about your understanding of the subject matter and your abilities to teach it to students:

1. Do I articulate evidence of my understanding of major concepts, assumptions, debates, processes of inquiry, and ways of knowing that are central to my discipline(s)?
   - Do I represent and use differing viewpoints, theories, ways of knowing and methods of inquiry in my teaching of subject matter concepts? Do I effectively use multiple representations and explanations of disciplinary concepts that capture key ideas and link them to my students' prior understandings?
   - Do I engage students in generating knowledge and testing hypotheses according to the methods of inquiry and standards of evidence used in my discipline(s)?

2. Do I reveal evidence of understanding how my students' preconceptions and misconceptions influence their learning?
   - Do I evaluate teaching resources and curriculum materials for their comprehensiveness, accuracy, and usefulness for representing particular ideas and concepts? (You will take up this question again in Principle 7.)

3. Do I create interdisciplinary learning experiences that facilitate my students' integration of knowledge, skills, and methods of inquiry from several subdisciplines within my field and from several different subject areas?

4. Do I reveal a belief in the complex and ever-evolving nature of knowledge?
   - Do I reveal evidence of my appreciation of multiple perspectives and my ability to convey to learners how knowledge is developed from the vantage point of the knower?
   - Do I connect my discipline(s) to students' and adults' everyday lives?
   - Do I develop and use curricula that encourage my students to see, to question, and to interpret ideas from diverse perspectives?

5. Do I reveal evidence of keeping abreast of new ideas and understandings in my field(s)? (You will take up this question again in Principle 9.)

6. Do I reveal enthusiasm for my discipline(s)?

DISCUSSION QUESTIONS

1. Define *central concepts*, *tools of inquiry*, and *structures of the discipline*. How do these components interact to define a content area?
2. How can a teacher make content *meaningful* to students?
3. How can an educator determine the most important parts of a content area to teach? How can an educator determine the stumbling blocks for students within a content area?
4. Look up Shulman's conception of "pedagogical content knowledge." How does it differ from other forms of content knowledge? Why is it important to teaching? What is the value of relating one discipline to another (i.e., interdisciplinary teaching)?
5. Why is it valuable to help students approach learning from multiple perspectives? From what perspectives might any given discipline be approached?
6. Why is it important for educators to continue to learn more about their disciplines and the teaching of those disciplines?
7. What has enthusiasm got to do with effectively teaching a content area?

Implementing INTASC Principle 2 in Your Portfolio

5

You should examine yourself daily. If you find faults, you should correct them. When you find none, you should try even harder.

Xi Zhi

Woichek sifted through a stack of lesson plans from his high school student teaching in social studies. His eyes settled on one particular lesson and the attached reflection. It would be a good document to show his understanding of learning theories. In this one, he specifically applied Bruner's constructivist theory to create a situation that would allow his students to determine the issues they would be addressing in the class. He then developed the means and approach for the students to explore *their issues* that would allow him to present and reinforce content knowledge by having the students gathering, simplifying, and manipulating information and phenomena and then generating new ways of explaining the phenomena. The students wanted to engage the issue of race and diversity since their community was becoming increasingly diverse. In that context, they were interested and empowered and, therefore, ready to learn. In the process Woichek provided the students multiple opportunities to explore different racial groups from around the world, to place them on a map, and to think about the location of the groups and their respective skin colors. The students pulled in geographic knowledge and biology to determine that skin color is an issue of location relative to the equator and so tied to amount of sunshine and melatonin production in the skin rather than issues of intelligence, ability, and values. The lesson was his first real application of constructivist theory, and his students' success and active involvement convinced him to take the extra time needed to infuse constructivism as much as possible into his lessons.

QUESTIONS FOR CONSIDERATION

- What theories of learning and development have helped you understand student learning and behavior?
- How do learning and development impact how students learn and how a teacher teaches?
- How may educators use their understanding of student readiness to improve student learning?
- What part do teachers play in their students' intellectual, social, and personal development?
- What may a teacher learn from patterns of student errors that may be useful in better facilitating students' learning?
- How may children's development differ and yet still be within normal expectations? How can a teacher deal with differences in development and readiness when preparing to teach?

Good teachers are incredibly observant and flexible. They draw on their knowledge of each student's development, experience, intelligences, learning preferences, culture, and much more to ensure each child has the opportunity to learn to her or his potential. That's no easy task, but it is what good educators do every day. While preservice teachers don't have the same depth of knowledge and experience as veteran teachers, they still need to demonstrate their knowledge of child and adolescent development and theories of learning, as well as their ability to consider these important resources when creating learning opportunities for their students. Your portfolio must give evidence that you both know the developmental and learning theories and consciously apply that knowledge when considering classroom challenges and when creating learning activities, classroom management plans, lessons, units, and assessments for the classroom.

Teaching is a complex task that involves much problem defining and problem solving. Across the range of artifacts and reflections you place in your portfolio, you must demonstrate your ability and willingness to put your understanding of student learning and development to work toward clarifying and solving the complex problems inherent in the teaching and learning environment.

UNDERSTANDING PRINCIPLE 2

Principle 2: The teacher understands how children learn and develop, and can provide learning opportunities that support their intellectual, social, and personal development.

Principle 2 asks for evidence of two things:

1. Understanding *of theories of learning and child/adolescent development*
2. The ability to use that understanding to *provide learning opportunities that support the intellectual, social, and personal development of all students*

Principle 2 and Principle 3 work together to address the learning of all children from two perspectives: the former paints a picture of how groups of learners at different ages and stages of development and cognitive makeup tend to develop and approach learning; the latter focuses on individuals within the group making finer distinctions about individual students' approaches to learning, experiences, abilities. Principle 2, then, expects you to know broadly how students learn and develop and to apply this knowledge consciously in the creation of developmentally appropriate learning opportunities for your students. In other words, Principle 2 expects you to reveal your understanding of where your students have come from before entering your classroom and where they might be headed after they leave your classroom.

LEARNING THEORIES

"By making them write, as well as discuss, I was able to reinforce what they had learned in a concrete way, and I had a nice assessment of what they learned and what they still did not understand."

Much research and theory is available to support teachers as they endeavor to facilitate learning among their students. Learning theories and their proponents (from behaviorism to information processing to social constructivism to theories about the very nature of intelligence) have developed a foundation that speaks broadly about how children and adolescents learn. Theories, however, are derived from large numbers of cases rather than the specific learning behaviors of an individual student or even a single classroom of students. Thus, learning and development theories propose general tendencies for how students learn and grow and broad principles upon which teachers may create the best opportunities for students to learn.

In your portfolio artifacts and reflections, you are expected to reveal explicitly your understanding of the theoretical foundations of learning and development and your conscious application of these theories in the context of your classroom. Context here is a key issue. You must explore the concepts you are trying to teach, weighing them against the ways your students learn, to determine where students might have difficulty and where misconceptions might occur. Then you must show how you used this knowledge to determine how the target concepts might best be taught.

"It is difficult to motivate high school students, so a teacher has to find out what makes them interested. Wlodkowski talks about the motivating ability of moral issues related to real phenomena. This gives students a sense of power and involvement that makes them interested in the content."

Is direct instruction most appropriate? Perhaps cooperative groups and social learning might be better given the complexity of the issues being taught. Or given the nature of the students in your class, maybe a more constructivist exploration would be most effective. Whatever your ultimate choice, your portfolio reviewer should see you wrestling with the content to determine the best approach and then *consciously* applying the theoretical framework to developing learning opportunities and in evaluating the resulting lessons, activities, units, assessments, and so forth.

CHILD AND ADOLESCENT DEVELOPMENT

Principle 2 also expects you to reveal your understanding of intellectual, social, and personal development in a number of domains (cognitive, social, emotional, moral, and physical). As with learning theory, you must *consciously* apply theoretical and practical knowledge of developmental patterns in creating learning that not only teaches content but also helps students develop their complex reasoning skills, their social (interpersonal) skills, their physical skills, their character (moral), and their personal (intrapersonal) skills.

"These courses, by helping me understand the nature of high school learners, what motivates them, and how they may or may not be comfortable with Piaget's formal operations or abstract principles, gave me a solid theoretical foundation on which to build my lessons and units."

Again, much research has been done in these areas. Development theorists (Piaget, Erickson, Kohlberg, Krathwohl, etc.) have given us a specific—albeit sometimes contradictory—body of theory to help us understand how students construct knowledge, acquire skills, and develop habits of mind. Knowing the stages or phases that come before and after the age/development of your students can help you tailor instruction and adjust expectations for individuals. Knowledge of development helps determine the method and context for learning.

WHAT ARE THE IMPLICATIONS OF THIS KNOWLEDGE BASE FOR MY PORTFOLIO?

In your portfolio you must be able to document a working knowledge of relevant theories/theorists and show how you consciously use that knowledge to build lessons, instructional activities, and assessments. Your reflections, journal entries, and commentaries must draw explicitly from these theorists and theories as both a source for instructional designs and actions and for reflecting on and modifying instruction after the fact. Your lesson design and classroom management choices must also clearly exhibit your consideration of and reflection on these theories and their practical application to your specific students' learning needs. Your documentation should reveal your ability to use formal and informal assessment data and personal interaction with your students to determine their developmental level and favored approaches to learning. It should also reveal your ability to use what you know about your students to judge whether or not the content, activities, and strategies you are employing are developmentally appropriate. Furthermore, you must also exhibit your ability to encourage students to monitor and reflect on their own learning, as well as your ability to access that assessment information and use it to refine, modify, and/or redirect your instruction.

Principle 2, then, begs for a rich understanding of students and how they learn and develop. Let's review the knowledge, skills, and dispositions presented with Principle 2:

Knowledge

- The teacher understands how learning occurs—how students construct knowledge, acquire skills, and develop habits of mind—and knows how to use instructional strategies that promote student learning.
- The teacher understands how students' physical, social, emotional, moral, and cognitive development influences learning and knows how to address these factors when making instructional decisions.
- The teacher is aware of expected developmental progressions and ranges of individual variation within each domain (physical, social, emotional, moral, and cognitive), can identify levels of readiness in learning, and understands how development in any one domain may affect performance in others.

Dispositions

- The teacher appreciates individual variation within each area of development, shows respect for the diverse talents of all learners, and is committed to help them develop self-confidence and competence.
- The teacher is disposed to use students' strengths as a basis for growth and their errors as an opportunity for learning.

Performances

- The teacher assesses individual and group performance in order to design instruction that meets learners' current needs in each domain (cognitive, social, emotional, moral, and physical) and that leads to the next level of development.
- The teacher stimulates student reflection on prior knowledge and links new ideas to already familiar ideas, making connections to students' experiences; providing opportunities for active engagement, manipulation, and testing of ideas and materials; and encouraging students to assume responsibility for shaping their learning tasks.

■ The teacher accesses students' thinking and experiences as a basis for instructional activities by, for example, encouraging discussion, listening and responding to group interaction, and eliciting samples of student thinking orally and in writing.

From these statements, we can distill the following six issues that need to be addressed in your reflection and the artifacts you choose:

■ Applying developmental theory (physical, social, emotional, moral, and cognitive) consciously in the instructional decision-making process
■ Showing respect for the diverse talents of all learners and a commitment to helping them develop self-confidence
■ Assessing students' prior knowledge and experience and using students' strengths as a basis for growth and their errors as an opportunity for learning
■ Stimulating student reflection on prior knowledge and linking new ideas to already familiar ideas
■ Providing opportunities for active engagement, manipulation, and testing of ideas and materials, and encouraging students to assume responsibility for shaping their learning tasks
■ Encouraging discussion, listening and responding to group interaction, and eliciting samples of student thinking orally and in writing.

At a minimum, your reflection and artifacts ought to address some combination of these issues (though it is not likely you will deal with all of them).

ARTIFACT SELECTION

When deciding which artifacts to include in your portfolio, you must ask yourself at least the following questions:

1. Which artifact(s) reveal my understanding of student learning and development?
2. Which artifact(s) reveal my appreciation for student developmental differences and learning styles as beginning points for developing lessons and activities?
3. Which artifacts show that I know how to find out about students' prior knowledge and experience and translate that into meaningful learning opportunities?
4. Which pieces of my work show that I am conscious of the various domains of student development and my ability to build instruction to support student growth in each domain?
5. Which artifacts reveal my ability to give my students a role in developing instruction as a means of individualizing instruction, promoting self-awareness, and enhancing their self-confidence?
6. Which artifact(s) show my ability to encourage discussion, listen and respond to group interaction, and elicit samples of student thinking orally and in writing?

TYPES OF ARTIFACTS

As sources for documenting your knowledge and skills relevant to development and learning theory, the following categories of artifacts will be particularly fruitful:

■ *Lesson plans and unit plans* clearly revealing attention to development issues, student experience/knowledge levels, meaning construction, student engagement, and adaptations for diverse learners
■ *Assessments* (both formal and informal) revealing your ability to gather meaningful and useful information about student knowledge and development and your use of this information/data to build meaningful learning experiences for diverse students

■ *Reflections and journal entries* showing your reflection before and after instruction, especially reflection informed by theories and theorists, leading to thoughtful planning for future instruction or professional growth

■ *Essays or projects* from professional courses exhibiting your understanding of development and learning theories

■ *Case studies* revealing your application of theoretical knowledge to interpret student behavior and achievement and form plans based on appropriate theoretical and practical knowledge

■ *Evaluations* from your cooperating teacher and clinical experience supervisor revealing others' recognition of your ability apply appropriate theory to classroom practice

EXAMPLE ARTIFACT

Now let's review an artifact and reflect on what it reveals about the teacher's knowledge, dispositions, and performance skills relevant to Principle 2. The lesson plan that follows was one of several artifacts offered to document one teacher's having met the expectations of the principle.

LESSON PLAN FOR CHEMISTRY IN THE COMMUNITY

Level: High School

Unit: Petroleum

Lesson: Exxon *Valdez* Oil Spill

Objectives:

1. Students will be able to express chemistry principles evident in media, explain how they are being used, and determine whether such principles are being used correctly.
2. Students will be able to analyze opposing viewpoints presented in visual and written forms for accuracy and bias.
3. Students will be able to apply their knowledge of chemistry principles to draw conclusions from various presentations by comparing and evaluating their content and use of scientific facts/concepts.
4. Students will be able to express and support their findings orally and in writing.

Materials:

Exxon *Valdez* video

Copies of Web page, www.exxonvaldez.org

Teaching Sequence:

1. Lead discussion of students' knowledge of oil spills and their potential effects on the environment.
   What do we already know about the Exxon *Valdez* oil spill, in particular? What are some chemical properties at work in such an incident?
2. Have students watch the movie (22 minutes) with the following questions in mind (on handout):
   a. What principles of chemistry are presented in the video?
   b. How is scientific information presented in the video?

     c. What is the perspective of the producers of the video?

     d. How would you rate the reliability of the information/perspective presented in the video? Why?

3. Discuss the movie.

     a. Make sure students understand the process that occurred after the spill: oil recovery and cleanup, including bioremediation; wildlife rescue; long-term impact assessment.

     b. Ask students to assess the impact of the spill based on the information given in the movie.

     c. Ask students if their opinions of oil spills changed in light of the movie.

     d. Ask the students who produced the movie and if this has any impact on their response to it.

4. Have students read the Web article.

5. Discuss the article and ask students the following questions:

     a. How would you assess the impact of the spill based on the information given in the article?

     b. What principles of chemistry are presented in the article?

     c. How is scientific information presented in the article?

     d. Has your opinion of oil spills changed in light of the article?

     e. Who produced the article and does this have any impact on your response to it?

     f. How would you compare and contrast the viewpoints presented in the video and article?

     g. How might the video have been different if it had been produced by the organization producing the article?

6. Assess student learning by asking students to complete the following freewrite: How does one's purpose determine one's approach to presenting "the facts" of one's case?

Accommodations, Modifications, and Adaptations: For students with limited language proficiency, have another student read the focus questions and Web article to the students. Monitor student participation and check with special-needs students to ensure they comprehend the materials before going on. In special instances, allow students requiring more time to have access to materials ahead of time for early viewing and to preexpose students to the concepts. Allow students with difficulty writing to dictate their freewrite or give them to the teacher orally.

    This artifact contains evidence to support the teacher's case for having met the expectations expressed in Principle 2. The objectives outlined in the lesson are appropriate for high schoolers and challenge the students to employ higher level thinking skills. Depending on the time of year or the level of the students, the lesson is heavily scaffolded (one might argue, too heavily scaffolded) to guide students in thinking about the source materials. The teacher appears to understand the social and cognitive development of his or her students and the influence these have on learning—hence the inclusion of both Web-based and video texts to which the students must respond, as well as the sociomoral issues the lesson engages. Moreover, the inclusion of written and discussion components in the instructional activities address the understanding of how the social aspects of learning may be utilized and the value of "writing to think" among adolescents (i.e., having students write as a means of making thinking more concrete and generating reflection on ideas gathered from sources). The lesson indicates to some degree the teacher's willingness to encourage discussion and group interaction, as well as student thinking via discussion and in writing.

In another respect, the lesson shows the teacher's ability to individualize instruction, promote self-awareness, and enhance students' self-confidence. The use of both written and video components allows students with different strengths an opportunity to engage with the materials in meaningful ways and to express their personal understanding and findings in a safe forum. The use of specific questions supports all learners because it helps students with underdeveloped abilities focus their attention on specific issues and look for key words or topics in the source material. The lesson also asks students to apply their content knowledge to real-world situations, in this case the evaluation of propaganda using relevant content knowledge.

The preceding example addresses several areas within the expectations set for Principle 2. For example, the teacher appears to do the following:

- Appreciates "individual variation within each area of development, shows respect for the diverse talents of all learners"
- "Stimulates student reflection on prior knowledge and links new ideas to already familiar ideas; making connections to students' experiences; providing opportunities for active engagement, manipulation, and testing of ideas and materials; and encouraging students to assume responsibility for shaping their learning tasks"
- "Accesses students' thinking and experiences as a basis for instructional activities by, for example, encouraging discussion, listening and responding to group interaction, and eliciting samples of student thinking orally and in writing"

A reviewer would like to see more attention to all of the developmental domains, as well as more attention to assessment as an instructional tool. More evidence of accessing and using student prior experience to develop lessons would also be valuable to fully address the issues inherent in the principle.

WRITING A REFLECTION FOR PRINCIPLE 2

Now let's look at the reflection accompanying the previous artifact. How does it work as a reflection, and how well does it support the case for the teacher having met the expectations outlined in Principle 2?

RATIONALE FOR PRINCIPLE 2: HUMAN DEVELOPMENT AND LEARNING

Principle 2 states that teachers need to understand how children learn and develop, and they must be able to provide learning opportunities supporting intellectual, social, and personal development. Humans develop in much the same way but not always to the same level or at the same rate. Cognitive skills, social skills, and morality may vary from student to student and from group to group. I try to use this knowledge to help me cope with student behavior and to help me build lessons that will fit my students' capabilities and also challenge them.

In my professional course work, I had several classes that addressed the topic of student learning and development. These courses are listed on my transcript (*Artifact 1*):

Introduction to Learners and Learning, Adolescent Psychology, Psychology of Teaching and Learning, Psychology of the Exceptional Child, and Curriculum and Methods of Teaching Physical Science (Sec Ed 240). I earned an "A" in Ed Psych 312, Psychology of Teaching and Learning. Topics covered in this class included learning and cognitive processes, knowledge construction, higher level thinking skills and various theories of learning, including behaviorist and social-cognitive views. These courses—by helping me understand the nature of high school learners, what motivates them, and how they may or may not be comfortable with Piaget's formal operations or abstract principles—gave me a solid theoretical foundation on which to build my lessons and units. This knowledge was really refined by the Curriculum and Methods of Teaching Physical Science course, which gave me more specific information related to science instruction, as well as practical tools relevant to knowledge construction and discovery learning in the sciences. Though I do not view these models of teaching as complete pictures of how to teach science, I do believe that much of value can be applied from them.

I have done several groups of lessons based on the learning cycle, including my introduction to the gas laws lesson (*Artifact 5*), a learning cycle exercise using syringes with rubber stoppers to study Boyle's law, which states the relationship between pressure and volume for an ideal gas. My supervising teacher confirms in his supervisory reports that my instructional methods are appropriate for teaching high school science (*Artifact 6*). One will note his specific interest in and approval of my use of a variety of inquiry and cooperative education techniques during my student teaching role in his classes.

In my Chemistry in the Community class (the lower level chemistry course), we concluded our unit on petroleum with two activities intended to reinforce student learning by asking students to apply their knowledge in real-world situations. The first was the Exxon *Valdez* Oil Spill Lesson (*Artifact 12*), which asked students to apply their knowledge of the chemistry of petroleum to interpret and critique propaganda about the oil spill in video and Web-based texts. This critical thinking activity asked students not only to think chemically but also to use their moral judgment. It is difficult to motivate high school students, so a teacher has to find out what makes them interested. Wlodkowski talks about the motivating ability of moral issues related to real phenomena. This gives students a sense of power and involvement that makes them interested in the content. In the activity, I tried to bring out what students had already learned about the chemistry of petroleum and their knowledge of the oil spill before going into the actual analysis of the propaganda pieces. This did two things. First, it let students recall things they would need to apply while it reinforced what they had already learned and gave them some context before the activity began. Second, it tied the experience to existing knowledge from the news for those who knew, and it gave those people with no prior knowledge a context with which to understand the informational pieces. I scaffolded the students with a series of questions to help them engage in their analysis. I did this because the students were not used to thinking in this kind of way in a science class or asking these sorts of questions. The students were involved in lively discussions during the activity and ended up writing about what they discovered. By making them write, as well as discuss, I was able to reinforce what they had learned in a concrete way, and I had a nice assessment of what they learned and what they still did not understand.

All in all, the lesson was a success. The students learned a great deal about the nature of propaganda and how knowledge of chemistry can help them really think about and question what people say and recognize how people can misuse or misrepresent facts and principles to support their side of an argument.

When I introduced the Web page project (*Artifact 15*), I used the students' experience with our Exxon *Valdez* Oil Spill lesson as a jump-off point for thinking about how one might construct a Web page. I next gave the students my basic expectations for the setup of the pages. I figured they might be somewhat intimidated by the task of constructing their own Web pages, so I related the software that we would be using

(Netscape Communicator Page Composer) to something that they were already familiar with: word processors. Entering basic text for a Web page works the same way as it does in Claris Works, which is the word processor that the high school has on its computers. The only new skill the students would have to learn would be saving and inserting images and creating links to other sites on the World Wide Web. I assured them that these tasks would not be difficult and that I would help them out.

I knew that a few students already knew how to compile rather sophisticated Web pages. I wanted to make sure that these students, as well as all of the others, understood that a sophisticated Web page would not be effective if it did not clearly communicate the content of the report. As an analogy that most of them could relate to, I asked the students to name their favorite commercials from the Super Bowl, which occurred the day before. They mentioned several commercials. For most of the commercials, students were able to name the company being advertised. But there were some very memorable commercials (such as the "herding cats" commercial) for which no one could remember the company or product. I then brought the discussion back to Web pages: if the students produce pages with all kinds of neat pictures, backgrounds, animations, and movies but do not have good textual content or do not clearly communicate that content, they will not have met the objectives of the project.

It has been especially challenging to motivate the students in Chemistry in the Community to be responsible for their own learning. Many of them usually put forth little effort in the classroom and will do nothing for the class outside of the classroom. One thing that encouraged more of them to be responsible for their own learning was the student-produced Web pages. A few of the students put in little effort again, but other students worked very hard and produced excellent Web pages. There are several reasons why this project motivated many of the students. First, it gave them some variety. We had just completed what was for many of them a difficult unit on chemical reactions, and this was quite different. Second, this project gave them the opportunity to be creative. Some students were concerned about every aesthetic detail of their pages, and this often led to a more clear presentation of the science content as well. Third, I think this project involved a number of Gardner's multiple intelligences, including linguistic and spatial intelligences, in ways that students had not been able to use them in this class before. *Artifact 18* shows some examples of pages that were produced by students in both Chemistry and Chemistry in the Community.

In the Chemistry in the Community unit on chemical formulas, we used a number of different approaches to teaching about how ions combine to form ionic compounds because it is difficult for students at this age to understand these concepts in the abstract. We built on what we had already done with the Bohr model of the atom, and we used manipulatives, did labs, and discussed the topic in class. One activity that was both fun and effective was a card game called Formula Rummy (*Artifact 7*). We had the students play mostly in pairs to encourage cooperative learning. As some of the groups gained a better understanding of how to create valid ionic compounds with the cards, their level of interest increased. One group especially played Formula Rummy with intensity and enthusiasm. Students enjoy games because games do not feel like "school." But by associating learning with fun, a teacher can open students up to learning and motivate them to engage with materials that may seem abstract and irrelevant if presented in traditional ways. Interestingly, after the game of Formula Rummy, several students who had not fully understood the concept of ionic compounds did a lot better on their unit exam than they or I expected based on their earlier difficulty.

Teaching chemistry is a complex task when students are interested; when they are not, the task becomes even more difficult. I really need to spend more time developing my range of instructional strategies and my understanding of what motivates and interests high school–aged students, what they know and what they can do. I know this will make me a better teacher and help my students learn better. I am more convinced that students need to have their different intelligences addressed in every subject, so I need to find out what other successful teachers at the high school level are doing to make science more meaningful and engaging for their students. I know I have a long way to go, but I already have some success under my belt to help me know what sorts of techniques can work for teaching high school science.

First, let's compare this reflection with the elements of a good reflection:

Identification of context. The writer begins by restating of the principle. While the reflection offers little real explication of the principle, references to theories and the discussion of development and learning issues give some sense that the teacher appreciates the intent of the standard and seems comfortable thinking about developmental issues and learning theory when planning and evaluating lessons and student learning. One would like, however, to see more discussion of what the teacher knows about development, especially about the grade level he or she is preparing to teach. It would also be helpful to have a more explicit discussion of the choice of theoretical bases for instructional decisions. When taken holistically, one might give this teacher a nod in favor of "good reflection" with a leaning toward the "weak reflection" category on the reflection rubric.

Observation and description of artifact (experience or document). The writer offers a variety of artifacts (teaching, experiential, and third party) to support his or her claim of having met the expectations set by Principle 2. The teacher is somewhat inconsistent with regard to how much descriptive detail he or she offers the reviewer when presenting the context and processes responsible for the artifact. In some places, a reviewer needs more to work with; in other places, there is too much detail. For the most part, however, it is easy to understand what is going on throughout most of the reflection despite sometimes limited detail. One might again come down on the low side of the "good reflection" category for this portion of the rubric, suggesting that the teacher discuss his or her artifacts consistently in more explicit detail.

Application of theories or principles of effective practice. One would like to see greater evidence of the theoretical background the teacher is using to make his or her instructional decisions. While a couple of theorists are named in the reflection and their influence is reflected in the instructional activities and decisions, the references seem more like window dressing than a serious expression of theoretical thinking. Here a reviewer might favor the "weak reflection" category of the rubric (i.e., "a reviewer might question depth of understanding"). However, the references made to theorists are neither incorrect nor exactly narrow, so the reflection does not fall neatly into the category. On the positive side, the teacher presents ample evidence for making good decisions relative to instruction and keeping his or her students' prior knowledge, experiences, and development in mind when choosing instructional strategies and developing lessons. The impression left with a reviewer is generally positive though somewhat shallow. Evaluating this reflection is a tough call, then, but in keeping with the rubric, a reviewer would probably have to conclude that it falls into the "good reflection" slot on the rubric.

Identification, analysis, and interpretation of causes and effects. Again, a reviewer would like to see more evidence or analysis and interpretation. There is only one good example of this in the reflection, when the teacher explains three reasons why the Web page assignment was somewhat successful. A little later, the teacher offers some analysis and interpretation about the success of the Formula Rummy game. Interestingly, and somewhat troubling, the teacher tends to explain only the successes among the students, while not analyzing why other students did not do well. Candidates tend to focus only on the positive within portfolios, but a thoughtful, research-informed recognition and analysis of failures is a powerful part of reflection and supports the belief that the teacher is indeed reflective. Failures and mistakes are our greatest sources of learning and professional growth. They should not be ignored. Based on this analysis, one is compelled to place this example in the "weak reflection" category because its analysis is somewhat superficial and narrowly focused on only the successful students' behavior.

Projection from observations toward problem solving and lifelong learning. The teacher offers at least some evidence of having thought about professional growth in the area of instructional strategies and Gardner's theory of multiple intelligences (i.e., theory into practice). In the language of the rubric, the teacher "acknowledges professional development needs without necessarily identifying the means for addressing those needs." Lacking, however, is evidence of refinement of practice based on past experience within the classroom (i.e., what the teacher would do differently next time based on weaknesses discovered in student performance or instructional practice). Again, we might place the reflection in the "good reflection" category with some weakness.

Based on the previous analysis and applying the rubric holistically, we can say that although the reflection is not strong, it is by and large a good reflection, giving the reviewer enough evidence to judge that the student is performing appropriately well when measured against the rubric for reflection.

But what about the expectations of Principle 2? Are they sufficiently met by the evidence? We cannot be absolutely sure because we have not seen all the evidence. However, based on this one lesson and the reflection, where would you tend to place this teacher on the following rubric:

Meets the Standard	*Not Yet Meeting the Standard*
The preservice teacher applies knowledge of how students learn and develop to create developmentally appropriate learning opportunities that not only strengthen prior knowledge and encourage student responsibility, but also support the intellectual, social, and personal development of all students.	The preservice teacher demonstrates or implies a basic knowledge of some theories and principles of human development and learning (e.g., paraphrases the most major developmental and learning theorists). However, there is little or superficial evidence of using this knowledge to create developmentally appropriate instruction.

While not a perfect performance, the teacher is tending toward the "Meets the Standard" column of the rubric. The preceding lesson and those referred to in the reflection appear to be developmentally appropriate and take into consideration how students learn. There is ample evidence the teacher knows how to and is inclined to "strengthen prior knowledge and encourage student responsibility." Moreover, evidence exists to reveal that the teacher supports at least the intellectual and social development of his or her students.

SUMMARY

Becoming a professional educator is a complex task that involves both the mastery of theory and practice and the application of both in an even more complex reality called the classroom. Principle 2 demands a working knowledge of the theories that undergird the profession. Your portfolio, then, must meet that demand by showing both an understanding of the theories informing the profession and the ability to apply those theories consciously in the endeavor to help students learn and achieve. Here are some questions to help you gather your evidence and prepare your reflection:

1. Where and how do I articulate evidence of my understanding of how students learn and develop?

   - How do I represent and use differing viewpoints, theories, ways of knowing, and methods of inquiry in my teaching? How do I effectively use multiple representations and explanations of disciplinary concepts that capture key ideas and link them to my students' prior understandings?
   - How do I provide students with opportunities to actively engage, manipulate, and test ideas and materials, and encourage students to assume responsibility for shaping their learning tasks?
   - How and where do I consciously apply developmental theory (physical, social, emotional, moral, and cognitive) in the instructional decision-making process? Where is this reflected in my choice of teaching strategies, classroom management decisions, assessment, and curriculum planning?

2. Where and how do I reveal my understanding of how my students' prior knowledge and experience can influence and inform their learning?

   - When and how have I assessed student prior knowledge and experience, and how have I used students' strengths as a basis for growth and their errors as an opportunity for learning?
   - When and how have I supported student reflection on prior knowledge and their ability to link new ideas to already familiar ideas?
   - When and how do I connect my discipline(s) to students' and adults' everyday lives?

3. When and how have I analyzed teaching strategies and resources for their developmental appropriateness and meaningfulness for my students and their ability to engage students in the curriculum?

4. Where and how have I provided learning opportunities that support the intellectual, social, and personal development of my students?

   - When and how have I encouraged discussion, listened and responded to group interaction, and elicited samples of student thinking orally and in writing?
   - Where have I evidenced my respect for the diverse talents of all learners and a commitment to helping them develop self-confidence?

5. Where and how do I reveal a belief in the complex and ever-evolving nature of our understanding of human development and learning?

   - Where do I reveal evidence of my appreciation of multiple perspectives and my ability to convey to learners how knowledge is developed from the vantage point of the knower?

- When have I developed and used curricula that encourage my students to see, question, and interpret ideas from diverse perspectives?

6. Where do I have evidence of keeping abreast of new ideas and understandings in development and learning?

   - What professional development have I accessed to support my continued professional growth?
   - When have I analyzed my performance and that of my students as a way to focus my professional development?
   - What gaps do I see in my professional practice and development that might guide my future professional development planning?

Discussion Questions

1. What are developmental and learning theories? Why are they important to consider when preparing learning opportunities for students?
2. What major developmental and learning theories seem relevant for teachers today? Which do you agree with and why?
3. How might knowing the developmental level of students, their preferred way of learning, and their prior experiences with a concept impact the way the concept is taught?
4. Why is it important for students to engage in reflection and self-assessment as part of learning?
5. What roles does social interaction play in the learning process and learning environment?
6. Why is active engagement and motivation important to teaching and learning? How may a teacher promote and support active engagement and motivation?
7. How may diverse experiences among students be used to benefit all students?
8. What role does self-confidence play in learning?

Implementing INTASC Principle 3 in Your Portfolio

6

Multicultural is not a philosophy or a strategy, or for that matter, a choice. In a society where there are many cultures, multicultural is simply a description. Similarly, as resistance theory makes clear, the power of students is not something for adults to bestow or deny, or debate whether it is a good idea to have. Where there are students, they have power—although that may be power to act out and disrupt; power to shut down and withdraw; or power to learn, care, and contribute. The question worth asking, then, is "What shall students and teachers make of these multicultures and power?"

Jeannie Oakes and Martin Lipton

Henry looked across the students seated in his classroom. There were seven African American students, three Hispanic students, four students from Bosnia, one student from the Dominican Republic, two Vietnamese students, and the remaining students visibly fit into the Caucasian category, whatever that meant. From among these he had a list of students with a variety of learning and behavioral difficulties that would impact their ability to keep up with the rest of the class. What's more, since he was student-teaching in an urban school, the range of socioeconomic levels was extreme. Some students were poor and transient; others were middle-class and had lived in the district all their lives. And clearly, given his experience with them so far, he was aware that they differed greatly in terms of how they learned, their strengths and weaknesses, and what they already knew about the range of subjects he was charged with teaching in the sixth grade. True, it was a challenge to daily come up with ways to individualize the learning for these students. Some days it just didn't work, but Henry knew a lot about his students already, and he was comfortable letting them guide the direction of their studies to a great degree. He knew that if he tried to control everything in his classroom, he would be lost. As it was, he and the students cooperated pretty well to get the learning done.

QUESTIONS TO CONSIDER

- ■ What is diversity? How can it impact teaching and learning experiences?
- ■ Why does a teacher need to identify differences in approaches to learning and performance among her or his students?
- ■ How may a student's learning be influenced by individual experiences, talents, and prior learning? How can a teacher use these issues to strengthen learning opportunities and performance?
- ■ Why should a teacher understand cultural and community diversity, and why or how should the teacher incorporate that understanding into classroom activities?
- ■ What tools and resources are available for designing learning opportunities to address the diverse needs, cultures, experiences, communities, and learning modalities of students?
- ■ How does one create a learning community in which individual differences are respected? Why is it a desirable thing to do?

Some people refer to this principle as the *diversity principle,* but they often hold a narrow definition of diversity. Some think it refers to students of color; others believe it refers to students with physical, emotional, or behavioral disabilities. Both definitions are too narrow, and both deny the diversity inherent in every culture. Diversity means more than color or disability; it encompasses socioeconomic background, language, ability, sexual orientation, and gender, as well as ethnic origins, abilities, and how these can impact learning and instruction. Thus, meeting the first expectation of understanding (how students differ in their approaches to learning) requires you to reveal the depth and breadth of your understanding of how diversity affects the ability of individual students to learn—both positively and negatively.

The heart of Principle 3 and the dispositions it promotes is the belief that all children can learn challenging curricula to a high level and that persistence will help all children achieve success. Simply asserting your belief that all students can learn is not sufficient, however, to demonstrate your commitment to Principle 3. The principle requires you to demonstrate your inclination to understand the kinds of diversity present in your classroom and community and your ability to use that understanding to improve the learning of every student in your class. Moreover, you must exhibit the personal mindset necessary to use this knowledge consciously to build a safe and supportive learning environment in the classroom, including varied opportunities for every student to achieve to her or his potential.

Your choices of evidence for this disposition must reveal your recognition of and appreciation for diversity as a resource (rather than as a deficit or an accommodation) and how that appreciation consciously tempers every instructional decision you make—from daily lesson planning to classroom management choices.

UNDERSTANDING PRINCIPLE 3

Principle 3: The teacher understands how students differ in their approaches to learning and creates instructional opportunities that are adapted to diverse learners.

This principle expresses two expectations:

1. Your *understanding of how students differ in their approaches to learning*
2. Your *ability to create learning opportunities that can be adapted for diverse learners*

UNDERSTANDING HOW STUDENTS DIFFER IN THEIR APPROACHES TO LEARNING

There are two sources for knowledge and understanding of how students differ in their approaches to learning: (a) knowledge gained from reading and study about the different areas of diversity and (b) data gathered from students themselves and one's experiences with them. Your portfolio entries (artifacts and reflections) for this principle must reveal both of these knowledge bases and your ability and inclination to use them in designing and carrying out instruction and classroom practice.

I reflected on what I had learned from the students about their home culture, the community they live in, and their experience. I realized that this was an important lesson but not in the form the text and curriculum was presenting it; therefore, it would have to be modified to allow all the students to relate to it and learn from it.

Theoretical foundations for practice. As we discussed in chapter 5, developmental theorists give the teacher a framework for understanding the tendencies learners exhibit at different ages or developmental stages. As you discovered in responding to Principle 2, these tendencies help teachers design a practice that is appropriate to the age or developmental level of most students. In the context of Principle 3, however, you must focus on how students may differ in relation to the benchmarks presented by development theories. Your portfolio must reveal by explicit statement and by evidence within lesson plans, reflections, classroom management decisions, and classroom practice that you have consciously considered these theories and their thinking when developing and implementing instruction.

Data from students and personal experience. An important and useful source of evidence of your understanding and application of this principle is your ability to gather and use data or information (including observational data and personal experience) from and about students, their environment, and their community. This information can help you to develop classroom practices that help individualize instruction to meet the motivational and learning needs of all students. Necessarily, you must show you are disposed to finding out about your students, how they are similar and how they differ, and what they bring with them to the learning situation.

Your portfolio must provide specific examples (through both artifacts and reflections) of your gathering and using knowledge about students to create learning opportunities that help all students learn and achieve to their potential. This includes the inclination and ability to modify, accommodate, replace, and enrich curriculum, instruction, and the classroom environment to reflect and make use of your students' diversity. Although your artifacts should demonstrate your ability to accommodate or seek specialized services, they must also demonstrate your ability to identify and build on students' rich and varied prior experience; their differing approaches to learning; and their family, culture, and community.

WHAT ARE THE IMPLICATIONS OF THIS KNOWLEDGE BASE FOR MY PORTFOLIO?

Principle 3 begs for a rich definition of diversity, one that addresses the expectations established by the principle and its indicators. Let's review the knowledge, skills, and dispositions presented within Principle 3:

Knowledge

■ The teacher understands and can identify differences in approaches to learning and performance—including different learning styles, multiple intelligences, and performance modes—and can design instruction that uses students' strengths as the basis for growth.

■ The teacher knows about areas of exceptionality in learning—including learning disabilities, visual and perceptual difficulties, and special physical or mental challenges.

■ The teacher knows about the process of second language acquisition and about strategies to support the learning of students whose first language is not English.

■ The teacher understands how a student's learning is influenced by individual experiences, talents, and prior learning, as well as language, culture, family, and community values.

■ The teacher has a well-grounded framework for understanding cultural and community diversity and knows how to learn about and incorporate students' experiences, cultures, and community resources into instruction.

Dispositions

■ The teacher believes that all children can learn at high levels and persists in helping all children achieve success.

■ The teacher appreciates and values human diversity, shows respect for students' varied talents and perspectives, and is committed to the pursuit of "individually configured excellence."

■ The teacher respects students as individuals with differing personal and family backgrounds and various skills, talents, and interests.

■ The teacher is sensitive to community and cultural norms.

■ The teacher makes students feel valued for their potential as people and helps them learn to value each other.

Performances

■ The teacher identifies and designs instruction appropriate to students' stages of development, learning styles, strengths, and needs.

■ The teacher uses teaching approaches that are sensitive to the multiple experiences of learners and that address different learning and performance modes.

■ The teacher makes appropriate provisions (in terms of time and circumstances for work, tasks assigned, communication, and response modes) for individual students who have particular learning differences or needs.

■ The teacher can identify when and how to access appropriate services or resources to meet exceptional learning needs.

■ The teacher seeks to understand students' families, cultures, and communities and uses this information as a basis for connecting instruction to students' experiences (e.g., drawing explicit connections between subject matter and community matters or making assignments that can be related to the students' experiences and cultures).

■ The teacher brings multiple perspectives to the discussion of subject matter, including attention to students' personal, family, and community experiences and cultural norms.

■ The teacher creates a learning community in which individual differences are respected.

We can distill the following issues from the preceding knowledge, skills, and dispositions that need to be addressed in your reflection (and in the artifacts you choose):

■ Identifying differences in approaches to learning and performance
■ Recognizing and addressing exceptionality in learning

- Understanding and addressing second language acquisition
- Recognizing how a student's learning is influenced by individual experiences, talents, and prior learning
- Understanding cultural and community diversity and incorporating that understanding into classroom activities
- Designing learning opportunities to address the diverse needs, cultures, experiences, communities, and learning modalities of students
- Creating a learning community in which individual differences are respected

Your reflection and artifacts must, at a minimum, address a preponderance of these issues, although it is not likely you will deal with them all in one section of your portfolio. Remember that each principle acts like a lens, refocusing your perspective from something you were writing about in another principle. Therefore, you should ensure that you reveal Principle 3 knowledge, dispositions, and performances throughout your portfolio.

ARTIFACT SELECTION

When deciding which artifacts to include in your portfolio, you must ask yourself at least the following questions:

1. Which artifacts will best demonstrate my understanding of the theoretical foundations for recognizing and dealing with the range of diversity found in the classroom?
2. Which artifacts will best show my inclination to think about diversity as an important resource and challenge when I am selecting instructional strategies and when I am planning short- and long-term learning opportunities?
3. Which artifacts will best demonstrate my ability to accommodate, individualize, and adapt for the diversity present in my classroom?
4. Which artifacts will best reveal my disposition toward enabling and empowering diverse learners?
5. Which artifacts will best document my understanding of my students' development and its impact on instruction?

TYPES OF ARTIFACTS

As sources for documenting your knowledge and skills relevant to diverse student populations, the following categories of artifacts will be particularly fruitful:

1. *Case studies* of diverse learners and conclusions drawn from those case studies
2. *Lesson/unit plans and assessments,* especially those clearly revealing your attention to diversity, offering choices and options for approaching subject matter, showing adaptations for students with special needs, and using the diverse cultures of your students as foundations for instruction and learning
3. *Student work samples* showing expectations and adaptations for diverse learners
4. *Documentation of classroom diversity,* of your ability to interact successfully with diverse student populations, and of your ability to help these students learn (however, do not rely on photographs to reveal diversity in your classroom)
5. *Questionnaires, surveys, and other investigative tools* used to identify the diversity of your students and the resources that diversity represents (including conclusions drawn from the information gleaned from these tools)
6. *Evidence of your understanding of IEPs or IAPs* for students in your classrooms and how those affected your instructional practice
7. *Evaluations* from your cooperating teacher and student teaching supervisor

8. *Journal entries, reflective essays, or course assignments* revealing your knowledge and dispositions relevant to diverse learners
9. (potentially) *Transcripts and test scores, citations of achievement or honors,* though less valuable, may help document your basic grasp of the area and show that you have taken relevant courses

EXAMPLE ARTIFACT

Look at the following artifact (a questionnaire from a second grade class), and reflect on what it reveals about the teacher's knowledge, dispositions, and performance skills relevant to Principle 3.

Name: George X
Age: 7

SPACE QUESTIONS

1. What is your definition of outer space?
   Lots of stars, lots of people go at there sometimes. It looks like your going slow but are going fast.
2. How many planets are there? 500
3. What are the names of the planets?
   Pluto, Sun, Mars, Earth, and Venus. There are more but I can't think of them.
4. How would you describe a planet? Round, light because if it was heavy it would fall.
5. What is the order of the planets from the sun? Don't know.
6. Do you think we can live on other planets? Why or why not?
   No, because not big enough for all the people and it doesn't have oxygen.

Some people will ask what this artifact has to do with diversity. But if you look at the principle and what it requires, you will note that it talks about "students' stages of development" and diversity (knowledge). In this example, the beginning teacher is apparently trying to learn what students already know about the content she or he wishes to teach (disposition); moreover, this artifact reveals the kinds of misconceptions characteristic in young learners that can influence their learning and understanding (knowledge). For example, it reveals the student's misconception about the number of planets in the solar system—or even the galaxy for that matter; it reveals misconceptions about the size and weight of planets and what keeps them in space. This artifact, then, might work within a package of artifacts intended to reveal a multifaceted approach to dealing with student diversity.

Would it be sufficient on its own to reveal the teacher's understanding and appreciation of diversity among her or his students? Not likely, because it reveals only one aspect of diversity: development and prior knowledge. However, if combined with a lesson plan, for example, that uses the information gleaned from this survey and that exhibits the teacher's ability to adapt a lesson to meet the needs of diverse students, then the package would better validate the teacher's knowledge, dispositions, and skills. Even better, however, would be the addition of a third piece—a journal reflection, for example—showing the teacher's interpretation of the survey findings, her or his thinking on how best to deal with the students' misconceptions, and her or his thinking about what adaptations, accommodations, or substitutions might be necessary to teach the content to diverse students.

The principles are rich in their intent and the expectations they are setting for you. Make sure you have included enough evidence to document your having met all or most of what the principle has set out for you.

WRITING A REFLECTION FOR PRINCIPLE 3

Once you have chosen the artifacts to highlight in your reflection statement, you need to explicate them for your reader to clearly document your understanding and mastery of the knowledge, skills, and dispositions that principle requires. Chapter 3 gives you a set of specific topics that need to be addressed for each artifact in your reflection:

1. Identification of context
2. Observation and description of artifact
3. Application of theories or principles of effective practice
4. Identification, analysis, and interpretation of causes and effect
5. Projection from observations toward problem solving and lifelong learning

After the first two topics on this list, you should find yourself citing or applying specific theories and theorists. Moreover, you ought to be using the language of the principle and its knowledge, skills, and dispositions.

EXAMPLE REFLECTION

Now let's look at a portfolio reflection written for Principle 3. What does it reveal about the high school English teacher and her or his understanding of diversity? Is it sufficient to meet the expectations set by the principle?

> Principle 3 states that the preservice teacher "understands how students differ in their approaches to learning and creates instructional opportunities that are adapted to diverse learners." We live in a global community. Our students live in a global community. They rub shoulders every day with students who are different from them, speak different languages, are from different countries, and have different cultures.
>
> As teachers, we are aware that our students are multiethnic, and we need to promote a general understanding of one another. It is only with knowledge that one can begin to understand. So in my teaching, I focus on introducing my students to as many ethnic-based, multicultural literatures as I can. When introducing ethnic literature to young people, we have to make special effort because the students may be totally unfamiliar with the experiences and the culture of the protagonist in the piece of work. As teachers, if we accept the challenge of introducing minority literature in our classroom, we will have to invest more time and energy into the project than normal, but the end result will be worth it. When introducing minority literature in our classroom, we have to help our students identify with the ethnic group that is the focus of the book. I learned that once students get to experience something, they no longer fear it. Once they approach the subject hands-on and get into the thick of it, they become active learners not passive onlookers. They are no longer outsiders looking on, but they become one of them.

The reflection and introduction of artifacts continues in this same vein and gives a nice picture of a teacher who is well versed in ethnic diversity and its implications on the high school literature classroom. This teacher explores the issue of ethnic diversity from various angles and even talks about adapting and individualizing lessons to meet the needs of her or his "ethnically diverse" students.

What is the problem then? The conception of diversity is too narrow to work in a twenty-first-century classroom where not only are the students ethnically diverse, but they are also socially and economically diverse and bring to the classroom a range of un-developed abilities or physical and mental disabilities. While this teacher appears to be sensitive to language and culture, is he or she capable or inclined to individualize in-struction for students with a broader range of diversities and abilities? Has she or he the knowledge, skills, and dispositions set forth in the standard? It is not at all clear from this reflection—nor is it clear from the selection of artifacts:

- List of activities for introducing students to diverse cultures
- Personal essay, "The Other Story: The Culture I Bring to My Classroom"
- The presentation for *Shabanu, the Daughter of the Wind*
- Individualized lesson plan for practicum experience: *Antigone*
- Professional reading critique: *Harvard Education Review,* "Moving Beyond Polite Correctness: Practicing Mindfulness in the Diverse Classroom"

Even in this selection of artifacts, the teacher has limited himself or herself to issues related to ethnic or cultural diversity—or, at most, language diversity. Again, this is not sufficient to address issues such as "how students differ in their approaches to learning" and creating "instructional opportunities that are adapted to diverse learners," especial-ly if the definition of diversity expressed and implied by the principle and its indicators (knowledge, dispositions, and performance skills) includes more than ethnic diversity—which it does.

In this instance, the teacher needs to broaden his or her conception of diversity and use the reflection to present the definition in clearer more detailed terms. Then he or she needs to align the selection of artifacts with the broader conception and expand the reflection to include evidence to support her or his recognition of and response to diversity in its vari-ous manifestations. Finally, the teacher needs to enrich the selection of artifacts to convince portfolio readers that he or she has indeed met the expectations expressed in the principle.

ANOTHER EXAMPLE REFLECTION FOR PRINCIPLE 3

Let's look at another reflection and evaluate it against the criteria for effective reflections and the rubric for Principle 3:

PRINCIPLE 3: INDIVIDUALIZATION AND DIVERSITY

Artifact 8: "Journey to the Stars Lesson"
Artifact 9: "Sailing Lesson"
Artifact 10: "School Personnel Interview
Artifact 21: "Comparison Chart of 4th Hour Test Scores"

Principle 3 deals with diversity and the teacher's ability to understand the needs and abilities of diverse learners and create lessons and units that make use of the diverse back-grounds students bring with them and to individualize instruction when necessary to as-sist students with different ability levels to achieve to a high standard. The artifacts I have chosen document my experiences in diverse classrooms and my ability to recognize diversity and reflect it in my classroom.

During my first placement at Carver Junior High School (Fall 1999), I was fortunate to be assigned to a classroom with very diverse students. Not only did I have African American students and Asian students, but also two of my students were from Bosnia. In addition to the cultural diversity, several of my students qualified for special services.

Moreover, over 90% of the students qualified for free or reduced lunch because of the lower socioeconomic level of the neighborhoods surrounding the school. Working with the students gave me the opportunity to learn how to identify and plan for their special needs in the classroom. It is important to challenge "lower ability" students to achieve to their full potential, which is often more than most teachers believe they can achieve.

For students to accomplish this goal {of reaching their potential], I often had to modify lesson activities. This individualization was in the form of reteaching, teacher-picked groups, and modified activities and worksheets. An example of this individualization is evident in Artifact 8: "Journey to the Stars." The assessment worksheet would have been difficult for English as a second language (ESL) or learning disabled (LD) students to complete. For this reason, I modified their copies by including page numbers next to the answer blank. This allowed them to narrow the focus of their searches for the answers to the review questions. By the time I left Carver Junior High, I was completely used to always modifying the assignments for my diverse students. Although it took me only a few extra minutes to prepare the modification, I am sure that it made a world of difference to the students.

While preparing a lesson plan on energy, forces, and motion, Artifact 9: "Sailing," I realized that the students would most likely not be able to relate their prior experiences to an activity in the textbook that required some knowledge of sailing. I was even more concerned about the likelihood of my ESL and voluntary transfer students (VTS) students having had opportunities to sail. This made a simple writing activity about a sailing experience impractical and probably not very productive. I reflected on what I had learned from the students about their home culture, the community they live in, and their experience. I realized that this was an important lesson but not in the form the text and curriculum was presenting it; therefore, it would have to be modified to allow all of the students to relate to it and learn from it. I went to work, then, adding hands-on activities and work sheets that drew from activities the students were more likely to have experienced, like using a hammer, rolling a ball, sweeping, playing basketball or football, dancing, flying a kite or holding a balloon in the wind. These stations and examples allowed the students to engage in "complex" tasks that connected the ideas we were learning (along with the vocabulary) to their own daily experiences. By changing the assignment, I was able to acknowledge the students' multiculturalism and diversity in learning abilities. This allowed the students to be engaged in the lessons and the learning. Based on the pretest and posttest data I gathered and graphed (Artifact 21: "Comparison Chart of 4th Hour Test Scores), all my students increased their understanding of forces and motions and increased their scores by an average of 43 points.

Artifact 10: "Interview" presents my summary of an interview I had with the school specialist at St. Alphonse School (Spring 1999). I spoke with Amee McRee, who is one of four resource teachers on staff at the school. Through the interview, I gained valuable knowledge about the student referral process and the kinds of services available for students in schools, especially students with special needs or giftedness. I also learned about different strategies that could be employed by a teacher and specialist to meet the needs of these students while not causing them embarrassment or unnecessary stress. One such strategy was using read-aloud with tests to assist limited reading proficiency students and visually impaired learners. After discussing this strategy with my cooperating teacher, I tried it with one of my students, an ESL student with limited reading ability. I used the strategy twice during my placement and the student's test scores did improve by 20 to 30 points. Through this experience I learned that many resources exist in the school to assist students with special needs. I also learned that there are a lot of good, practical ideas out there among other teachers that I can draw on to help my students. All I have to do is ask.

I am still not comfortable that I know enough about how to work with the diverse students I will meet in my classroom. Inclusion and the increasing ethnic diversity of the

United States guarantees that I will be faced with many interesting and challenging students. In the future, I will need to continue to learn new ways of finding out about my students and tapping the wealth of knowledge they already have. I will also have to seek new and better ways of giving all my students access to learning and success through better instruction and the resources available to me in my school.

Identification of context. In the first portion of the reflection, the student restates the principle for which the artifacts have been chosen. In other places within the reflection, the teacher gives additional insights into her or his own definition of diversity and its importance to teaching and learning. Moreover, in the context statement, the teacher clearly presents the kinds of students she or he worked with while serving as a student teacher. The teacher reveals a broad and inclusive definition of diversity: ethnic, language, socioeconomic, and ability. The teacher takes time to find out about the makeup of her or his classroom population. She or he also reveals the belief that diversity is not necessarily a deficit for students or learning: "It is important to challenge 'lower ability' students to achieve to their full potential, which is often more than most teachers believe they can achieve." It is clear this preservice teacher knows the meaning and intent of Principle 3.

Observation and description of artifact (experience or document). The teacher offers four artifacts to support having met the expectations of Principle 3. For each artifact, we find a brief description of what led to its creation or the experience it represents. More important, however, the teacher gives us some insight into what he or she was thinking while the experience was occurring or the artifact was being created. This allows the reviewer to see the teacher's thinking and decision-making processes. Descriptions offer much detail to give background to the reviewer.

Application of theories or principles of effective practice. The teacher has chosen several artifacts that offer a range of evidence to demonstrate having met the principle. The only thing lacking is clear evidence that the teacher has filtered her or his planning and decision making through the lens of theory. While a theoretical knowledge base may be implicit in the comments the teacher makes, the addition of appropriate references to theorists and their work would strengthen this teacher's case.

Identification, analysis, and interpretation of causes and effects. The teacher offers the reviewer some evidence of thinking about causes and effects in the discussion of Artifact 9: "Sailing." The teacher explains his or her decisions relevant to the appropriateness of the lesson for diverse students. Further, the teacher explains the results of modifying the lesson to match better the student's range of experiences and the resulting gains in test scores.

Projection from observations toward problem solving and lifelong learning. Finally, the teacher ends the reflection by broadly expressing the need to continue seeking new knowledge, skills, resources, and tools to better serve the needs of diverse learners.

This is moderately good reflection, based on the rubric given in chapter 3. It presents an insightful explication of the principle, as well as the teacher's dispositions relevant to the intent of the principle. Additionally, the teacher does a good job of describing the teaching events. The reflection is somewhat weak, however, in the area of analyzing the interconnections among classroom practices, though evidence exists to suggest the teacher has considered this issue to a limited extent. Moreover, the reflection reveals the teacher's ability to gain insights from critical analysis of practice, make changes in instruction, and plan for further professional development. Finally, the reflection offers, implicitly at least, some evidence of the teacher's understanding of the knowledge base and theoretical base that the principle requires.

Let's see how this reflection works relative to the following rubric for Principle 3:

Meets the Standard	*Not Yet Meeting the Standard*
The preservice teacher demonstrates the ability to adapt instruction and assessment to meet the diverse physical, intellectual, and cultural needs of individual students. Based in high expectations, activities connect with and build on students' individual strengths, prior experiences, family, culture, and community heritages. The candidate demonstrates knowledge of when and how to access specialized services.	The preservice teacher demonstrates a recognition that students have different approaches to learning but offers only occasional or narrow evidence of the ability to implement even the most basic adaptations to meet the needs of individual learners. Alternatively, the preservice teacher may assert a belief in the individuality of learners (possibly considering only ability differences), but instruction appears predominantly designed for the whole class. Overt knowledge of when and how to access specialized services is superficial or absent.

Does this reflection and range of artifacts perfectly address the expectations of Principle 3? The teacher demonstrates "the ability to adapt instruction and assessment to meet the diverse physical, intellectual, and cultural needs of individual students." Moreover, she or he obviously holds high expectations for students but makes sure "activities connect with and build on students' individual strengths, prior experiences, family, culture, and community heritages." The teacher also exhibits knowledge of when and how to access specialized services. All in all, she or he does a fairly good job of presenting the case for having met the standard set by Principle 3.

Summary

Knowing and understanding are two different though related things. When reviewers approach your portfolio, they will be seeking evidence of both knowledge of the theory and practice of education for diverse learners and the ability and disposition to apply that knowledge to support the learning of all students. You must give both in order to convince a reviewer that you have the knowledge, skills, and dispositions required by Principle 3.

The following list presents some of the questions reviewers will be asking as they explore your portfolio. You should be asking yourself the same questions as you prepare yourself to be a teacher and as you prepare your professional portfolio for review:

1. Does this teacher see diversity as a deficit or as a resource for teaching and learning?
2. Does this teacher recognize that students bring a wealth of knowledge, culture, and experience to the learning situation?
3. Does this teacher recognize the importance of empowering all students to participate in defining and guiding the learning process and goals?
4. Does this teacher understand how to employ knowledge gained about students and their milieu to create meaningful learning experiences for all students?
5. Does this teacher understand how students develop and does the teacher consciously consider development when designing instruction appropriate to students' stages of development, learning styles, strengths, and needs?

6. Does this teacher use teaching approaches that address different learning and performance modes?

7. Does this teacher understand about areas of exceptionality in learning, and does she or he make appropriate provisions (in terms of time and circumstances for work, tasks assigned, and communication and response modes) for individual students who have particular learning differences or needs?

8. Can this teacher identify when and how to access appropriate services or resources to meet the learning needs of exceptional students?

9. Can this teacher build a community of learners based on mutual understanding and respect?

DISCUSSION QUESTIONS

1. How may students differ in their approaches to learning and performance? What implications might that have for the classroom?

2. What is the range of possible exceptionalities among students? How may a teacher accommodate these in her or his classroom?

3. What impact may individual experiences, talents, and prior learning have on how students learn?

4. How may cultural and community diversity be used as a resource to enrich the classroom experiences of all students?

5. What is a learning community? What can an educator do to create and support a learning community in the classroom and school? How can an educator promote respect for diversity in his or her classroom?

Implementing INTASC Principle 4 in Your Portfolio

7

If one component among many for effective teaching practice can claim to be the most important, engaging students in learning with a multitude of strategies is the one.

Charlotte Danielson

Caroline was in a quandary, and her teaching journal reflected it: "How can I create a lesson about interpreting poetry that the students will enjoy while still making it academically rigorous? I really want them to think about the poetry, not just roll their eyes and play along. Direct instruction is obviously not the answer—another poetry lecture on rhyme and meter and symbols just won't cut it. I really need the students to dig into the poems on their own. I want them to think like a poet, to understand the processes a poet goes through to create a poem. What's the point otherwise? The curriculum demands they study poetry, its form and content, but the form is so foreign to them. It just doesn't relate to their world and realities. But that's what poetry's supposed to do—reflect the world (personally or globally) in images and language. It is like painting, in a way, but with words and images—and sometimes with rhyme and meter. I wonder if I could get them to adopt a poet, maybe as teams. Dividing up the work seems to make it more palatable for the kids because they can work from positions of expertise (each will have a job in the group that the student, I hope, will feel comfortable doing), and cooperative groups help get more knowledge out there for the whole class without saddling one person with a whole topic. They can even choose their own poets, maybe working up a proposal for approval."

QUESTIONS FOR CONSIDERATION

- What is the difference between an instructional strategy and a fun activity?
- What range of instructional strategies have I used in my teaching?
- What does it mean to *facilitate* learning?

■ What are the characteristics of critical thinking? How do I know my students are engaged in higher order thinking?

■ What is the difference between problem solving and solving problems?

■ What are performance skills? How can I best teach them?

Like a carpenter or a doctor, a teacher has a tool chest or a repertoire of instructional strategies she or he can draw on to help students learn the range of knowledge and skills expected by the curriculum. Your portfolio (across a set of artifacts) needs to show that you possess and know how to implement this range of strategies to help your students achieve. Moreover, your portfolio needs to demonstrate that you value and understand the nature of critical/creative thinking and problem solving. Bloom's taxonomy is not a flat plane; rather it represents increasingly complex levels of thinking your students must move up and down in the course of your lessons. Direct instruction, once the mainstay of teaching, while safe, is no longer adequate or acceptable as the primary mode of teaching. Teachers play several roles in the classroom; disseminator of knowledge is only one—and a small one at that. You need to demonstrate your ability to move from teacher to facilitator to coach. You need to show you are a creator of opportunities to learn—and sometimes a discoverer and utilizer of opportunities that present themselves, often by the students themselves.

Instructional strategies are not just fun activities; rather they are proven approaches to structuring classroom work and interaction to help students learn. These strategies include cooperative learning, direct instruction, discovery learning, whole-group discussion, Socratic seminar, independent study, and interdisciplinary instruction, among others. Your professional course work will likely discuss each of these strategies in more or less detail; you may also have practice in using each for simulated teaching and for lesson construction. You should make sure you are familiar with each of these strategies and try to have examples of your successful use of them. More important, you should have evidence of having chosen the strategy for a particular teaching purpose, for a particular body of knowledge and skills, and for particular student needs.

UNDERSTANDING PRINCIPLE 4

Principle 4: The teacher understands and uses a variety of instructional strategies to encourage students' development of critical thinking, problem solving, and performance skills.

Principle 4 asks for evidence of two things:

1. Your understanding of *a variety of instructional strategies*
2. Your ability to use those strategies to *encourage students to develop critical thinking, problem solving, and performance skills*

Instructional strategies are methods for delivering instruction intended to help students to achieve instructional objectives. You can think of these as a set of vehicles to achieve a particular end: *students' development of critical thinking, problem solving, and performance skills* (within the context of content knowledge and basic skills). Instructional strategies range from prescriptive and teacher directed (direct teaching) to less explicit and student centered (indirect teaching). Teacher-centered instruction tends to address lower order thinking and memorization; student-centered instruction tends to deal with higher order thinking skills and the application of knowledge. Realistically, a teacher will move up and down this scale, depending on the nature of the materials being taught, students' prior knowledge, and the level of thinking and application being

"This lesson helps my students become better learners in a number of ways. By working in groups to develop a time line, they practice collaboration and cooperation. They engage in active discussion with each other rather than being passive observers/listeners to my instruction."

modeled or promoted. Along with these strategies comes a range of technologies that may help students to develop these skills and abilities. A thoughtful teacher will think about the value of technology at the same time she or he is thinking about strategies. Principle 4 expects you to have practiced a broad range of teaching strategies and to be able to move back and forth among them as the demands of the classroom and content change.

In creating the mobile, they are actively and independently researching information through a number of different sources, giving them experience in how to identify and select appropriate resources.

Students' development of critical thinking, problem solving, and performance skills is the end to which instructional strategies are directed. While content knowledge and basic skills are important, in fact essential, the application of those skills and the use of that content knowledge in the service of critical thinking, problem solving, and performance skills is the desired end of teaching. These three categories of developed abilities are actually a complex set of interconnected skills and abilities. Critical thinking includes analysis, invention, induction/deduction, causal analysis, and so on. Problem solving is a form of critical thinking focused on identifying and addressing problematic situations, frequently using a standard set of steps. Performance skills are a grab bag of abilities students need to develop and use, such as communication skills, symbolic representation, and thoughtful reading. Effective teachers use many teaching strategies and resources as a means to differentiate their instruction and to engage students in the learning process. Mere activity, however, will not necessarily engage students' minds. Simple participation is not sufficient either. Students require intellectual engagement with the content and active construction of understanding, which requires the active and invested participation of all students.

WHAT ARE THE IMPLICATIONS OF THIS KNOWLEDGE BASE FOR MY PORTFOLIO?

In your portfolio you must be able to document your skill at engaging students through multiple teaching strategies. Specifically, your portfolio artifacts and reflections must reveal your ability to select appropriate teaching strategies, materials, and technology and arrange them to achieve your instructional objectives and to meet your students' needs. Your documents also need to show how you structure learning opportunities to engage students in active learning via critical thinking, problem solving, and performance capabilities. You must also demonstrate through your artifacts and reflection how each of the instructional strategies matches the requirements of the content and the development of the learners, including students with special needs. Your reflections, journal entries, and commentaries on this standard must also make explicit reference to student engagement.

The following are the knowledge, dispositions, and performances outlined in Principle 4:

Knowledge

- The teacher understands the cognitive processes associated with various kinds of learning (e.g., critical and creative thinking, problem structuring and problem solving, invention, memorization, and recall) and how these processes can be stimulated.
- The teacher understands principles and techniques, along with advantages and limitations, associated with various instructional strategies (e.g., cooperative learning, direct instruction, discovery learning, whole-group discussion, independent study, and interdisciplinary instruction).

■ The teacher knows how to enhance learning through the use of a wide variety of materials as well as human and technological resources (e.g., computers, audio-visual technologies, videotapes and discs, local experts, primary documents and artifacts, texts, reference books, literature, and other print resources).

Dispositions

■ The teacher values the development of students' critical thinking, independent problem solving, and performance capabilities.

■ The teacher values flexibility and reciprocity in the teaching process as necessary for adapting instruction to student responses, ideas, and needs.

Performances

■ The teacher carefully evaluates how to achieve learning goals, choosing alternative teaching strategies and materials to achieve different instructional purposes and to meet student needs (e.g., developmental stages, prior knowledge, learning styles, and interests).

■ The teacher uses multiple teaching and learning strategies to engage students in active learning opportunities that promote the development of critical thinking, problem solving, and performance capabilities and that help students assume responsibility for identifying and using learning resources.

■ The teacher constantly monitors and adjusts strategies in response to learner feedback.

■ The teacher varies his or her role in the instructional process (e.g., instructor, facilitator, coach, audience) in relation to the content and purposes of instruction and the needs of students.

■ The teacher develops a variety of clear, accurate presentations and representations of concepts by using alternative explanations to assist students' understanding and presenting diverse perspectives to encourage critical thinking.

Principle 4 asks for evidence of the following four issues that need to be demonstrated within your artifacts and reflections:

1. Understanding a wide range of teaching strategies, materials, and technologies to achieve multiple learning goals, instructional purposes, and to meet student needs (e.g., developmental stages, prior knowledge, learning styles, and interests).
2. Knowledge of and ability to use various strategies and instructional roles to engage students in active learning that promotes the development of critical thinking, problem solving, and performance capabilities.
3. Ability and inclination to constantly monitor and adjust strategies in response to learner feedback.
4. Ability to develop a variety of clear, accurate presentations and representations of concepts by using alternative explanations to assist students' understanding and presenting diverse perspectives to encourage critical thinking.

ARTIFACT SELECTION

When deciding which artifacts to include in your portfolio, you must ask yourself at least the following questions:

1. Which documents and other artifacts (e.g., a videotape of a class, a unit plan) reveal your understanding of the whats, hows, and whys of choosing and implementing multiple teaching strategies to achieve instructional objectives more effectively?

2. Which documents reveal your ability to choose appropriate teaching strategies, materials, and technologies and their impact on diverse learner needs and development?
3. Which artifacts show your skills to implement activities to help students engage deeply with challenging subject matter?
4. Which pieces show your skill in grouping students in many different ways to enhance the level of student engagement?
5. Which documents show your ability to design different activities to enhance problem-based and inquiry-based learning?

TYPES OF ARTIFACTS

Possible portfolio artifacts for this standard include the following:

- *Lesson and unit plans* demonstrating a variety of instructional strategies
- *Videotapes* of a lesson that includes a variety of teaching strategies and illustrates your ability to engage students in higher order thinking, learning, and performance
- *Clinical experience observations and evaluations* commenting on your use of varied instructional strategies and student engagement in critical thinking, problem solving, and performance skills
- *Self-assessment* of your instructional practices after watching your teaching techniques on the videotape of your class
- *Reflections* on your instruction focusing on your activities in relation to the principle's performance indicators and student engagement with an assessment result that may show the success of your teaching strategies
- *Student work* demonstrating students' engagement in higher order thinking, problem solving, and other performance skills
- *Transcripts* (optional) showing the instructional methods course you have taken

EXAMPLE ARTIFACT

Now let's review an artifact to see what it reveals about the teacher's knowledge, performances, and dispositions relevant to Principle 4.

LESSON TOPIC: COMMUNICATION TOOLS AND INVENTIONS

Grade 2

State Content Grade Level Expectation: Social Studies 5—Elements of Geographical Study and Analysis

Concept 5—Relationships between and among places

Grade 2 Benchmark: Describe different types of communication and transportation and identify their advantages and disadvantages

Objective: After identifying and discussing communication inventions, the students will assemble a time line of all of the inventions and create a mobile of one of the inventions that includes the year it was invented and at least two features, two advantages, and two disadvantages of the invention.

Duration: Two to three class periods (assume 40 minutes per period)

Materials Needed:
Teacher: Activity Sheet "Great Moments in Communication" (one per student)

Time line materials: Yarn/paper clips (enough for each pair of students)
Mobile materials: One coat hanger, yarn, paper clips, six index cards per student
Resource materials: Resource books, magazines, newspapers, Internet access to relevant bookmarked sites
Students: Pencil, crayons/markers, scissors, glue

Anticipatory Set:
Explain the following situation to the students: "Our principal has some exciting news to tell. How could he/she communicate the news to the students? To teachers? To parents? To the neighborhood?" List the students' ideas on the board, encouraging them to consider the best method for each audience.

Input/Activities:

1. Ask students to reflect on the meaning of the word *communicate*. On the chalkboard, summarize the student responses that convey information (e.g., to tell, to announce, to speak, to write). Clarify the definition of communication: Communication is the way people share ideas, thoughts, or information with each other.

2. Ask students to brainstorm about the kinds of information that people exchange (e.g., news [local, national, global], weather, community events, births, deaths, items for sale, new inventions, relating experiences [stories]). List their ideas on the board.

3. Ask students to brainstorm about how people long ago (hominids, Indians, pilgrims, pioneers) may have communicated with each other. List their ideas on the board.

4. Distribute the modified activity sheet "Great Moments in Communications" to each student (www.cybersmartcurriculum.org/act_sheets/CY00_Stdnt_G68_L23a.pdf). Read and discuss each activity with the students, providing additional details or clarification as needed (make sure students understand the meaning of "B.C." in the date). Discuss the different ways these developments allow people to communicate (written, visual, vocal, signs, etc). *Note:* Modify activity sheet as appropriate for grade level.

Activity 1: Divide the students into four groups (five students in each of the four groups). Assign each group one of the following time periods, which coincide with the communication developments on the activity sheet: 45,000 B.C.– A.D. 900, 1450 A.D.–1837 A.D., 1876 A.D.–1928 A.D., 1970 A.D.–2003 A.D.

Instruct each group to arrange each communication moment into a chronological time line using yarn and paper clips. Visit each group, ensuring that they are working cooperatively and that they understand the assignment.

Once each group of students has arranged its time line, have student link it in the correct order with the other groups' time lines, resulting in one time line of all of the communication developments. Reflect with the students about the communication advances that occurred in each time period, comparing the features, advantages, and disadvantages of the various inventions in each time period with the other time periods.

Activity 2: Assign each student one of the following means of communication invented by humans: cave paintings, fire beacons, books, pony express, telegraph, telephone, computer, billboards, television, newspaper, and radio (some students will have the same invention). Explain that students are to create a mobile that has the following specifications:

Include at least six pictures or photographs of the communication tool, glued onto index cards. Each picture or photograph must show a different type or a different version of that particular tool (e.g., for types of telephone could include rotary dial, push-button, cell, and cordless).

On the back of each picture, the student must write the year the communication was invented, the name of the communication tool, and a feature, advantage, or disadvantage of this invention. Students must list at least two features, two advantages, and two disadvantages of the communication device in the mobile.

Review the following example with the students to be sure that they understand what is needed in the mobile:

Telephone: Invented in 1876 (with picture of a phone)
Feature: Signals communication with sound, like a ring or a beep.
Advantage: Sends communication over long or short distances.
Disadvantage: Long distance communication can be expensive.

Provide each student with materials for making the mobile (reference material list) and review the proper way of constructing a mobile (punch hole in index card, hang with paper clip by yarn strand to coat hanger). Make resources for finding pictures or photographs and conducting further research of the invention accessible to each student:

- Reference/resource books
- Magazines/newspapers
- Internet access to relevant sites concerning communication inventions

As students work independently, visit them periodically to make sure they understand the assignment and to answer questions as necessary. When completed, have each student present his or her mobile to the class, sharing the pictures and information found for the communication tool.

This activity is part of a second grade social studies unit plan on communication tools and inventions. The artifact has a clear link to state and district curricula, being aligned to state social studies content grade level expectations and benchmarks. The artifact describes both direct and indirect instructional strategies. The strategies used for the direct instruction include questioning and brainstorming (e.g., definition of communication, types of information to communicate, and historical methods of communication); the indirect instructional activities include cooperative group work and individual analysis/interpretation/presentation. The opening activity is a good example of the teacher activating students' prior knowledge. Once the teacher has done this, she or he moves into indirect instructional strategies (i.e., hands-on and group activities). In this part of the lesson, the teacher clearly assumes the role of facilitator and coach. This shows that the teacher can shift between strategies and roles based on the requirements of the content and the needs of the students (in this case, the need for social interaction and hands-on activities to reinforce learning).

Within the lesson, the teacher taps several resources, including the Internet, to provide activities for the lesson and materials for students to use in their projects. These activities, including the more teacher-centered opening, give students the opportunity to think critically and to problem-solve. The students must also do research, communicate (with each other, though not in any more coherent written form), and be creative (building the mobile). The lesson plan also gives ample details regarding what the teacher did (provided information, materials, resources, directions, and guidance) and what the students did (participated in discussion, made time lines as a group, and created a mobile independently).

One would like to see the activity sheet and perhaps samples of student work to give a fuller picture of the lesson. Having these additional artifacts available would also help the reviewer determine how much of the lesson the candidate actually developed and how much came from the downloaded worksheet. Moreover, a reviewer would probably like to see more performance skills required in the lesson (e.g., more writing and more explicit research). Finally, one would like to see what criteria the teacher held for scoring the time lines and mobiles. It is not clear what he or she is looking for from the student products.

WRITING A REFLECTION FOR PRINCIPLE 4

The following is the reflective statement written by the same teacher about the instructional strategies of the lesson.

The following lesson is intended to demonstrate my accomplishments relevant to IN-TASC Principle 4. The activities in the lesson address the principle's performance indicators because they incorporate a variety of teaching strategies, materials, and technology, which engage students in active learning. The strategies evident in the artifact include a combination of cooperative learning, direct instruction, problem solving, creation and presentation of a product, questioning, and researching using multiple materials and resources including the Internet.

This lesson helped my students become better learners in a number of ways. By working in groups to develop a time line, they practiced collaboration and cooperation. They engaged in active discussion with each other rather than being passive observers or listeners to my instruction. In creating the mobile, they were actively and independently researching information through a number of sources, giving them experience in how to identify and select appropriate resources. They applied what they learned to a visual product (the mobile), allowing them to utilize their creative skills to convey their knowledge of the subject. By actively creating a physical product rather than only reading from a textbook, students were more likely to retain what they learned. Students also had an opportunity to practice their speaking and presentation skills when they presented their mobile to the class.

This lesson helped me become a more effective teacher because in it I provided students with opportunities to be actively engaged in the lesson (time line and mobile creation) rather than passively listening to a lecture. By the nature of the activities and the discussions in this lesson, I was effective in reaching the objective and meeting the standard because I am encouraging and challenging students to think about not only the simple facts about communication inventions but also the impact (advantages and disadvantages) these inventions had/have on people's ability to communicate. In the discussions, I asked both lower and higher level questions to challenge and motivate the students.

Identification of context. The candidate never really describes the context for creating the lesson, what it was intended to accomplish, how it fit into the curriculum, or how he or she came up with the idea to teach the content in the way chosen. The candidate alludes to the principle being addressed, using some of the language of the principle and its performance indicators ("a variety of teaching strategies, materials, and technology, which engage students in active learning"). The reader is left in the dark about when, why, and how the lesson was created. Therefore, without the lesson close by, the comments make little sense to a reader, forcing him or her to find the artifact and continue to reference it while reading the reflection.

Observation and description of artifact (experience or document). This reflection is much less detailed than others we have seen so far—and it is less detailed than we would normally advocate. The teacher tries to explain about preparing multiple activities and resources to meet student needs, but the description lacks detail and sounds like mere assertion. The reflection is too dependent on having the artifact immediately available to make it understandable. The teacher then asserts that the lesson plan includes various instructional strategies (direct instruction, hands-on, and cooperative learning activities) and materials to help students become problem solvers and critical thinkers, again with little detail offered (though later in the reflection, she or he mentions time line and mobile creation). All in all, a reviewer will find the reflection less informative than needed.

Application of theories or principles of effective practice. When the candidate talked about student learning relevant to the lesson, he or she wrote, the students "are applying what they have learned to a visual product (the mobile) allowing them to utilize their creative skills to convey their knowledge of the subject. By actively creating a physical product rather than only reading from a textbook, students are more likely to retain what they have learned. Students also have an opportunity to practice their speaking and presentation skills when they present their mobile to the class." Within this discussion, a reviewer may get an impression that the candidate is applying a learning theory or best practice, but the connection could be more clearly and convincingly documented. As always, a direct reference to a theorist or learning theory is more powerful and serves the purposes of the portfolio better. The candidate does not talk about students' prior knowledge or experience, neither does he or she mention how the nature of the content affected instructional choices.

Identification, analysis, and interpretation of causes and effects. The candidate discusses minimally the advantages of the hands-on activities (mobile and time line making) compared to a traditional lecture. However, she or he did not discuss whether or not students retained the knowledge and skills better because of the choice and arrangement of activities. The reflection doesn't present assessment data or discuss student responses or learning.

Projection from observations toward problem solving and lifelong learning. The reflection does not deal with the issues of problem solving or lifelong learning at all. One wonders if the candidate really reflected on the lesson, its implementation, and its impact on students. An essential element of reflection is the projection to the future: What could I have done better to make the lesson more effective? It is not clear the candidate engaged in any critical evaluation of the lesson.

All in all, this is a weak reflection. It hints at many things but never gives the detail or depth required to substantiate the assertions it makes. In addition, one lesson is probably not sufficient to prove one's proficiency relevant to any principle. The single artifact coupled with this reflection is not likely to impress a portfolio reviewer.

The following is the summative evaluation rubric of Principle 4. How well would this candidate score given the evidence she or he has provided?

In light of the single artifact (lesson plan) and the rather sparse reflection, it is difficult to judge the candidate's ability or proficiency relevant to Principle 4. While

Meets the Standard	*Not Yet Meeting the Standard*
The preservice teacher uses and subsequently evaluates the impact of a variety of instructional strategies, materials, and technologies to meet individual student needs and to encourage students' development of critical thinking, problem solving, and performance skills. Although artifacts reveal the use of a variety of strategies, reflections may not clearly establish the candidate's ability to match specific strategies with the content or skills to be taught. The candidate uses student work in the evaluation of a strategy's impact on student learning.	The preservice teacher uses a limited set of instructional strategies, materials, or technology to create lessons mostly at the recall/recognition level; the candidate may not distinguish multiple activities using the same strategy from those using different strategies. There is little or no evidence of either the ability to create learning opportunities that encourage students' development of critical thinking, problem solving, and performance skills or the ability to align instructional strategy with content or skills to be taught. The candidate reveals only limited evidence of the ability to engage each student in active learning; rather, instructional artifacts emphasize a frequently teacher-centered, whole-class approach to instruction. The candidate tends to assert the positive impact of a strategy rather than provide evidence via student work.

there is evidence the candidate can employ different instructional strategies, he or she does not seem inclined to reveal a theoretical foundation for or evaluate the effectiveness of those strategies. While he or she asserts "the lesson helped my students become better learners," no proof appears to support this statement. One might infer that the candidate can employ varied instructional strategies, little evidence exist for her or him having consciously selected the strategies to match student development or approaches to learning. One might ask how the candidate knows the lesson "encourages development of critical thinking, problem solving and performance skills." With such limited detail and lack of depth in the reflection, a reviewer will necessarily be left with some doubts. One hopes other examples in the portfolio documenting other principles will help prove the candidate's case. However, a reviewer should not have to work to find support. These gaps leave the reviewer at a loss to make a clear-cut final evaluation. Some evidence arises from the artifact but is not supported or proved by the reflection. Therefore, one is compelled to determine that this candidate does not yet meet the expectations set by Principle 4.

SUMMARY

Teachers are professionals; however, they are still much like technicians in the sense that they need a wealth of technical information and expertise to perform their professional roles and responsibilities. This technique should include a broad range of instructional strategies suited to a variety of subject-area content, a diverse range of student ability and backgrounds, and the expectations that students must be trained in and engage in critical thinking, problem solving, and other performance skills. Will you have a full "tool chest" when you complete your initial training to become a teacher? No, but you should have enough of a range to keep learning interesting and keep the class moving. Moreover, you need to be able to assume more than just an instructor's role in the classroom; you must also be able to be a coach, a facilitator, and an observer, giving students increasing responsibility for their own learning.

Here are a few questions to further guide you as you begin to document your proficiency in Principle 4:

1. What instructional strategies have I mastered? How do I decide which ones to use given my goals, the content, and my students?
2. What is critical thinking? How do I engage students in that mode of cognitive activity?
3. What is problem solving? What parts or steps are involved in that process? When and how have I engaged students in that form of cognitive activity?
4. What other higher-order performance skills must I help my students master?
5. How do I find out what my students already know about a topic? About their personal environments and experiences? About their strengths and areas of needed improvement?
6. What roles have I assumed in my teaching? What roles have I observed other teachers assuming in their classroom practice?
7. How do I get students to take responsibility for their own learning?
8. How do I exhibit flexibility in my teaching? How do I monitor the classroom interaction to know when I need to adapt my strategies?

DISCUSSION QUESTIONS

1. What alternatives to lecture or discussion do teachers have for creating learning opportunities for their students? Why might other approaches to teaching be more successful for different students and different content?
2. How do students' prior knowledge and experiences have an impact on teaching and learning?
3. What is active learning? Why is it preferable to passive learning?
4. What are the characteristics of critical thinking and problem solving? Why are these so important to teaching and learning? How does one go about teaching these capabilities?
5. Why should a teacher constantly monitor and adjust strategies in response to learner feedback? What sorts of feedback might one find available for this purpose?
6. What is the value of presenting concepts and content in multiple ways and from multiple perspectives?

Implementing INTASC Principle 5 in Your Portfolio

The whole art of teaching is only the art of awakening the natural curiosity of young minds for the purpose of satisfying it afterwards.

Anatole France

Professor Karson flipped peevishly through another portfolio, looking for some evidence that students understood what a classroom management plan was. "I can't understand why they all seem to confuse it with a discipline plan or with behavior management. It's so much more than that. Sure it includes behavior management, classroom rules, and discipline plans, but these things are just small features. If you are really going to talk about classroom management, you need to consider motivation and instructional strategies, heck, the whole philosophy and theoretical foundation of the classroom. Classroom management should be a positive proactive approach to engaging students in meaningful learning. When they are engaged, there is little need for disciplinary actions. When they are invested in what goes on in the classroom and feel some ownership, again there is little need for discipline. Depending on how empowered the students are, they frequently become a self-monitoring and self-disciplining group. But why can't I get my preservice teachers to see this? I really need to work on this and on helping them identify portfolio artifacts that will help them document their understanding."

QUESTIONS FOR CONSIDERATION

- How can motivation and motivating practices have an impact on the classroom environment?
- What motivates individuals and groups to learn, behave appropriately, and interact positively?
- What are the features of "positive social interaction"?

- What constitutes active engagement in learning? How can a teacher get students to actively engage in learning?
- How may a teacher help her or his students become self-motivated?
- What features of a classroom management plan can support individual and group motivation?

Effective teachers bring to the classroom a range of skills and tools to help build an environment that will support meaningful learning for all students. Much of that environment building goes beyond rules, seating charts, calendars, and the other individual ways of structuring the school day. More important than these are the ways a teacher creates a community in the classroom: a group of people who work and play together, who respect and support each other as they learn and achieve. This latter effort is what Principle 5 is setting as an expectation for beginning teachers. The principle also asks that the preservice teacher reveal understanding of and ability to apply theories of motivation and group dynamics. It is really an instructional issue at play here, as well as classroom management (also confused with discipline by many preservice teachers). Via various artifacts, the preservice teacher needs to reveal this understanding and demonstrate some ability to consciously manage time, space, transitions, and activities to keep students engaged and motivated and, when necessary, to deal with behavior issues. This will likely demonstrate at least some encouragement of student self-responsibility for learning.

UNDERSTANDING PRINCIPLE 5

Principle 5: The teacher uses an understanding of individual and group motivation and behavior to create a learning environment that encourages positive social interaction, active engagement in learning, and self-motivation.

Here again, the principle asks preservice teachers to exhibit two traits:

1. Understanding of *individual and group motivation and behavior*
2. The ability to use this understanding to *create a learning environment that encourages positive social interaction, active engagement in learning, and self-motivation*

For many beginning teachers, classroom management is merely another word for behavior management, which is merely a euphemism for discipline; similarly, motivation for many beginning teachers means compliance. For these teachers, motivated students are those who do what they are told to do when they are told to do it. These beginning teachers frequently find their early experiences in the classroom disappointing. What the teacher finds interesting and worth knowing and doing is frequently very different from what his or her students find worth knowing and doing.

The extent to which students become actively and productively engaged in an activity is based on at least three conditions:

1. Whether they believe they can be successful at the task
2. The degree to which they value the rewards associated with successfully completing the task
3. The climate, or the quality of relationships, within which they are asked to engage in the task[1]

---

[1]Feather, N. (1982). *Expectations and actions.* Hillsdale, NJ as cited in Jones, V., & Jones, L. (1995). *Comprehensive classroom management: Creating positive learning environments for all students.* Boston: Allyn and Bacon.

In other words, students will be motivated when they *expect* they can complete the task, when they find *value* in the task, and when they complete the task in an environment supportive of their basic personal needs (e.g., their need to exercise some degree of control over their environment, to belong to a community, to feel safe to explore, and even to make mistakes).

Creating an environment that encourages **positive social interaction** refers to a classroom in which students are comfortable and feel safe interacting with the teacher and, even more important, comfortable and feel safe interacting with their peers. One researcher refers to this kind of environment as one that is providing "social support for student achievement."[2] You would recognize this classroom as one in which the teacher and the students hold high expectations for the quality of their work and their behavior. They exhibit mutual respect for each other and provide assistance to each other in completing challenging and meaningful work.

Creating an environment that encourages **active engagement in learning** refers to a classroom in which everyone believes the goal is achievable *and* values the goal itself. Teachers who create such environments have taken into account their students' interests, backgrounds, opinions, and developmental characteristics when designing the instructional activity. Although students may be moving around the room and the room itself may even appear chaotic to the outsider, closer examination reveals that most of the students are on task. The task they have been challenged to complete holds some intrinsic value for most of the students, frequently because it involves them in creating something "important" rather than merely completing an assignment to please the teacher. For that reason, they choose to complete the task rather than disturb or distract others.

Creating an environment that encourages **self-motivation** refers to an environment in which students complete their work because it is important to them rather than to comply with someone else's expectations or a set of classroom rules. Students become increasingly self-motivated as their feelings of *significance* (the sense of being valued gained from being involved in a positive two-way relationship), *competence* (being able to perform a socially valued task as well as or better than others of one's age level), and *power* (ability to control one's physical, emotional, and intellectual environment) increase.[3] Where an elementary teacher's understanding of young children might lead him to build instructional activities around novelty, a secondary teacher might recognize that students are less motivated by novelty than they are by complexity, incongruity, and functionality; therefore, instructional activities might focus on the application of knowledge and skills to the solution of real-world problems.

No one will dispute that individual and group behavior play a role in the degree to which a classroom can be supportive of all students, can be engaging to all students, or can be personally motivating to individuals within the class. Even the most experienced teacher will sometimes need to intervene when one or more students' behaviors are distracting enough to warrant the intervention. Where the experienced teacher might look for an explanation of the behavior problem in terms of unmet needs or unshared values, the inexperienced teacher might simply demand compliance with class rules on penalty of removal from class. Furthermore, experienced teachers will readily acknowledge that the more engaged the students, the more self-motivated the students, and the more the students feel safe and competent, the less they create behavior problems.

"The purpose of our classroom management plan is to provide a framework by which we may build an environment conducive to teaching and learning."

"I promise to only assign homework that has a purpose and will benefit your learning. I will not assign busywork just so you have something to do. I know you are busy and have many commitments with family, sports, music, church, etc. With that understanding, I expect you to complete the homework you are assigned to the best of your ability. I promise I will respect your time at home, so out of courtesy please complete each assignment thoroughly and accurately."

"In a well-managed classroom students have input in the decisions that are made. They desire to experience a sense of control and power over their environment. Involving students in the decision-making process and giving them choices can be very impacting. I must be sure that the classroom objectives are being met, but overall students should be given input on classroom rules and procedures, because if they feel like they helped create them, they are more likely to abide by them."

---

[2]Newmann, F., & Wehlage, G. (1993). Five standards of authentic instruction. *Educational Leadership 50*(7), 10.
[3]Coopersmith, S. (1967). *The antecedents of self-esteem.* San Francisco: W.H. Freeman as cited in Jones, V., & Jones, L. (1995). *Comprehensive classroom management: Creating positive learning environments for all students.* Boston: Allyn and Bacon, p. 39.

WHAT ARE THE IMPLICATIONS OF THIS KNOWLEDGE BASE FOR MY PORTFOLIO?

In your portfolio, then, you must gather and present evidence of what you know about motivation and classroom management, both theories and practices, and what you can do with that knowledge. Artifacts and reflections should reveal your tendency to design lessons and activities based on the needs and interests of your students while still addressing the curriculum you are charged with teaching. A reviewer should see your classroom management efforts as community building with emphasis on communication and self-motivation/regulation. To understand the implications of Principle 5 in greater detail, review the following list of knowledge, skills, and dispositions identified within the INTASC principle document:

Knowledge

- The teacher can use knowledge about human motivation and behavior drawn from the foundational sciences of psychology, anthropology, and sociology to develop strategies for organizing and supporting individual and group work.
- The teacher understands how social groups function and influence people, and how people influence groups.
- The teacher knows how to help people work productively and cooperatively with each other in complex social settings.
- The teacher understands the principles of effective classroom management and can use a range of strategies to promote positive relationships, cooperation, and purposeful learning in the classroom.
- The teacher recognizes factors and situations that are likely to promote or diminish intrinsic motivation and knows how to help students become self-motivated.

Dispositions

- The teacher takes responsibility for establishing a positive climate in the classroom and participates in maintaining such a climate in the school as a whole.
- The teacher understands how participation supports commitment and is committed to the expression and use of democratic values in the classroom.
- The teacher values the role of students in promoting each other's learning and recognizes the importance of peer relationships in establishing a climate of learning.
- The teacher recognizes the value of intrinsic motivation to students' lifelong growth and learning.
- The teacher is committed to the continuous development of individual students' abilities and considers how different motivational strategies are likely to encourage this development for each student.

Performances

- The teacher creates a smoothly functioning learning community in which students assume responsibility for themselves and one another, participate in decision making, work collaboratively and independently, and engage in purposeful learning activities.
- The teacher engages students in individual and cooperative learning activities that help them develop the motivation to achieve, by, for example, relating lessons to students' personal interests, allowing students to have choices in their learning, and leading students to ask questions and pursue problems that are meaningful to them.

- The teacher organizes, allocates, and manages the resources of time, space, activities, and attention to provide active and equitable engagement of students in productive tasks.
- The teacher maximizes the amount of class time spent in learning by creating expectations and processes for communication and behavior along with a physical setting conducive to classroom goals.
- The teacher helps the group to develop shared values and expectations for student interactions, academic discussions, and individual and group responsibility that create a positive classroom climate of openness, mutual respect, support, and inquiry.
- The teacher analyzes the classroom environment and makes decisions and adjustments to enhance social relationships, student motivation and engagement, and productive work.
- The teacher organizes, prepares students for, and monitors independent and group work that allows for full and varied participation of all individuals.

These statements may be distilled down to the following strands:

- Creating a smoothly functioning learning community in which students assume responsibility for themselves and one another, participate in decision making, work collaboratively and independently, and engage in purposeful learning activities.
- Relating lessons to students' personal interests, allowing students to have choices in their learning, and leading students to ask questions and pursue problems that are meaningful to them.
- Managing the activity in the classroom by organizing, allocating, and managing the resources of time, space, activities, and attention to provide active and equitable engagement of students in productive tasks.
- Developing shared values and expectations for student interactions, academic discussions, and individual and group responsibility that create a positive classroom climate of openness, mutual respect, support, and inquiry.
- Ordering factors and creating situations that are likely to promote intrinsic motivation and knowing how to help students become self-motivated.

Your reflection and artifacts, at a minimum, ought to address some combination of these issues (though it is not likely you will deal with all of them).

TYPES OF ARTIFACTS

Possible portfolio artifacts include the following:

- *Classroom management plans* revealing your ability and efforts to create and support learning communities in your classroom
- *Reflections and journal entries* on classroom management issues and observations
- *Projects or assignments* from professional course work relevant to classroom management and student motivation
- *Lesson plans and unit plans* (especially those using a variety of instructional strategies to engage students in active learning, and to promote effective communication, group and individual responsibility, and respect for oneself and others)
- *Evaluations* from the cooperating teacher and student teaching supervisor
- *Transcripts (optional)* showing course work you have taken in the areas of motivation and classroom management

EXAMPLE ARTIFACT

Now let's review an artifact and reflect on what it reveals about the teacher's knowledge, dispositions and performance skills relevant to Principle 5. The classroom management plan that follows was one of several artifacts offered to document one teacher's having met the expectations of the principle.

CLASSROOM MANAGEMENT PLAN

PHILOSOPHY

The purpose of our classroom management plan is to provide a framework by which we may build an environment conducive to teaching and learning. The expectations and procedures for our class will allow me to teach effectively and will allow you to learn. The classroom expectations and procedures are for your benefit because you and I want to be successful!

EXPECTATIONS

The list that follows is a beginning set of classroom rules. In the next few days, we will work together as a class to understand these rules and add others you think are important. Since we all share this classroom, we must work together to establish our rules so we can all agree to them and use them.

Beginning Rules

- Be in class on time and ready to learn!
- Be respectful and kind toward other students with both your actions and your words.
- Listen, stay focused, and be respectful in class.
- Keep the room clean and orderly.
- Be willing to try new things.
- Be in your seat ready to work when the bell rings.

PROCEDURES

Attendance. I will do my very best to be in class at all times. I expect the same from you. I understand that sickness occurs, and family priorities can take you away from school. I do expect you to do your best to be here every day. If you have an excused absence (accompanied by the appropriate documentation from the office) you will be able to make up missed assignments or tests. You will not be able to make up for unexcused absences. I will do my best to make every class meaningful so that you want to be here.

Tardies. Being on time is very important. It helps you because you don't miss out on learning, and it helps me because I am able to focus on the lesson. If you are tardy, come in quietly and join the class without disruption. At the end of class it is your responsibility to come to me with your pass or reason for being tardy. Unexcused tardies will be dealt with according to school policy.

Homework. I promise to only assign homework that has a purpose and will benefit your learning. I will not assign busywork just so you have something to do. I know you are busy and have many commitments with family, sports, music, church, and so on. With that understanding, I expect you to complete the homework you are assigned to the best of your ability. I promise I will respect your time at home, so out of courtesy please complete each assignment thoroughly and accurately.

Grading. I hope all students will learn. You will have challenging goals set before you with each unit of study. I will assign grades frequently, so you know how well you are doing at meeting the goals and so I know how I am doing at teaching. As the school policy states, the percentage range for each letter grade is as follows:

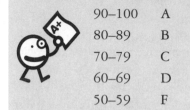

90–100	A
80–89	B
70–79	C
60–69	D
50–59	F

Assistance. If you ever have a question in class about an assignment you are working on, first ask a classmate next to you for clarification. Often your peers are great tutors, and they may be able to explain something clearer than I can. If your classmate is unable to help you, please raise your hand and I will call on you or come to your desk and help.

Several things are at work here. First the teacher put the classroom rules and expectations in the context of learning and success for the students. This personal approach is reinforced in several ways, including the use of the second person *you* throughout the document as a way of investing each student with the responsibility and ownership of the class and its management. This is a positive approach to classroom management. The rules and expectations are clearly laid out for the students but with some room for their input into the refinement and further development of the rules. The statements are direct, informative, and reasonable but made less threatening by the use of clip art within the body of the document as a way of making it more child-friendly and pleasant.

This artifact gives us a beginning idea of this candidate's attitudes and beliefs about classroom management. Clearly it is more than an issue of managing behavior, though that is a significant focus of the document. It attempts to establish a collaborative environment among both students and teacher. It is clearly not sufficient to document all of the expectations of Principle 5, but the document begins to reveal a disposition and hints at a knowledge base relevant to classroom and behavior management. In addition, it reinforces evidence of technology competence, as well as communication skills. It is, therefore, a useful artifact for the portfolio.

Writing a Reflection for Principle 5

Now let's look at the reflection accompanying the previous artifact. How does it work as a reflection, and how well does it support the case for the teacher having met the expectations outlined in Principle 5?

TEACHING COMPETENCY REFLECTION

CLASSROOM AND BEHAVIOR MANAGEMENT

INTASC Principle 5 says "The teacher uses an understanding of individual and group motivation and behavior to create a learning environment that encourages positive social interaction, active engagement in learning, and self-motivation." The research by Wang, Mararegt, Haertel, and Walberg has concluded, after reviewing 11,000 pieces of research that spanned 50 years, that the most important factor governing student learning is classroom management! Wow! This research can either place a huge burden of guilt on teachers who are not good classroom managers or it could excite them to become better classroom managers. To know that it is me as the teacher who makes the difference in the classroom is motivating.

Classroom management by Harry Wong's definition refers to "all of the things that a teacher does to organize students, space, time, and materials so that instruction in content and student learning take place." Wong, an expert on classroom management, wrote, "Classroom management includes all of the things a teacher must do toward two ends: To foster student involvement and cooperation in all classroom activities, and to establish a productive working environment."

It is comforting to know that if I create in my classroom an environment that is welcoming, safe, organized, and consistent, my students will learn and I will love teaching. I found during student teaching that if I was excited to see the students, presented them with a safe and organized environment and was fair with them in my discipline, they were with me all the way (Artifact: tab #3, Positive Behavior Intervention System).

I believe that one key to having an effectively managed classroom is having high expectations. Students thrive off of being challenged and pushed to succeed. In Foundations of Education, I was taught that students will only achieve as high as you expect them to. The expression, "Shoot for the moon, and even if you don't reach it you will land among the stars" gives me a mental picture of what I want for my students. In my classroom management plan my expectations are clearly stated (Artifact: tab# 3, Classroom and Behavior Management Plan). During student teaching I found that if I stuck to my guns and remained consistent with the level of expectation then my students rose to the task, were generally well behaved, and productive.

Understanding and applying motivational theory is essential to an effectively managed classroom. I have read theories posed by Wigfield, Ford, and Brophy, but the one that explains motivation the best is the theory by Vernon and Louise Jones. "Motivation = expectation × value × climate." In other words, motivation equals the belief that "I can do this," "This is important," and "I feel supported by those around me." Currently in my classroom, I communicate my positive expectations to my students, I help them to see that what they are learning is important and beneficial, and I ensure that the students feel supported by their classmates and me.

In a well-managed classroom, there are procedures for everything! I have thought through how I want everything done in the classroom so as to leave minimal room for distraction. Procedures help the day go by with a minimum of wasted time and confusion. I personally have a procedure for beginning the period, taking roll, students asking questions, turning in homework, quieting the class, dealing with absences, grouping, and the list goes on. If I explain, rehearse, and reinforce these procedures, my classroom will run smoothly and both the students and I will get the job done. During student teaching, I found that rehearsing the "quiet down" strategy of dimming the lights was quite effective. I explained the strategy, modeled it, and we rehearsed it a few times. After that, the students knew what their expected behavior was and they followed through and quickly were able to quiet down.

In a well-managed classroom, students have input in the decisions that are made. They desire to experience a sense of control and power over their environment. Involving students in the decision-making process and giving them choices can be very impacting. I must be sure that the classroom objectives are being met, but overall students should be given input on classroom rules and procedures, because if they feel like they helped create the rules, they are more likely to abide by them.

If a classroom is managed well, then there will be little need for behavior management. A well-managed class keeps students on task and thus minimizes misbehavior. However, "Peoples is peoples" as the *Muppets Take Manhattan* would say. We are all human. Life is complex and draining and at times students are just going to misbehave. There are, of course, varying degrees of misbehavior such as misbehavior to get attention, to avoid or escape a problem, to control events, or to get revenge (Toppers, 1994). There are also students who are diagnosed as behaviorally disturbed. Whatever the case, I must not overreact and calmly be prepared to handle misbehavior as it arises.

I must be aware of the different possibilities for analyzing and understanding misbehavior (such as behavioristic, constructivist, psychodynamic, and environmental approaches) so that I diagnose and treat the misbehavior correctly. In student teaching, I found that much of the misbehavior was a desire to get a rise out of another student or distract someone else, or it was due to the student's environment (such as who the student was sitting next to). I did, however, deal with a few instances where the student's family life struggles were, as you would say, "throwing more wood on the fire."

The Circle of Courage is a behavior management program I have implemented with great success. After watching videos and reading the handouts on the program in Classroom and Behavior Management class, I am very interested in implementing its principles in my classroom. The plan states that students have four needs: belonging, independence, mastery, and generosity. Students in my classroom will know that they are special and that they are an important part of the group. Cooperative learning can help meet this need. My students will be able to exercise independence in the choices I offer them. All of my students will experience a high degree of mastery with every objective. All students will be empowered to achieve and will taste success. I will provide many opportunities for my students to be generous as well. Service learning projects are a wonderful way to get students to focus on the needs of others instead of being egocentric (Artifact: tab #3, Service Learning Project).

I have talked with friends and relatives who are currently teaching, and they all said they were *not* prepared to manage a class. I know that I have learned valuable theories and have been forced to think through tough situations by means of case studies and student teaching experiences. I do, however, believe that continual teaching experience is what is going to make it click. By nature teenagers are changing every day; therefore, I must be flexible. I believe one of the best ways for me to grow as a teacher in the area of classroom and behavior management is to step back and reflect each day. "What worked?" "Why didn't this work?" "What was going on with this student that might have caused him or her to act out?" "Am I being consistent?" I will practice reflection because questions such as these keep teachers honest and moldable.

Identification of context. The candidate spends a good deal of time talking about the expectations of the principle and some of the classroom management theories and theorists. This gives the reviewer a considerable amount of evidence of theoretical knowledge and dispositions. In other parts of the reflection, one finds a few nuggets of information about the candidate's application of this theoretical knowledge.

Observation and description of artifact (experience or document). There is surprisingly little description of the artifacts or experiences in this reflection. If one believes a portfolio reflection is intended to give the reviewer insight into the artifacts within the context of theory, then this reflection, while informative and lengthy, does not really satisfy its purpose. This leaves the reader with the notion that the candidate has a lot of theoretical knowledge and maybe some dispositions, but that the skills and performances may still be lacking. One will hope the artifacts reveal a more practical knowledge of classroom management. This is perhaps the weakest part of a promising reflection.

Application of theories or principles of effective practice. The candidate provides ample evidence of his or her knowledge of theories and theorists. One does not, however, find much application of that theoretical knowledge although, presumably, the artifacts will provide evidence of application. Certainly the classroom management artifact presented earlier gives some evidence (albeit limited) of the candidate's ability to apply what she or he has learned.

Identification, analysis, and interpretation of causes and effects. This reflection spends a lot of time projecting what will happen in the candidate's classroom but little time on what has happened. Artifacts are listed but not really reflected upon. Only once does the candidate reveal an instance of having actually applied his or her learning to the classroom: "During student teaching, I found that rehearsing the 'quiet down' strategy of dimming the lights was quite effective. I explained the strategy, modeled it, and we rehearsed it a few times. After that, the students knew what their expected behavior was and they followed through and quickly were able to quiet down." Here is a good example of applying a strategy. Having too little of this type of reflection weakens the overall impact of the reflection and puts enormous weight on the artifacts to reveal application without benefit of commentary.

Projection from observations toward problem solving and lifelong learning. We find the candidate projecting about the future but not really in the context of the expectations of Principle 5, student learning or professional development. Rather she or he uses the final paragraph of the reflection to talk about the values of classroom experience and reflection. While these are good things to think about and do, they do not constitute a projection toward problem solving and lifelong learning. Add this to the fact that the reflection almost never reflects on practical application of the knowledge base, and one begins to wonder whether the candidate has actually applied anything he or she has learned in training. A reviewer will certainly be impressed with the candidate's discussions of the theory but will likely feel slightly unsatisfied and eager for the artifacts.

All in all, this might be judged a passable reflection, revealing a fair amount of knowledge and disposition. Still, if a reviewer is eager to see reflection on action and in action, this will not satisfy that expectation. The reflection needs much more specific reflection on the artifacts offered within the context of the theoretical knowledge so nicely presented.

A rubric for the expectations presented in Principle 5 follows. Using that rubric, and based on the contents of the reflection and the one artifact you have seen, where would you place this candidate?

Meets the Standard	*Not Yet Meeting the Standard*
The preservice teacher provides evidence of not only knowing but also applying motivation theories and behavior management strategies and techniques to create a collaborative, participatory, and individualized learning environment that encourages positive social interaction, active engagement in learning, and self-motivation. The preservice teacher demonstrates the capacity to actively engage students in their own learning and the effort to encourage all students to set, monitor, and adjust their learning goals and behavior.	The preservice teacher may recount the principles (or theorists) of individual and group motivation and behavior management but offers little or no evidence of the ability to design and implement a collaborative, participatory, or individualized learning environment that encourages positive social interaction, active engagement in learning, and self-motivation. Maintaining control may be emphasized over student empowerment.

This candidate, based solely on the reflection and one artifact, seems to fall more into the "not yet meeting the standard" column of the rubric. We get a lot of information about theorists and theories but little practical application. Of course, this might change with the review of more artifacts.

SUMMARY

Too many educators get bogged down in the effort to control their students rather than empowering them to control themselves and to contribute positively to the community of their classroom. Many young teachers are more worried about systems of punishment than they are about communication systems and collaboration. If one puts education in the context of preparing productive citizens for a democratic republic, then such approaches to classroom management are contradictory, at best. Professional educators must see classroom management as much more than behavior management and work to make their classrooms miniature communities where their students can learn and practice self-management, good citizenship, effective communication, and positive work habits.

Here are some questions to spark your thinking and help you identify and select effective artifacts for your portfolio:

1. When have I been a part of creating a learning community?
    a. In what ways and with what tools have I helped students assume responsibility for themselves and one another?
    b. What examples do I have of letting my students participate in decision making in the learning process and environment?
    c. What activities, lessons, and procedures have I devised to help students learn to work collaboratively and independently?
2. What examples do I have of having created and implemented purposeful learning activities?
    a. Relating lessons to students' personal interests?
    b. Allowing students to have choices in their learning?
    c. Leading students to ask questions and pursue problems that are meaningful to them?
    d. Getting students to actively and equitably engage in productive, meaningful learning activities?

3. How do I manage my classroom's activity (time, space, resources, activities, and attention)?
4. What examples do I have of helping students develop shared values and expectations that create a positive classroom climate of openness, mutual respect, support, and inquiry?
   a. Classroom interaction?
   b. Academic discussions?
   c. Individual and group responsibility?
5. When and how have I gone about ordering factors and creating situations that are likely to promote intrinsic (self) motivation?

DISCUSSION QUESTIONS

1. What is a learning community, and why is it so important to effective teaching and learning?
2. Why is it important for students to take responsibility for themselves and one another, to participate in decision making, and to work collaboratively and independently?
3. What is meant by "purposeful learning activities"? Why is this idea important for motivating learners?
4. Why should students have choices in their learning? What is the value of leading students to ask questions and pursue problems that are meaningful to them?
5. Why are organizing, allocating, and managing the resources of time, space, activities, and attention essential to classroom management and to motivating learners?
6. How is classroom management supported by developing shared values and expectations for student interactions, academic discussions, and individual and group responsibility? How might these help create a positive classroom climate of openness, mutual respect, support, and inquiry? Why are these important?
7. What is intrinsic motivation, and why is it good for teachers to foster this in their students?

Implementing INTASC Principle 6 in Your Portfolio

Communication is an essential skill utilized by any teacher. It is important to be a culturally competent communicator. It is also important to identify the belief systems of both the student and teacher in order to spot blocks to communication.

Unknown

Keisha sat quietly viewing and reflecting on the videotape of her lesson. What did it show about her knowledge of communication and how she supported good communication in the classroom? As the moments passed, she began to see a pattern of behavior among her students and herself that she hadn't noticed before: There was a respect and civility that had not been evident when she first began working with her class. How had they gotten to that point? As she reflected, she began to trace the actions she had taken to rein in a rampant disrespect among many of the children, especially in their relationships with other students. A big part of the solution was getting the students to begin using appropriate language rather than abusive language and physicality to express their frustrations and concerns. Over several weeks, there was a shift from loud, disturbing behavior to a calmer, more thoughtful atmosphere. Sure there were still problems, but she and the other class members could easily handle those. The video clearly showed her modeling the desired respectful behavior. With a good reflection to trace her decisions and actions leading up to it, this might be a good artifact for her portfolio.

QUESTIONS TO CONSIDER

■ How do you communicate with your students? How do they communicate with each other?

■ How would you describe the culture of your classroom?

- How does one go about establishing a supportive and collaborative culture in the classroom? What does such a culture look like?
- What are the characteristics of active inquiry?
- What other ways of communicating exist outside of written and oral communication? How can these other forms of communication impact teaching and learning?
- Why is communication outside the classroom so important?
- How can a teacher model and use communication to empower students?
- What role does communication play in development and thinking?

Communication is a key performance skill every successful person possesses. It involves much more than correct grammar, spelling, and word usage. What's more, it may not even be verbal language at all. Communication is interaction in all its forms, and it is an essential element of effective classroom cultures. How you speak with students, how and in what forms you communicate with parents and others, and how you help students learn to communicate and work together in your classroom community are all the purview of this standard. But how do you *communicate* your abilities relevant to this principle? To do so, you need to give evidence of the different ways you communicate and that you are effective in doing so. Moreover, you need to let the portfolio reviewer see into the classroom to understand how you influence the communication flow. We are models for our students, and much of what they learn about social interaction is based on what they see adults do in school. At base, then, the portfolio needs to reveal the effective use of various forms of communication in the classroom. The artifacts must also reveal that students are practicing, *in all content areas,* the communication skills the teacher is modeling, in groups, within class discussion, and in presentations (traditional or technology enhanced). This is a good place for the teacher also to reveal the ability to effectively communicate with parents and colleagues.

UNDERSTANDING PRINCIPLE 6

Principle 6: The teacher uses knowledge of effective verbal, nonverbal, and media communication techniques to foster active inquiry, collaboration, and supportive interaction in the classroom.

Principle 6 expects you to exhibit certain knowledge and skills:

1. Demonstrated knowledge of *"effective verbal, nonverbal and media communication techniques."*
2. The use of this knowledge to *"foster active inquiry, collaboration, and supportive interaction in the classroom."*

This principle is often called the communication principle. That may be too limiting because while the standard does ask the preservice teacher to demonstrate his or her *knowledge* of various forms of communication, it more specifically requires the use of that knowledge to *foster* certain behaviors integral to effective classrooms: *active inquiry, collaboration, and supportive interaction.*

Effective verbal, nonverbal and media communication techniques encompass a number of important issues, including the following:

- Understanding how communication and miscommunication occurs
- Understanding the qualities of good writing and speaking
- Understanding how people may use nonverbal communication for various purposes, both positive and negative

■ Understanding how communication issues impact the development and support of effective communities

■ Understanding how to use various forms of media communication, including written communications, public speaking, electronic communications, and presentation programs. (*Note:* In the early 1990s when INTASC developed its principles, technology in the service of teaching and learning was still fairly young. Since the mid-1990s, the amount of software, hardware, and Web tools available to teachers and students has exploded, as federal, state, local, and foundation money is poured into schools to increase student and teacher access to these tools. The INTASC principles, to date, have not been revised to reflect this growth in the importance of technology. However, the National Education Technology Standards for Teachers [NETS•T, see chapter 14] give excellent guidance on what teachers and students ought to know about technology and be able to do with it.)

The intention of this knowledge base is to create and support a community of learning involving the following three key activities:

■ *Active inquiry* suggests students be involved in question generation and exploration. They are not just passive receivers of information, but they are also actively involved in discovering and constructing knowledge.

■ *Collaboration* is more than just cooperating, (i.e., working side by side); it is working together to achieve a common goal important to all participants. One would expect, then, to see students engaged in learning teams actively working together to solve problems, to accomplish shared tasks, or to develop shared products. The implications are important for social development among students and their success throughout their lives.

■ *Supportive interaction* is more difficult to define. It is as much about community building in the classroom as it is about sharing ideas. In a supportive classroom, one would expect to see communication being used as a tool for problem solving and mediation. Respect is a key feature of the classroom culture, demonstrated by both the teacher and the students. The entire classroom recognizes, supports, and models the diversity of ideas, experiences, cultures, and values.

WHAT ARE THE IMPLICATIONS OF THIS KNOWLEDGE BASE FOR MY PORTFOLIO?

Principle 6 really defines culture building in the classroom, so that is what your portfolio has to reveal. First you need to demonstrate an understanding and effective use of communication in all forms. Then you must demonstrate that your teaching and your students' behaviors model and reflect that understanding in ways that represent a learning community in action. Your portfolio needs to show that you understand the integral relationship between communication and cognition and that you actively and consciously model and support the kind of communication that contributes to building this community. Moreover, the activities and strategies in which you and your students engage—as evidenced by your lesson plans, unit plans, projects, evaluations, and so forth—reveal an active community of learners engaged in critical processes, self-reflection, inquiry, and collaborative work. Anyone who reviews your portfolio must come away with the clear impression of a teacher who facilitates learning by creating the atmosphere and conditions necessary for effective communication and, therefore, successful learning and achievement.

To further clarify the implications of this principle, look at the following performance indicators:

Knowledge

- The teacher understands communication theory, language development, and the role of language in learning.
- The teacher understands how cultural and gender differences can affect communication in the classroom.
- The teacher recognizes the importance of nonverbal as well as verbal communication.
- The teacher knows about and can use effective verbal, nonverbal, and media communication techniques.

Dispositions

- The teacher recognizes the power of language for fostering self-expression, identity development, and learning.
- The teacher values the many ways in which people seek to communicate and encourages many modes of communication in the classroom.
- The teacher is a thoughtful and responsive listener.
- The teacher appreciates the cultural dimensions of communication, responds appropriately, and fosters culturally sensitive communication by and among all students in the class.

Performances

- The teacher models effective communication strategies in conveying ideas and information and in asking questions (e.g., monitoring the effects of messages, restating ideas and drawing connections, using visual, aural, and kinesthetic cues, being sensitive to nonverbal cues given and received).
- The teacher supports and expands learner expression in speaking, writing, and other media.
- The teacher knows how to ask questions and stimulate discussion in different ways for particular purposes, for example, probing for learner understanding, helping students articulate their ideas and thinking processes, promoting risk taking and problem solving, facilitating factual recall, encouraging convergent and divergent thinking, stimulating curiosity, and helping students to question.
- The teacher communicates in ways that demonstrate sensitivity to cultural and gender differences (e.g., appropriate use of eye contact, interpretation of body language and verbal statements, acknowledgment of and responsiveness to different modes of communication and participation).
- The teacher knows how to use a variety of media communication tools, including audiovisual aids and computers, to enrich learning opportunities.

These knowledge, skills, and dispositions can be distilled in six issues that should be demonstrated by the artifacts and reflection(s) included in your portfolio:

- Knowing and applying communication theory, language development, and the role of language in learning to support student learning and positive student interaction
- Communicating (via both listening and responding) effectively with a variety of audiences for a variety of purposes tied to professional practice
- Using media and communication tools to enhance professional practice and student learning
- Encouraging communication and higher-order thinking processes in the classroom by using active, thoughtful inquiry, collaboration, problem posing, and problem solving

- Modeling and creating an environment for the effective, supportive, and nonbiased use of language and communication in the classroom and school environment
- Recognizing and building on the connections between language, culture, and personal identify and how the effective use of language can support personal student development and success
- Initiating, monitoring, and sustaining cognitively stimulating discussions that encourage student-to-student conversation, risk taking, problem solving, and critical thinking; and that demonstrate sensitivity to such discussion-related issues as wait time and gender bias.

ARTIFACT SELECTION

When deciding which artifacts to include in your portfolio, you must ask yourself at least the following questions:

1. What documents or other artifacts show me using effective communication for a variety of purposes with a variety of audiences?
2. What evidence do I have that I can create a positive and supportive classroom environment for all students?
3. What lessons and units reveal my ability to use communication, collaboration, and active inquiry to enrich my students' experience and challenge them to extend the range of their critical abilities?
4. What documents do I have that reveal my ability to use media communication tools not only to enhance my own teaching but also to support my students' cognitive development and level of achievement?

TYPES OF ARTIFACTS

As sources for documenting your abilities to use effective communication to create a positive and supportive classroom environment, the following categories of artifacts will be particularly fruitful:

- *Classroom communications,* notes/newsletters to parents, media presentations (may include video clips), videotapes of classroom communication and culture
- *Reflections* on communication issues inside and outside the classroom, as well as one's own communication performance
- *Action research* you have conducted to examine and improve your classroom communication abilities
- *Projects or assignments* from professional course work
- *Lesson plans and unit plans,* especially those using various forms of communication in the classroom to promote effective communication, responsible group and individual interaction, and media communication skills
- *Professional development opportunities* you have taken to better understand and improve your communication skills and your teaching environment
- *Evaluations* from faculty, cooperating teachers, and the student teaching supervisor reflecting upon and evaluating your communication knowledge and practices
- (potentially) *Transcripts and course grades* indicating you have successfully completed courses in communication theory and practice.

EXAMPLE ARTIFACT

Look at the artifact displayed in Figure 9.1 and reflect on what it reveals about the teacher's ability relevant to the professional knowledge and behaviors demanded by Principle 6.

THE FRESHMAN ENGLISH NEWS

Keisha Forrester, Editor and Teacher
4th Hour Freshman English Class

Volume 2, Number 4:   October 12, 2004

What's Happening Next Week?

In Class
October 15th: Finish Reading Poe's "Masque of the Red Death" and turn in analysis and reflection journals
October 16th: Group Selection of Poe Story for Radio Theatre
October 17th: Radio Theatre Examples and the Scriptwriter (guest)
October 18th: Group Work Day on Radio Theatre Script
October 19th: Submit Draft of Script in Conference

In the School
Auditions for Thornton Wilder's *The Skin of Our Teeth:* Tuesday, 4:00 p.m. in the auditorium. Audition for a part in this rollicking, absurd comedy that follows the trials and tribulation of the Anthrope family.
Math Club Bake Sale! Friday Be sure to bring some extra "dough" to buy some goodies. All proceeds go to help pay for the Math Club members' participation in the city-wide Math Olympiad.
Music Assembly on Friday: Senior Choir will perform works they will be taking to the State Music Competition
Parent-Teacher-Student Conferences! *Wednesday Night, 4:00 'til 9:00* Here's a great opportunity to get together the whole family to look our work and set goals for the rest of the year (see story for more details).

How To Contact Ms. Forrester:
School Number: 555-9000
Classroom Phone: 555-9980
E-mail: kforrester@shs.edu
Regular Mail: Shenandoah High School, 2199 South Jefferson, Erewhon, MO 64039

Students Explore Eerie World Of Edgar Allen Poe

(Shenandoah High School) Freshman English students in Ms Forrester's Freshman English class have spent the last week involved in may projects and activities designed to help them understand, appreciate and even enjoy the writings of one of America's best-known and most frightening writers, Edgar Allen Poe.

The students read and discussed a number of Poe's writings, including his short stories and poems.

Poe is considered the "father of the modern short story" by many critics and is believed to be the author of the first murder mystery, "Murders in the Rue Morgue." A number of his short stories have been adapted for movies, many of them starring the late Vincent Price, who

The Reading List
- "The Cask of Amontillado"
- "The Pit and the Pendulum"
- "The Black Cat"
- "The Telltale Heart"
- "Murders in the Rue Morgue"
- "The Raven"
- "Lenore"

lived in St. Louis, Missouri, before moving to Hollywood. Many authors owe a debt to Poe for paving the way for the beginnings of the horror story. Stephen King, among others, has openly expressed his debt to Edgar Allen Poe, saying his early exposure to Poe's works help to shape his own macabre imagination and storylines.

During the study of Poe's works, your children have been memorizing poetry, creating posters and PowerPoint Presentations and Poe, his work and the time in which he wrote.

The students have identified and used the elements of the short story, often using these elements to analyze other short stories we have read thus far in the class and that we have found in other sources. The students have used these elements and structures to create their own stories, poems, and artworks, which are being collected into our own literary magazine (coming out just in time for holiday giving).

Ask your child about Edgar Allen Poe and the things he has written. You are sure to be amazed at what we have learned so far. *Coming Next Week: Some Thrilling and Scary Poe Radio Theatre!*

Parents, Teachers and Students Make Plans

(Shenandoah High School) Parents, Teachers and Students will meet Wednesday evening (4:00 to 9:00) to review student work and to set goals for the coming year.

Parent-Teacher-Student Conferences give everyone an opportunity to have input into what our class' goals will be for the rest of the year. These important events help you get acquainted with your child's teachers, to communicate your expectations for what your child will learn at school, and help your child understand and share in setting personal goals for the rest of the year. This is one of many ways you can support your child's success in school, so please plan to attend and reserve a time by calling Ms. Forrester at 555-9980 before 8:30 a.m., between 1:00 and 2:00, or after 3:30 p.m. I can also meet with parents and students at other times and places by appointment. *Please take time to be a part of your child's success in school!*

FIGURE 9.1

Communication Skills Artifact

The artifact in Figure 9.1, a classroom newsletter, is typical of those often included in a portfolio because such newsletters (and other pieces of written text) are the easy examples of communication skills. They are, by their very nature, limited, however, so a reviewer will expect to see much more than this as documentation of one's ability to use *"knowledge of effective verbal, nonverbal, and media communication techniques to foster active inquiry, collaboration, and supportive interaction in the classroom."* This is not, however, an empty artifact. One can glean from it a number of inferences about the teacher and her or his communication skills and how she or he uses communication to foster collaboration, at least between the teacher and the parents. First, it is well written and clearly keeps its audience in mind. The amount of important information is relevant. In it the teacher includes homework assignments as a reminder for both the parent and for students. In this way the teacher keeps the parents informed not only about what is going on but also about what their child should be doing at home and in class. Moreover, the teacher connects the parents and students to what is going on in other areas of the school, giving parents and students at least the knowledge of events to allow them the opportunity to participate if they wish.

By discussing in some detail the Edgar Allen Poe unit, including giving the list of readings from the unit, the teacher gives the parent some insight into classroom objectives, content, and activities. This gives the parents information that may be used to promote conversation at home about what is going on at school. The story even prompts parents to ask their children about the unit. The mention (in more than one place) of the radio theater activity also helps connect parents to activities and sets additional expectations for what the students should be able to talk about at home.

The story about parent-teacher-student conferences gives the parents a well-worded reminder about the event and offers them the chance to make alternate arrangements if desired. The contact information in the sidebar gives parents a number of ways to connect with the teacher. One gets a clear sense that this teacher recognizes the value of collaborating with parents to support student learning and is capable of developing ways to support and promote this collaboration.

Is this artifact sufficient to meet the standard? Probably not. A reviewer would likely want to see other evidence, especially evidence from lesson plans and reflections about how the teacher encourages good communication in the classroom, active inquiry, and a supportive atmosphere. A classroom management plan that talks about communication in the classroom would be a good artifact, as would an evaluation of the communication patterns apparent in the teacher's classroom interactions. A video clip revealing classroom discussion skills would also be a good artifact, particularly if it shows giving students time to think and involving many students in the discussion.

WRITING A REFLECTION FOR PRINCIPLE 6

The following is a reflection for Principle 6. How does it work as a reflection, and how well does it support the case for the teacher having met the professional expectations outlined in the principle?

PRINCIPLE 6: TEACHER AS AN EFFECTIVE COMMUNICATOR

Artifacts:

E: Parent Newsletters, January–October 2004 (Publisher).

F: Classroom Management Plan (Microsoft Word)

G: Methods Class PowerPoint Presentation: Communication Issues in the Classroom

H: Communication Flow Case Study Analysis (PowerPoint)

Principle 6 sets a high standard for communication in the classroom. Within the standard are a number of issues that extend beyond just verbal and nonverbal communication. The principle states that the preservice teacher "models effective verbal, nonverbal, and media communication techniques to foster active inquiry, collaboration, and supportive interaction in the classroom." Therefore, the teacher must demonstrate not only the use of appropriate language and communication skills, but also the ability to create a climate in the classroom that promotes those same skills among the students. But the standard does not stop there; it also expects the teacher to create a high-level learning community to engage students actively in learning, in inquiry, and in the sorts of social experiences that support this kind of learning community.

Artifact E consists of several newsletters I designed and wrote to parents during my student teaching. The newsletters demonstrate my ability to clearly communicate, both visually and in written form, about the activities in our classroom to foster supportive interaction between parents, students, and the teacher. I created the newsletters using Publisher, which I learned how to use during a teacher in-service workshop in February. I enjoy writing and creating things on the computer, so I volunteered to be responsible for the newsletter for my cooperating teacher. I collaborated with her regarding what topics to cover in each issue; then I organized the layout, wrote the text, and inserted pictures and clip art. By using the Publisher program along with pictures that I took with my digital camera, I demonstrate my ability to use a variety of media tools for communication.

The newsletters were a valuable tool for communicating to parents about what the students were learning in the different subjects and encouraging them to ask their teenagers about our classroom activities. The intent was to facilitate the connection between what the students were learning at school and their everyday lives. The students were eager to receive the newsletter and to show it to their parents. We (myself and my cooperating teacher) received comments from a few of the students' families that they appreciated being updated about their child's school activities via the newsletter.

In January, before I had learned how to use the Publisher program, I created the newsletters on Word. Looking back, I admit that they did not have much pizzazz; they did not include any graphics or pictures, only typed information under various headings. I bought a digital camera and began taking pictures of the students and their activities at about the same time I learned about the Publisher program. This technology greatly enhanced the visual appeal of the newsletters and increased the effectiveness of the communication. I definitely plan to use a newsletter program like Publisher when I become a teacher.

Artifact F is a classroom management plan for my English classes. This plan demonstrates the sort of classroom atmosphere I wish to create to motivate my students to actively engage in meaningful learning in a safe, respectful, and stimulating environment. The plan includes an analysis of the characteristics of adolescents and young adults, focusing on the ways they interact, the things they value, their way of looking at the world, and what motivates them. Against this background, I then explore what I learned about my students from their teacher and from them, their specific interests, talents, beliefs, experiences, cultures, and so on that they will bring with them into the classroom. Based on these, I determined that my classes needed to allow students to somewhat direct what we were to explore, while still addressing the district curriculum. This took the form of the authors we read, the kinds of writing we did, the amount of group work we undertook, and the kinds of projects they completed. I even gave them input into the classroom rules and consequences for breaking them.

While there were still problems from time to time, I found that the students were truly up to the task of managing themselves once I created the kind of interesting and engaging learning activities that would keep them on task. That was the hardest part of the whole plan, keeping up with the need for creative and motivating experiences that were tied to the curriculum and yet were consistent with what I knew would best motivate the students. I found early on that technology is a great tool for supporting this kind of classroom interaction and inquiry. But I still need to learn more about co-operative groups, other forms of technology, and how to manage the Internet within the context of a high school classroom. I have already signed up for an advanced technology in teaching and learning workshop for this summer in hopes that I will have more things to use in my own classrooms when I begin teaching in the fall.

Artifact G is a PowerPoint presentation that I created in my English/Language Arts methods course. The purpose was to use a medium other than print to communicate to my classmates about the various issues relating to supporting communication and interaction in the classroom. In the presentation, I began by discussing cognitive development issues such as the relationship between discourse and thinking skills (Rowe 1987) and Vygotsky's belief that "social interaction with others spurred the construction of new ideas and enhanced the learners' intellectual development" (Arends 1997). With this background, I then discussed a number of topics including "wait time" (Rowe 1987) or "think time" (Stahl 1990), the impact of questioning strategies on "substantive conversation" and "social support for student achievement" (Newman and Wehlage 1993), and Sadkers' research on gender bias in the classroom (1995). For each of these issues, I gave an example of what and what not to do.

This presentation shows that I have a theoretical foundation on which I may develop and support communication structures and practices in my classroom. Social interaction is an important component of learning but only if it is safe, respectful and purposeful. In my classroom, as you can see from the classroom management plans, I try to utilize these ideas. In particular I apply procedural elements such as wait/think time, cooperative grouping, questioning strategies, and consciously addressing questions and accessing responses evenly across my students, both male and female. Moreover, I utilize a number of techniques in addition to cooperative grouping to support positive social interaction and learning. For example, I use reciprocal teaching techniques to strengthen student comprehension of their reading. This interaction technique calls on students to help each other build and utilize comprehension strategies to get more from their reading. This technique pairs students as reading partners and asks them to take responsibility for each other's understanding of reading assignments.

After I implemented these strategies in my student teaching, I immediately noticed more thoughtful discussion of reading assignments. I also noticed fewer students not reading the assignments. I have found cooperative learning groups to have the same impact. Moreover, students improved their scores on comprehension tests as well as constructed response tests, which asked them to explain or apply what they had learned in their reading.

Artifact H is a Communication Flow Case Study Analysis. I did this analysis as part of my student teaching seminar. The study had me videotape a class I taught while I was student teaching. I and a partner reviewed our own and each other's videotapes, mapping the communication patterns for the hour. Therefore, I had to draw lines from me to the students, among the students, and back to me as a means of capturing the characteristic flow of the class discussion. I needed to answer questions such as "Who initiates most of the discussion in the classroom?" "How would you characterize the flow: Centralized? De-centralized? Organic? High structured? Spontaneous?" "Who controls the flow of information?"

What I found was a pattern of me asking a question, me recognizing a student, he or she answering the question, and me asking another question. I did not see much interaction among the students, so they were not really engaged in discussion; in fact, there was no discussion. This surprised me because I was so sure we were having a lively give and take. Not so. The case study was really an eye-opener for me. It showed me that even though I wanted an interactive classroom of motivated students, what I had was a class of students waiting for their chance to perform with me calling the shots. I have since worked very hard to develop discussions that are more student centered and less teacher centered. Cooperative group discussion with large-group reports work out well, as does asking different students to lead discussions. I have also gotten better at asking open-ended questions and then acting as a facilitator among the students, letting them guide the direction of the conversation. I have heard of the Socratic seminar, which is a good way to lead such discussions. I hope to get more information and training on this in the future, so I can continue to develop my ability to stimulate my students' interactions and thinking.

I believe I am a proficient communicator, and I am getting better at creating opportunities for my students to engage in the kinds of thinking, inquiring, and communicating that will help them become better learners and citizens. By providing students with varied methods of expression (speaking, writing, creating a physical product), I will be more effective in reaching these objectives and meeting the expectations raised by Principle 6 because I am fostering active inquiry, collaboration, and supportive interaction in the classroom. I believe it is important to provide students with experience speaking, writing, listening, and creating. I plan to incorporate all of these modes of communication in my teaching.

First, let's compare this reflection with the elements of a good reflection:

Identification of context. The preservice teacher begins by explicating Principle 6 for the reviewer, indicating that it is more than simply a requirement for writing and speaking proficiency. The teacher goes on to explain briefly the additional expectations given by the principle.

After this, and for each of the artifacts presented as documentation for Principle 6, the teacher gives a brief description of the context for the artifact, either the assignment that led to its creation or the teaching experience that necessitated its creation. Beyond that, however, we get only a little information about the students or the classroom environment, as appropriate. Still, the reader has at least a little context within which to interpret or evaluate the artifacts.

Observation and description of artifact (experience or document). Here the teacher gives us plenty to go on, describing in fair detail the artifact, its development, and its relevant features. For example, when talking about the newsletters, the teacher gives a reason for doing the newsletters, names the software used to develop them, identifies the kinds of stories and pictures included, explains how she or he took them, and lists other features (e.g., hyperlinks) included.

Application of theories and/or principles of effective practice. The evidence of reflection supported and informed by theory and professional literature is somewhat inconsistent in this reflection; however, the candidate's discussion of the PowerPoint presentation and the classroom management plan clearly have foundations in some of the literature on communication and classroom interactions, as well as motivation and management. Moreover, the teacher's reflection on the newsletters, while not citing research, mentions the need for and value of keeping parents abreast of what is going on in school so that they can interact with their children about the work and expectations. Additionally, the teacher reflects principles of effective practice and good reflection on action. For example, "I have since worked very hard to develop discussions that are more student-centered and less teacher-centered. Cooperative group discussion with large-group report outs works well, as does asking different students to lead discussions. I have also gotten better at asking open-ended questions and then acting as a facilitator among the students, letting them guide the direction of the conversation."

Identification, analysis, and interpretation of causes and effects. In a number of places, the candidate gives evidence of cause-and-effect thinking. For example: "What I found was a pattern of me asking a question, me recognizing a student, he or she answering the question, and me asking another question. I did not see much interaction among the students, so they were not really engaged in discussion; in fact, there was no discussion. This surprised me because I was so sure we were having a lively give and take. Not so. The case study was really an eye-opener for me. It showed me that even though I wanted an interactive classroom of motivated students, what I had was a class of students waiting for their chance to perform with me calling the shots." And "While there were still problems from time to time, I found that the students were truly up to the task of managing themselves once I created the kind of interesting and engaging learning activities that would keep them on task."

Projection from observations toward problem solving and lifelong learning. For nearly every artifact, the teacher talks about what she or he would do differently next time and what sorts of continued learning and professional development the teacher sees in the futures to enhance his or her teaching ability.

Based on this analysis and applying the rubric holistically, we can conclude that this reflection is somewhat successful. It gives the reviewer enough evidence to see the student performing appropriately when measured against the rubric for reflection.

What about the expectations of Principle 6? Are they sufficiently met by the evidence? We cannot be absolutely sure because we have not seen all the evidence. However, based on the reflection alone, where would you tend to place this teacher on the following rubric?

Meets the Standard	*Not Yet Meeting the Standard*
• The preservice teacher uses clear and articulate verbal, nonverbal, and media communication tools in all interactions with students, parents, colleagues, and the community. • The candidate uses these communication tools and techniques to support the learner's development of effective communication skills and to foster active inquiry, collaboration, and supportive interaction in the classroom. • Use of communication/media technology is appropriate and varied.	• The preservice teacher demonstrates effective personal oral and written communication skills and presentation techniques and may describe how these might be used develop learners' skills or to foster active inquiry, collaboration, and supportive interaction in the classroom without actually demonstrating the ability. • Interactions with students tend to be the same with no efforts to individualize. Evidence indicates limited knowledge of and use of media communication/media technology.

This teacher fits into the "Meets the Standard" column of the rubric. The reflection and the artifacts referred to in the reflection seem to reveal a teacher who can communicate well and is conscious of the need for students to have good models for communication within a learning community (i.e., "to support the learner's development of effective communication skills and to foster active inquiry, collaboration, and supportive interaction in the classroom"). Moreover, she or he is focused on student achievement and sees communication and student involvement as keys to success in the classroom.

SUMMARY

Professional educators must be excellent communicators and understand the role of communication and positive social interaction in effective teaching and learning. Communication in all its forms is key to making the classroom a safe place to inquire, develop, and test theories about how the world works. Developing such an environment is a complex task requiring a great deal of knowledge about how students learn in general and what individual learners know and have experienced before they enter the classroom.

Here are some questions to help you gather your evidence and prepare your reflection:

1. How do I communicate with my students, their parents, and my colleagues?
   - What examples do I have of these communications?
   - What have been the results, good and bad, of these communications?
   - What steps have I taken to improve the effectiveness of my communication abilities?
   - How do I know I am an effective communicator?

2. How do I build a classroom community that is supportive, active, and positive?
   - What is my definition of a learning community? When have I successfully created such a community?
   - What instructional strategies have I used to build learning communities and to support collaboration and positive engagement among my students?
   - When and how have I helped my students become better communicators, verbally, nonverbally, and interpersonally?

3. When and how have I used media communication and other technologies to support student learning and achievement?
   - In what lessons and instructional activities have I employed technology to teach complex concepts in ways that interest and motivate students to learn?
   - In what ways and in what situations have my students used these technologies to increase their own learning and achievement?
   - How have I used technology to support positive communication with students, their parents, and my colleagues?

DISCUSSION QUESTIONS

1. What kinds of communication go on in the classroom?
2. Why is it important for an educator to be a good communicator?
3. What kind of communication should a teacher model for students? How might he or she model such communication?
4. What role does communication play in active inquiry?
5. How might a teacher (and his or her students) create a positive, supportive environment in the classroom?
6. What sorts of communication does an educator engage in outside the classroom? How are these different from or the same as the communication that goes on in the classroom? How might these communications contribute to the supportive environment of the classroom?
7. How does an educator's communication style shift or change with regard to different audiences and purposes (e.g., to involve parents, to value students, to communicate negative information to a parent, to communicate with a mentor, to bring a complaint to the school principal, or to report to the Board of Education on a classroom project)?
8. How can an educator find out how well she or he is communicating?

Implementing INTASC Principle 7 in Your Portfolio

To begin with the end in mind means to start with a clear understanding of your destination. It means to know where you are going so that you better understand where you are now so that the steps you take are always in the right direction.

Stephen R. Covey

Professor VanderHaar flipped through the pages of the fourth portfolio he had read that day, trying to find just one good artifact that revealed the student's ability to create lesson plans and coherent unit plans. All he could find were lessons downloaded from the Internet and isolated instructional activities disconnected from each other and from any sort of coherent curriculum. "Doesn't Principle 7 specifically ask for evidence of the ability to plan with a curriculum in mind?" he said aloud. "I know we have talked about this again and again from the first class in the program till the end. We've given students multiple lesson formats, grounded them in the state content standards and curriculum frameworks, and even brought in sample district curricula. Why can't they make the connection? All I want is a coherent set of lessons tied to standards and the curriculum, plus evidence that the teacher has at least paid some attention to where the students are coming from. Why don't they get it?"

QUESTIONS FOR CONSIDERATION

- Why do I need to develop short-term and long-term plans? What kinds of planning does a teacher have to do?
- How do I plan lessons and activities to address the various learning styles of diverse learners?
- Why do I need to develop plans that are appropriate for curriculum goals and standards?
- What is the relationship between students, standards, community, curriculum goals, and instruction?

- Why do teachers need to plan assessment when they start planning their instruction?
- What community resources are available to enhance teaching and learning? How can teaching resources be part of lesson planning?
- What role does reflection play in lesson planning and instruction?

Principle 7 asks teachers to demonstrate four types of planning: curriculum planning, assessment planning, activity planning, and resource planning.

- The curriculum planner asks, "Which social studies subject knowledge, skills, attitudes, and values are essential?" "What are the performance-based instructional objectives?" "What content knowledge standards and performance standards are aligned with the objectives?"
- The assessment planner asks, "What evidence would indicate whether the essentials have been learned?" "What assessment plan is designed besides written tests, a checklist, or a rubric?"
- The activity planner asks, "What activities will engage my students' interest"—both physically ("hands on") and intellectually ("minds on")—"based on student needs for a sustained period of time?"
- The resource planner asks, "What resources do I need and what resources do my students need?" "Where are they, and how do I get them?"

Knowing how to fill out the template of ready-made lesson plans is far from sufficient to prove you know how to plan lessons and how to implement them under the auspices of curriculum goals and standards, especially as teachers are coming under growing pressure to increase the effectiveness of their teaching and their students' achievement. Merely printing prepackaged lesson templates from previous courses or the Internet shows nothing of your ability to harness the power of planning to actively engage students in learning activities and to challenge them to extend their understanding of the content beyond the basics.

An essential act of teaching is the design of curriculum and learning experiences or activities to meet specified objectives. Lessons and units ought to be clearly tied to your state's K–12 standards or grade-level expectations, at least, if not also to the district curriculum for the classroom(s) in which you may teach. Portfolio artifacts ought to reveal your understanding of the standards you are teaching, what they require of students, and how this may be reflected in and supported by classroom instruction and student achievement. Moreover, your instructional strategies and assessments ought to reveal a clear and conscious tie to these standards and expectations. Finally, you need to offer evidence that you can create thoughtful, standards-based lessons and unit plans that create a logical, useful, and realistic process for facilitating student learning.

Educators are also designers of assessments to diagnose student needs, to guide teaching, and to enable them, their students, and others (parents and administrators) to determine whether goals have been achieved. Did the students learn and understand the desired knowledge and skills? How do you know or what evidence do you have to prove that your students achieved the objectives you set? Clearly, students are your primary clients, given that the effectiveness of curriculum, assessment, and instructional activities is ultimately determined by student achievement. The artifacts for this principle, including assessment data and reflective writings, should document student achievement relative to the lesson objectives. Therefore, across the range of artifacts included in your portfolio, and within your reflective statement, you must show your understanding of both short- and long-range planning; interdisciplinary planning and teaching; meaningful activities that consider student needs and learning styles; higher order thinking;

and the ability to tie objectives, curriculum goals and standards, activities, and assessment together as a meaningful whole. You should orchestrate all of these components to achieve one goal: student learning.

UNDERSTANDING PRINCIPLE 7

Principle 7: The teacher plans instruction based upon knowledge of subject matter, students, the community, and curriculum goals

"For this lesson, I selected Social Studies Standards 2 and 6 because they require students to understand change in the history of the United States, in this case, as a result of the development of the continental railroad."

"The activity provides a developmentally appropriate experience for students by addressing a number of different learning needs (e.g., social, analytic, and artistic) to guide them in their study of the cattle kingdom and features of the westward expansion."

"To develop the unit, I had to first look at the district curriculum for this content and to determine exactly what the learning objectives were to be."

Principle 7 asks for evidence of a candidate's ability to plan instruction based on four important issues: (a) subject matter, (b) students, (c) the community, and (d) curriculum goals.

Subject matter refers to the actual content and content-related skills a teacher must teach. These pieces of content and associated skills are related in many ways to the *content knowledge* explored in Principle 1. The key here is to understand that the way we teach is substantially dictated by the material we are teaching. Different kinds of content may require very different instructional strategies.

Students, too, are a key consideration when a teacher is planning meaningful learning experiences. Different learners at different developmental stages, potentially with different abilities, experiences, conceptions of the world, and intelligences, are likely to require different instructional strategies.

Community can be broadly defined to include the school community; parents, guardians, and other relatives of students; the business and governmental community; and the community at large. These constituents of the community are resources, reality checks, and limiters. They are resources because they can provide teachers and students with excellent opportunities to enhance learning and to see content in context—that is, in action in the real world. However, communities also place limitations on schools and classrooms because "the community" clearly has a stake in what goes on in the school room. Achievement, socialization, community standards, and skill development all concern parents, governments, business, and the broader community whose taxes pay for public education. Moreover, research clearly indicates that the community needs to play an essential role in any successful effort to close the "achievement gap" and increase achievement overall.

Curriculum goals may have a number of sources: your own determination of what is most important for students to learn; what the school district has identified as curriculum appropriate for students in different subjects and at different grade levels; the state educational authority whose standards, grade-level expectations, and assessments invariably promote a particular set of curriculum goals; and, finally, national standards and expectations set by professional organizations and the federal government. These various "masters" generally inform each other and, therefore, have much in common. That said, there may be significant differences in the emphases with which educators must wrestle when determining what is most important for teachers to teach and students to learn.

WHAT ARE THE IMPLICATIONS OF THIS KNOWLEDGE BASE FOR MY PORTFOLIO?

In your portfolio, then, a reviewer will expect to see both individual lessons and long-term unit plans tied to at least a set of state goals, but preferably also to appropriate district curriculum goals and content expectations. These ties to external curricular goals must be explicit and appropriate. A lesson purporting to address a higher-order thinking goal while making sole use of rote memory and other lower order thinking skills does little to document alignment to established curriculum goals. Moreover, your portfolio will need to reveal your conscious accessing and consideration of the various communities in which your students and school reside. But most important, you must demonstrate two essential ways of thinking: one focuses on the abilities, needs, and backgrounds of individual students; the other focuses on the demands of the content you are teaching. Your reflections, journal entries, and other elements in your portfolio should reveal an educator who thinks about how his or her students' needs, prior knowledge and experience, as well as their abilities influence the way she or he teaches particular curricular issues. Also, your evidence must show that your choice of content, instructional strategies, materials, and so on arise out of both your understanding of your students and your understanding of the content you are teaching.

In your portfolio you must also document your knowledge of short- and long-range planning components, including the following:

- Curriculum goals and standards
- Objectives aligned with content standards
- Sequences of meaningful activities based on students' needs and instructional objectives
- Hands-on and minds-on assessments aligned with objectives
- Resources
- Reflections on the effectiveness of the lesson or unit with suggestions for improving it

Your reflections, journal entries, and commentaries on this standard must make explicit reference to student learning. The reviewer must see you using your short- and long-range plans as instructional tools as well as for assessment and evaluation. It would also be useful to see you communicating with a variety of audiences about instruction and student performance. Furthermore, you must exhibit your ability to encourage students to engage, explore, and access the content you are teaching.

Principle 7 expects the following knowledge, dispositions, and performance skills. You can use them as checklists when you reflect on your teaching in terms of student learning.

Knowledge

- The teacher understands learning theory, subject matter, curriculum development, and student development and knows how to use this knowledge in planning instruction to meet curriculum goals.
- The teacher knows how to take contextual considerations (instructional materials, individual student interests, needs, and aptitudes, and community resources) into account in planning instruction that creates an effective bridge between curriculum goals and students' experiences.
- The teacher knows when and how to adjust plans based on student responses and other contingencies.

Dispositions

- The teacher values both long-term and short-term planning.
- The teacher believes that plans must always be open to adjustment and revision based on student needs and changing circumstances.
- The teacher values planning as a collegial activity.

Performances

■ As an individual and a member of a team, the teacher selects and creates learning experiences that are appropriate for curriculum goals, relevant to learners, and based on principles of effective instruction (e.g., that activate students' prior knowledge, anticipate preconceptions, encourage exploration and problem solving, and build new skills on those previously acquired).

■ The teacher plans for learning opportunities that recognize and address variation in learning styles and performance modes.

■ The teacher creates lessons and activities that operate at multiple levels to meet the developmental and individual needs of diverse learners and help each progress.

■ The teacher creates short-range and long-term plans that are linked to student needs and performance and adapts the plans to ensure and capitalize on student progress and motivation.

■ The teacher responds to unanticipated sources of input, evaluates plans in relation to short- and long-range goals, and systematically adjusts plans to meet student needs and enhance learning.

Principle 7 therefore asks for evidence of the following broad areas:

1. Ability to plan lessons and activities to address variation in learning styles and performance modes, multiple development levels of diverse learners, and problem solving and exploration
2. Ability to develop plans that are appropriate for curriculum goals and rooted in effective instruction
3. Ability to adjust plans to respond to unanticipated sources of input or student needs
4. Ability to develop short- and long-range plans

Your reflection and artifacts, at a minimum, ought to address some combination of these strands (though it is not likely you will deal with all of them).

ARTIFACT SELECTION

When deciding which artifacts to include in your portfolio, you must ask yourself at least the following questions:

1. Which documents and other artifacts (lesson plans, unit plans) reveal my understanding of the whats, hows, and whys of planning in teaching and learning?
2. Which documents reveal my ability to develop rigorous, challenging lessons that use a variety of resources and are based on diverse learner needs?
3. Which artifacts show my skill in relating instructional objectives, standards, and assessments?
4. Which pieces of my work show my skill in choosing meaningful activities that help students engage in meaningful learning?
5. Which artifacts show what I take into consideration when choosing adequate resources to strengthen the activities?
6. Which documents show my ability to write learning objectives based on student outcomes directly related to the assessment strategies?
7. Which documents show my ability to match subject matter and instructional strategies and activities?

TYPES OF ARTIFACTS

Possible portfolio artifacts include the following:

- *Long-range unit plans and lesson plans* revealing ties to district and state as well as national standards for student learning and showing interdisciplinary approaches across the curriculum
- *Student work samples* demonstrating the results of lessons/assessments and the teacher's application of standards to score them
- *Assessments* tied to lesson objectives and content standards for student learning
- *Evaluations* from teacher education faculty, cooperating teacher, and student teaching supervisor
- *Reflections and journal entries* revealing your thinking on lessons and units, including modifications and adjustments made to enhance learning.

EXAMPLE ARTIFACT

Now let's review an artifact and reflect on what it reveals about the teacher's knowledge, dispositions, and performance skills relevant to the planning standard.

Topic: The Cattle Kingdom

Subject: Social Science

Grade Level: 5

Resources:
Unitedstreaming Video: *Real American Cowboy*

Subject: Social Science—Grades: 4–6

Synopsis: Looking through film clips, contemporary photos, and tools of the cowboy trade, learn how the real American cowboy led a tough and lonely life on the American plains. Produced by Discovery Channel School.

Children's Literature, Music, Drama, Other Disciplinary Areas, and Internet Links:

1. *Cowboys* (March 1996) by Lucille Recht Penner, Ben Carter (Illustrator), Grosset & Dunlap
2. *Rodeo-Ridin' Cowboy* (October 1999) by Andrea Davis Pinkney (Author), Brian Pinkney (Illustrator), Voyager Books; Reprint edition

Details

Behavior Objective: After using the text, video clips, children's literature, and a class discussion, the students will create a cow town that includes stockyards, hotels, stores, restaurants, and other businesses with 100% accuracy.

Standards:

- MO-SS.2: Continuity and change in the history of Missouri, the United States, and the world
- MO-SS.6: Relationships of the individual and groups to institutions and cultural traditions
- NCSS-1.1.a: Enable learners to analyze and explain the ways groups, societies, and cultures address human needs and concerns

- NCSS-1.5.b: Help learners analyze group and institutional influences on people, events, and elements of culture in both historical and contemporary settings
- NCSS-2.1 *Disciplinary Standard*—History: Teachers who are licensed to teach history at all school levels should possess the knowledge, capabilities, and dispositions to organize and provide instruction at the appropriate school level for the study of history. Teachers of history at all school levels should provide developmentally appropriate experiences as they guide learners in their study.
- NCSS-2.1.b: Enable learners to develop historical comprehension so that they might reconstruct the literal meaning of a historical passage, identify the central questions addressed in historical narrative, draw upon data in historical maps, charts, and other graphic organizers, and draw upon visual, literary, or musical sources.

Anticipatory Set:

- Students will watch the video clip, *Real American Cowboy*, which shows contemporary photos and tools of the cowboy trade, to learn how the real American cowboy led a tough and lonely life on the American plains.
- The teacher will read aloud *Cowboys* by Lucille Penner to lead the students to today's topic, "The Cattle Kingdom."

Materials:

- Class social studies textbooks
- Plain white paper
- A pencil
- Crayons, markers, or colored pencils
- The teacher will need to provide blank U.S. Maps for each student: www. eduplace.com/ss/maps/pdf/us_nl.pdf.

Procedure of Hands-On Activity:

1. The teacher will explain that today the class is going to talk about "The Cattle Kingdom," explored on Pages 482–485 in their social studies book. While speaking, the teacher will hand out the rubric for the lesson.
2. Next, the teacher will have the students read pages 482 through 485 with a partner. The teacher should explain that this reading is important because the students are going to use this information for their activity. (20 min)
3. The teacher will have the students discuss information from the text that they found to be new or interesting. The teacher can use the following questions as prompts for the discussion. (10 min)
   - What effect do you think the cattle drives and railways had on the Native Americans?
   - What is the difference between a railhead and a cow town?

4. Then the teacher will explain that today the students will illustrate a cow town. The teacher will pass out a map of the United States and the students will choose where on the map they want their cow town to be. It must be near a railroad, and the students must illustrate the railroad on the map as well. They can use the maps from their text on pages 478 and 485. (5 min)
5. The students will each receive a piece of paper to draw their cow town on. The teacher will explain that the cow town should include a stockyard, hotel, restaurant,

store, and other businesses. The students will then discuss what other businesses may have been in a cow town at the time seeing that these towns were for cowboys resting while waiting for the next train. (5 min)

6. The teacher will then pass out a bulleted list of these instructions titled "The Cattle Kingdom."

7. The teacher will discuss the rubric for this activity, asking students to explain the requirements and the differences between various points on the rubric.

8. The students will begin drawing their towns. After they are finished, they should illustrate their maps as well. They must draw a symbol for where their cow town is and draw a path of the railroad through the United States on their map. Then they will create a legend for their symbol and railroad. An example of where the railroads are on a map is shown on pages 478 and 485 of their social studies text. (20 min)

9. The students will then put everything away except their maps and cow town illustrations, and move on to the closure phase of the lesson.

Closure: Finally, the students will each discuss their illustrations and maps with the class. After each student talks about what he or she did, each will explain one new or interesting fact learned today.

Accommodated Plan for Students with Special Needs: If necessary, students can draw with a partner so that they can help each other.

Assessment: Throughout the entire lesson, the teacher should be monitoring the class and helping as needed. Student work will be assessed based on the rubric.

This lesson plan offers some evidence related to several issues from Principle 7. The artifact includes an instructional objective, content standards, resources, detailed procedures for the instructional activities, and an accommodation plan for special needs students—all things one would expect to see in a complete lesson plan. More specifically, the artifact demonstrates the candidate's ability to plan lessons and activities to address variations in learning styles by providing procedures for both hands-on and minds-on activities. Additionally, the plan leads the students to engage, to some extent, in critical thinking by having them explore multiple resources (e.g., the Internet, streaming video, children's literature, their textbook) to gather and synthesize information to successfully complete their work. Moreover, it includes appropriate topics for a fifth-grade curriculum with state and national social studies standards aligned with a somewhat narrowly written objective. It also reveals the teacher's inclination (though perhaps not clearly an adequate attempt) to adjust a lesson plan to accommodate students with special needs.

However, the artifact does not show the teacher's having addressed several other important issues from the standard. First, the artifact does not clearly demonstrate the link between this short-range lesson plan and a long-range plan (i.e., a unit plan). Teachers rarely teach lessons as single, one-time activities disconnected from a larger plan (usually tied to the district curriculum). This brings up another weakness—the lesson does not actually relate the lesson topic to district curriculum goals. It includes state standards and national standards, but it would be more effective to include district curriculum goals that may better demonstrate the appropriateness of the chosen topic in the context of the district's curriculum structure.

Finally, based on the lesson plan, the lesson appears to be more of a "fun activity" than a meaningful and important learning opportunity. The lesson does not demonstrate the teacher's ability to use a variety of assessment techniques to collect and analyze data, to interpret results, or to communicate findings to improve instructional practice and maximize student learning. The artifact refers to an assessment rubric for evaluating the "cow town," but the artifact does not demonstrate the ability to effectively assess the content knowledge expressed in the standards selected, especially relevant to Native Americans as part of American history (clearly part of the standards cited). One cannot be clear on what criteria the teacher holds for a project that successfully meets the standards or the objective. A reviewer would like to see at least the rubric, as well as graded samples of student work to complete the picture.

WRITING A REFLECTION FOR PRINCIPLE 7

Now let's look at the reflection that accompanies the artifact. How does it work as a reflection, and how well does it support or extend the case for the teacher having met the expectations outlined in Principle 7?

PRINCIPLE 7: CURRICULUM AND INSTRUCTIONAL PLANNING

Artifact N: Lesson Plan—The Cattle Kingdom
Artifact M: Unit Plan—Free Market Economy

Principle 4 requires that teachers know how to plan both long-term and short-term curricula and lessons to address the needs of their students, while also addressing the requirements set forth by the school district, the state, parents, and other members of the community. Teachers must be planners who think ahead about where they must get their students while keeping in mind where their students are at the moment. Many factors must be reflected in these plans: state and national standards, the district curriculum, the prior knowledge and experiences of students, the desires of their parents, and the resources available to help make the unit or lesson successful.

Artifact N: The Cattle Kingdom is a lesson I developed for my second student teaching placement in the fifth-grade class at Erehwon Elementary School. It is part of a larger unit on Westward Expansion and a good example of my ability to develop meaningful lesson plans based on state and district curriculum and standards. For this lesson, I selected Social Studies Standards 2 and 6 because they require students to understand change in the history of the United States, in this case, as a result of the development of the continental railroad. At the end of the lesson, we also discuss how this change affected the Native Americans and their lands. This can help the students better understand the relationships of the Native Americans to the U.S. government and the impact of government policies on Native American cultural traditions. Next I selected National Council for the Social Studies Standards 1.1.a, 1.5.b, 2.1, and 2.1.b because this activity will enable learners to analyze and explain the way the cow towns addressed the needs of the cowboys while they were traveling with their livestock on the railway. The lesson also helps students analyze the influence the cow towns had on the Native Americans and society today.

This lesson shows that I possess the knowledge and capability to organize and provide instruction at the fifth-grade level for the study of history because the activity provides a developmentally appropriate experience for students by addressing a number of different learning needs (e.g., social, analytic, and artistic) to guide them in their study of the cattle kingdom and features of the westward expansion. The activity of creating the towns helps them reconstruct the literal meaning of the text through tangible means. Students draw on data, such as maps, to locate their towns and identify central questions about the cattle kingdom, as well. I have organized the lesson so that everyone in the class can learn and benefit from it.

The students were motivated by the lesson and created detailed and accurate representations of cow towns and the functions they were designed to fill. While the students weren't initially excited about the research required for the activity, they soon got into it when they began to make connections between what they found out and the concrete representation they were required to create. The entire class stayed on task, and group members frequently helped each other out. The presentations and discussion afterward demonstrated the students' understanding of the material and their ability to make connections to content learned earlier in the unit and to experiences or knowledge they already possessed. The hands-on activity allowed the students to think about what they had read and discovered as they created the concrete representation. The drawing also gave the students a context for discussing differences of interpretation and helped all students refine their understanding of the content. On the unit test given later in the unit, students performed well above average on this and other content covered in the unit.

Artifact M: Free-market Economy Unit Plan was developed and taught during my first student teaching placement at Utopia Elementary School. My cooperating teacher suggested this topic because it was part of the economics portion of the district curriculum and because, as he clearly stated, he disliked and disagreed with this part of the curriculum. To develop the unit, I had to first look at the district curriculum for this content and to determine exactly what the learning objectives were to be. It was also important for me to know what the students had previously studied in the area of economics so that I could review and build on that previous learning. I, therefore, had to do a bit of research on the social studies curriculum at the lower grade levels as well. I designed the unit as a hands-on group activity in which we created and ran a microeconomy, with small groups developing businesses and acting as countries, and individual students maintaining personal finances. The unit required a lot of work to develop and implement, but the students found it interesting and exciting, and they really got into the roles they were asked to play. They also had to do a lot of research during the unit to gather and apply relevant economic information and data within their roles.

I have included the unit and corresponding lessons because they demonstrate that I am able to build on previously learned content and skills and to design and teach lessons that relate directly to the building/district curriculum. As well, the objective for each lesson is clearly aligned to the state standards for economics (Social Studies 8). Not critical to this standard, but important to me, is the fact that my cooperating teacher liked my unit so well that he plans to use it rather than what he has always used in the past. The students had more fun and demonstrated that they mastered more of the content than in previous years. Scores on their end-of-unit exams and projects showed that they learned more and performed better than any previous class, averaging 22% higher grades than prior classes.

Developing and teaching these lessons and unit helped me grow as a teacher because I have taken sometimes difficult content and created an original instructional activity that engages my students actively in the content they are responsible for learning. The experiences have reinforced my belief that hands-on, active engagement can better motivate students to learn and helps them reinforce and connect their learning. I have seen how these types of activities really get the students motivated and wanting to learn. I would like to explore other forms and resources for experiential and active learning, so I can make my units and lessons more coherent, more engaging, and academically richer. I have already signed up for a continuing education course on experiential learning at the university this summer and have plans to attend a constructivist teaching workshop and conference in the fall.

Let's compare this reflection with the elements of a good reflection:

Identification of context. For both artifacts, the candidate gives at least a cursory explanation of the context for the lesson and unit plan. In the case of the Cattle Kingdom lesson, we are also given detailed information about the standards and curriculum issues the lesson was intended to address. A reviewer would like to have received more reflection on the context for the free-market economy unit. The discussion of the research the candidate performed to determine where the content fit within the district curriculum and with his or her students' prior knowledge and experience gives good insight into the candidate's thinking processes and reinforces the impression of the candidate's professional preparation and practice.

Observation and description of artifact (experience or document). The candidate leaves the artifacts to speak for themselves and so spends little time describing what the reader will see in them. One would like to see more description of how each unit/lesson was created and how it unfolded, giving the reader a sense of how it supports the candidate's assertion of competence. Granted, we do not need a fully detailed narrative of all that went on; however, a reviewer will need enough information to see the principle in action. Remember, the reviewer does not necessarily have the artifact easily at hand when reading the reflection, so some description is necessary to provide background that will help the reviewer understand what the candidate is talking about. Moreover, the candidate asserts a number of conclusions about what the lesson addresses, about its developmental appropriateness, and about its meeting certain learning needs; however, these assertions are not born out by the lesson itself, nor are they explained in the reflection. This creates a contradiction in the mind of the reader, raising concerns about whether the candidate actually understands development and learning.

Application of theories or principles of effective practice. While specific theories are not identified within the reflection, it is clear the candidate is bringing theory into practice. References to hands-on, experiential learning, social/analytic/ artistic learning, developmental appropriateness, and critical reflection indicate the teacher's application of theory and principles of effective practice, at least for the lesson plan. For the unit plan, we get something of the same picture, but the connection to learning theory is less clear, so we are left needing to read the unit plan carefully to validate our impression.

Identification, analysis, and interpretation of causes and effects. The reflection for both the lesson and the unit plan gave some analysis of the effects of the candidate's planning/teaching on student performance. References to students staying on task, utilizing research, engaging in supportive behaviors, and assessment results give the reader a glimpse into the environment created for the learning opportunity as well as the student response to the learning. Still, these are just assertions, and the portfolio could benefit from student work samples showing what the students created within the lesson or unit and how the candidate assessed those products. This is somewhat mitigated by the candidate's mention of the increase in test scores compared to previous years.

Projection from observations toward problem solving and lifelong learning: At the end of the reflection, the candidate mentions one professional development goal arising from the experiences related in the reflection ("I would like to explore other forms and resources for experiential and active learning, so I can make my units and lessons more coherent, more engaging, and academically richer."). The candidate then identifies two plans for addressing this goal in the near term. The goal is tied somewhat to student learning and best practice.

Based on the artifact presented and the reflection, how would you rate the teacher against the following rubric for the principle?

Meets the Standard	*Not Yet Meeting the Standard*
• The preservice teacher demonstrates the ability to create and implement short-term curricular goals, the ability to set and to work toward long-term curricular goals, and the ability to evaluate the impact of a delivered curriculum.	• The preservice teacher demonstrates the ability to create and implement a short-term classroom curriculum without providing evidence of either the ability to set or to work toward long-term curricular goals or the ability to evaluate the impact of a delivered curriculum.
• The preservice teacher is aware of state and district knowledge and performance standards and considers those, as well as student needs, when planning lessons.	• Although lesson plans may include references to state knowledge and performance standards, references tend not to be reflected in what the K–12 students were actually asked to do.
• Instructional planning and implementation consider individual student learning styles and are constructed to build student skills in developmentally appropriate ways.	• Lessons tend to focus on whole-class instruction.
• During implementation, the preservice teacher demonstrates flexibility by evaluating and changing long- and short-term goals and instruction to meet student needs.	• Little evidence is available to indicate the teacher's ability or inclination to evaluate and change goals or instruction to meet student needs.

We may not be able to judge this candidate's performance without seeing the unit plan referred to in the reflection. The lesson plan is not as strong as we might like, though it has a number of elements one would expect to see in a lesson (e.g., goals, hands-on activities, performance activities). But we see some disconnect between the goals, the objective, and the instructional activities. In addition, we never fully understand the assessment for student work, so judging the alignment between goal/objectives and assessment is not possible. The candidate asserts in the reflection that he or she considered student development and learning styles in developing the lesson, but this is not necessarily clear from reading the lesson itself. Certainly the accommodation offered with the lesson is limited at best and is not likely to be effective for more than a narrow range of students—it only affects the construction of the cow town portion of the assignment. We see little evidence of the teacher demonstrating "flexibility by evaluating and changing long- and short-term goals and instruction to meet student needs." As a result, the lesson is not a strong artifact by itself. Even with the addition of the unit plan, without student work, assessment rubrics, and journal reflections on the lesson/ unit, it will be hard to fully evaluate the teacher's performance.

The reflection gives the reader considerably more to work on, with clearer insight into the creation of the lesson and a long-term curriculum unit. Here the candidate gives more consideration to what the students may already know, but we are given few details to illustrate how these findings are born out in the lesson/unit plans. We find more evaluation going on, with some good discussion of increases in student performance. Still, these appear to be assertions without clear evidence. A good bit of reflection on professional development goals and plans is evident.

Based on these findings, and without the unit plan, we cannot effectively judge the candidate's performance. Let us point out that in such cases, many reviewers are instructed to judge the portfolio as not having met the standard, so we must hope the candidate's unit plan is as powerful as the reflection asserts it to be.

SUMMARY

As the old saying goes, "If you don't know where you are going, any old place will do." Teachers have to know where they are going, not just in the short term but also in the larger scheme of things (i.e., within the context of a set of shared goals and expectations). If you have a clear sense of your destination, of the nature of the content you are planning to teach, of what your students know, and of how they best learn, then you are well on your way to creating a pathway to that end result. This kind of thinking, this drawing together of different pieces of the puzzle to create effective learning opportunities, is just what you will be expected to demonstrate within your portfolio.

To give you a little push in that direction, think about the following guiding questions:

1. What do I take into account when I am planning a lesson or a unit of lessons?
   - How do I consider the content?
   - How do I figure in my students?
   - Where do I come up with what I need or want to teach?
   - What external issues do I consider in the planning process?
   - What resources can I tap to enrich the experience?

2. How do I make sure my units and lessons are relevant, meaningful, and coherent?
3. What range of assessment strategies do I have in my toolbox to help me determine how well my students understand the content?
4. What is the theoretical basis for the choices I make in creating lessons and units?
5. How do I bring different content areas together to inform and strengthen one another?
6. How do I bring the community into the planning and teaching process?

DISCUSSION QUESTIONS

1. How might learners vary in their ways of learning? How can such variations be accommodated in classroom lessons and activities?
2. What are some sources for curriculum goals used to develop lessons? Why is it important to base instruction in such goals?
3. Why should teachers be flexible rather than tied slavishly to lesson plans or textbooks and teacher's editions? Why should they be able to adjust their plans to respond to unanticipated sources of input or emerging student needs or interests?
4. What are short-range and long-range plans? What is the difference between lesson plans and curricula?

Implementing INTASC Principle 8 in Your Portfolio

11

Assessment goes on continually in the classroom and is a natural part of the learning environment. The primary purpose of assessment is not to sort children or to compare schools; it is to improve teaching and learning.

Walter C. Parker

Beverly was assessing her students' map knowledge and skills before planning the geography unit. What had they learned in the unit? How deeply did they understand the concepts? Could they apply the concepts in situations other than those posed in the lessons? She began looking through her grade book, the students' test papers, her observational notes, and at the scoring guides for her assessments. She found a number of assessments: daily comprehension quiz grades, a paper-and-pencil test combining multiple-choice questions with some short-answer questions, a graded presentation of a group project, a graded diorama based on the unit information, and several pages of notes on what she had observed among the students as they interacted in class and in conversation with her. Reviewing what she had, she saw that most students had a clear grasp of the basic concepts of the unit, but only a couple of students scored well on the assessments requiring them to apply their knowledge. Moreover, her notes revealed that many of her students were inattentive during the times when they were supposed to be applying the knowledge in the group work and in the diorama work. She noted that many of the students seemed to be asking some of the same questions about the content in relation to these higher-level projects. Clearly, she could not easily go on to new concepts when her students did not have a clear understanding of the more basic concepts. How could she help them develop the higher-level understanding? Maybe a review of the kinds of errors they made in the assessments would give her some insights. With that in mind, she began to look again through the student assessments in her unit file.

QUESTIONS FOR CONSIDERATION

- What are the purposes of assessment?
- How do I incorporate formal and informal assessment strategies in my own teaching?
- How do I know if students have achieved the learning objectives of my lesson or unit?
- What are the principles of assessment?
- Why do I need to understand and be able to use various assessment strategies?
- How do I collect the assessment data to determine if my students have achieved the learning objectives I have set?
- How do I record the assessment data efficiently?
- How do I communicate meaningful assessment information to my students, their families, and my colleagues?
- How do I use assessment data to evaluate my own teaching?

Instruction and assessment are two sides of the same coin. A teacher must decide what she or he needs to teach (learning objectives based on curriculum goals), how to go about teaching it (instructional strategies), and then how to find out if the students have learned it (assessment). Assessment completes the process by helping the teacher (and others) find out if the students have actually learned what the teacher intended to teach them. Any good lesson or unit, then, will have an assessment plan built into it as a feedback loop to reveal learning.

One mark of an effective lesson plan is the link between each of the learner objectives and several assessments. Another mark is the appropriate selection of assessment types to match the level of the objective being assessed. The more diverse the types of instructional objectives, the more diverse must be the approaches to assessment. For example, a science unit may contain five instructional objectives: one related to factual knowledge, one to conceptual comprehension, one to data analysis, one to interpretation of findings, and one to collaborative skills. No single assessment approach is appropriate for all of these objectives. As a result, the teacher must devise several different assessments to get at the different objectives, from recall/recognition questions to application/synthesis questions or prompts. A simple written test may be appropriate for the factual knowledge, but the rest of the objectives need different assessment approaches that may not yield a single correct response.

Good assessment practice goes beyond traditional or even performance-based testing, with the shared goal of finding out what students learned. An effective teacher observes her or his class all the time, assessing where they are and the kinds of problems they are experiencing relative to the content. These observations are informal assessments intended to monitor learning as the lesson or unit is progressing. Such *formative* assessments allow the teacher to modify lesson plans and activities as the lessons unfold to meet the evolving needs of the students.

The full power of assessment is its use in providing feedback to students, reflecting on your teaching, and planning for the future. When used to inform the instructional process and plans for next steps, these assessment artifacts become examples of integrated teaching resources.

UNDERSTANDING PRINCIPLE 8

Principle 8: The teacher understands and uses formal and informal assessment strategies to evaluate and ensure the continuous intellectual, social, and physical development of the learner.

For my second-grade science unit on ecosystems, I created an assessment, which included multiple-choice and constructed-response questions, as well as a performance assessment.

Principle 8 asks for evidence of a candidate's ability to assess student achievement relevant to three important issues: (a) formal and informal assessment, (b) various assessment strategies or tools, and (c) the continuous intellectual, social, and physical development of the learners.

Formal and informal assessment refers the use of various means of evaluating and measuring the knowledge and understanding each student has gained relative to the instructional objectives targeted by the curriculum and the teacher. The assessment strategies run the gamut from traditional testing tools and more formalized alternative assessments to less formal assessments like classroom observation, student self-assessment, observational checklists, and questionnaires. Teachers do much of their evaluation of learning informally. Through daily observations and conferences with students, teachers can determine what gaps exist in their students' knowledge and understanding. Formal tests are more overt means of judging student progress; they yield quantifiable data for grades and other reporting purposes. Ranging from paper-and-pencil tests to performance assessments, these assessments require students to step outside the learning event and into the formal testing situation. Here they know they are being evaluated and having their performance noted. Whereas informal assessments primarily yield information of a formative nature about student progress, formal assessments tend to be summative, yielding data used to determine grades and final progress reports.

Topics covered in this class included formal and informal assessment, how to make objective and subjective written tests, validity and reliability of standardized tests, how to maintain the records using spreadsheets, and how to interpret standardized scores and communicate the data responsibly to students, parents, and community members.

Various assessment strategies refers to the many ways teachers may choose to evaluate student learning and the degree to which they have achieved the objectives. To have a clearer, more accurate picture of student achievement, teachers must collect multiple views of student knowledge and performance. These views may include informal assessment tools like observation logs and checklists of student collaboration, or they may include formal assessments, such as chapter tests, reading quizzes, reading logs, presentations, projects, and essays.

Additionally, teachers need to be aware of the assessments required by their states and districts as accountability measures of student achievement. Understanding the objectives of these assessments, their forms and structures, and their content will help you prepare your students to perform well on these tests. Students' being familiar with a test's format and expectations before taking it can make a big difference in their performance.

Students worked in cooperative learning groups, with partners, and individually. Considering their developmental levels and learning styles, students had opportunities during instruction to engage in hands-on, kinesthetic learning activities as well as to read, write, and draw about what they had learned.

Intellectual, social, and physical development refers to the different domains a teacher must assess to evaluate the development of the whole child. This may require teachers to broaden their assessment goals to include not only assessing students' learning at a single moment in time but also to evaluating their learning over time and assessing domains other than the cognitive. Most progress reports, especially at the elementary and middle school levels, include issues of social and physical development and issues of knowledge and skill development. These align to goals within state and district curricula and must be assessed. As we said earlier, instruction and assessment are two sides of the same coin; therefore, when teachers plan instruction relative to any of the domains, they must also think about how they will be assessing these same domains. Not all domains or goals may be assessed easily or effectively using formal paper-and-pencil tests. This requires teachers, then, to show the continuous, thoughtful use of a range of assessment types and the ability and inclination to collect and use assessment data to adjust, enhance, reinforce, or change instructional approaches to better support student learning.

WHAT ARE THE IMPLICATIONS OF THIS KNOWLEDGE BASE FOR MY PORTFOLIO?

In your portfolio you must document your knowledge of informal and formal assessment methods, including observation, conference, questioning, paper-and-pencil tests, and performance assessment, and your understanding of basic psychometrics (e.g., validity and reliability). Moreover, you must show how you have enhanced and monitored student learning, evaluated student progress and performances, and modified instructional approaches and learning strategies based on what you have learned from assessing your students. You must also demonstrate in your artifacts and reflection how you have involved learners in self-assessment activities to help them become aware of their learning behaviors, strengths, needs, and progress, and to encourage them to set personal goals for learning.

Although all classroom assessment is fundamentally about improving student learning, you must remember that assessment is not just about how students are performing; it is also about the effectiveness of your teaching. In your portfolio you need to include artifacts that demonstrate your ability to evaluate the effect of class activities on both individuals and the class as a whole. You also need to document how you keep records of student learning (e.g., your ability to use electronic grade books) and how you communicate student progress to students, parents, colleagues, and school administrators. Your assessment strategies and scoring guides must be explicitly designed to address student needs, collecting information on the instructional objectives identified for your lesson or unit.

Your reflections, journal entries, and commentaries on Principle 8 must make explicit reference to student learning. The reviewer must see you using your informal- and formal-assessment strategies as both a source for evaluating and improving student learning and for communicating with a variety of audiences about instruction and student performance. Furthermore, you must exhibit your ability to encourage students to assess their own progress, strengths, needs, and behaviors.

Principle 8, then, asks for evidence of the following broad areas:

1. Ability to employ a variety of formal and informal assessment techniques (e.g., observation, portfolios of student work, teacher-made tests, performance tasks, projects, student self-assessments, authentic assessments, and standardized tests) to enhance and monitor your knowledge of learning, to evaluate student progress and performances, and to modify instructional approaches and learning strategies

2. Ability to use assessment strategies to involve learners in self-assessment activities; to help them become aware of their learning behaviors, strengths, needs, and progress; and to encourage them to set personal goals for learning

3. Ability to evaluate the effect of class activities on both the individual and the class as a whole, collecting information by observing classroom interactions, questioning, and analyzing student work

4. Ability to maintain useful records of student work and performances and ability to communicate student progress knowledgeably and responsibly, based on appropriate indicators, to student, families, and colleagues

Principle 8 also expects the following knowledge, dispositions, and performance skills.

Knowledge

■ The teacher understands the characteristics, uses, advantages, and limitations of different types of assessments (e.g., criterion-referenced and norm-referenced instruments, traditional standardized and performance-based tests, observation systems, and assessments of student work) for evaluating how students learn, what they know and are able to do, and what kinds of experiences will support their further growth and development.

- The teacher knows how to select, construct, and use assessment strategies and instruments appropriate to the learning outcomes being evaluated and to other diagnostic purposes.
- The teacher understands measurement theory and assessment-related issues, such as validity, reliability, bias, and scoring concerns.

Dispositions

- The teacher values ongoing assessment as essential to the instructional process and recognizes that many different assessment strategies, accurately and systematically used, are necessary for monitoring and promoting student learning.
- The teacher is committed to using assessment to identify student strengths and promote student growth rather than to deny students access to learning opportunities.

Performances

- The teacher appropriately uses a variety of formal and informal assessment techniques (e.g., observation, portfolios of student work, teacher-made tests, performance tasks, projects, student self-assessments, peer assessment, and standardized tests) to enhance her or his knowledge of learners, evaluate students' progress and performances, and modify teaching and learning strategies.
- The teacher solicits and uses information about students' experiences, learning behavior, needs, and progress from parents, other colleagues, and the students themselves.
- The teacher uses assessment strategies to involve learners in self-assessment activities, to help them become aware of their strengths and needs, and to encourage them to set personal goals for learning.
- The teacher evaluates the effect of class activities on both individuals and the class as a whole, collecting information through observation of classroom interactions, questioning, and analysis of student work.
- The teacher monitors his or her own teaching strategies and behavior in relation to student success, modifying plans and instructional approaches accordingly.
- The teacher maintains useful records of student work and performance and can communicate student progress knowledgeably and responsibly, based on appropriate indicators, to students, parents, and other colleagues.

ARTIFACT SELECTION

When deciding which artifacts to include in your portfolio, you must ask yourself at least the following questions:

1. Which documents and other artifacts (lesson plans, unit plans) reveal my understanding of the whats, hows, and whys of assessing my students' achievement of instructional objectives?
2. Which documents reveal my ability to develop appropriate informal and formal assessment tools and activities based on diverse learner needs and instructional objectives?
3. Which artifacts show my skills in maintaining assessment records efficiently?
4. Which pieces show my skill in assessing students' behaviors and skills in each of the domains?

TYPES OF ARTIFACTS

Possible portfolio artifacts for Principle 8 include the following:

- *A range of formal and informal assessments* tied to lesson and unit objectives (paper-and-pencil tests, observation logs, scoring guides or rubrics, checklists, a list of questions)
- *Reflections on assessment data and actions* taken based on those data
- *Examples of record keeping and use of assessment data* (including a grade book, skills worksheets, and results of student assessments)
- *Lesson and unit plans* employing a variety of assessment tools (including student self-assessment) to gather data on student learning and instructional effectiveness
- *Evaluations* from your cooperating teacher and your student teaching supervisor regarding your assessment-related knowledge and skills
- *Written records* of students' progress and parent conferences, revealing your sensitivity to confidentiality

EXAMPLE ARTIFACT

Now let's review an artifact developed by a student teacher to see what it reveals about his or her knowledge, performance, and dispositions relevant to the assessment standard.

ASSESSMENT

Unit Topic: Ecosystems

Grade Level: Second Grade

Objectives

1. Students will be able to define the term *ecosystem* as a working unit made up of organisms interacting with each other and with nonliving factors.
2. Students will be able to describe ecosystems in their surroundings.

Assessment Methods

A. **Multiple-Choice Items (the keys for all but the first question are not included here.)**

1. A group of organisms of the same species living in the same area is called a (an)
   a. population.
   b. ecosystem.
   c. community.
   d. niche.
2. The source of all food in an ecosystem is
3. The living part of any ecosystem—all of the different organisms that live together in that area—is called a(n)
4. The ultimate source of energy for all living things are/is
5. An example of a decomposer is
6. These organisms kill and eat other organisms.
7. A forest is an example of a(n)
8. Liquid water changes into water vapor through

9. This is *not* one of the most important cycles of matter.
10. Within a food chain, there is _____ energy available at the higher feeding levels than there is at the lower feeding levels.

B. Constructed Response (12 points each)

Name and briefly describe the three basic energy roles in an ecosystem. For each role, give an example of an organism that plays that role.

How are a food chain, a food web, and a pyramid of energy different from one another? Describe the relationship among the three.

C. Performance Assessment (15 points)

Hold the mirror about an inch from your mouth (if not sure, contact the teacher). Say "Horace the horse hulas in Hilo, Hawaii." Pay attention to the mirror and explain what happens. Think about why this happens. Explain the water cycle and how this relates to what happened to the mirror. (Feel free to repeat the saying to the mirror in order to make your observation.)

ASSESSMENT RUBRICS

A. Multiple Choice (5 points each): 1. A, 2. C, 3. B, 4. D, 5. A, 6. B, 7. A, 8. B, 9. D, 10. C

B. Constructed Response Items (12 points each)

Points	Criteria for Constructed Response 1
4 points	Explains role of producers: Producers, such as plants, get energy from sunlight and turn this energy into food.
4 points	Explains the role of consumers: Consumers, such as animals, feed directly on producers.
4 points	Explains the role of decomposers: Decomposers, such as fungus and bacteria, break down the remains of dead organisms, releasing the nutrients back to the environment.

Points	Criteria for Constructed Response 2
4 points	Explains a food chain: A food chain describes a specific series of food and energy transfers from one organism to another in an ecosystem.
4 points	Explains a food web: A food web is made up of the overlapping food chains in an ecosystem.
4 points	A pyramid of energy describes the amount of energy that is available at each feeding level in an ecosystem. A pyramid of energy shows that energy is lost as you move along a food chain.

C. Performance Item (15 points)

Points	Criteria
11–15 points	Fully explains what happened when he or she breathed onto a mirror (mirror fogs up; water in breath cools as it reaches the outside air and condenses on the mirror). Accurately describes each step of the water cycle and relates that the water vapor he or she releases into the air when he or she breathes is part of this cycle.
6–10 points	Either explains the water cycle or observation of mirror effect, but not both.
0–5 points	Does not explain relationship between the mirror effect and the water cycle. Does not clearly explain the water cycle or the effect of breath on the mirror.

On one hand, this artifact contains evidence to demonstrate the teacher's ability to employ formal assessment techniques tied to instructional objectives (i.e., a teacher-made test involving multiple item types) to enhance and monitor student learning and to evaluate student progress and performances. On the other hand, this assessment artifact *by itself* does not show the teacher's ability to use informal assessment strategies; to use assessment strategies intended to involve learners in assessing their own learning behaviors, strengths, needs, and progress; or to encourage students to set personal goals for learning. Nor does it reveal the teacher's ability to evaluate the effect of class activities on either the individual or the class as a whole or the teacher's ability to assess other domains. By using these assessment rubrics, the teacher probably could maintain useful records of student work and performances; however, because the artifact is not accompanied by any student data, a reviewer could not be sure of the candidate's abilities to maintain records or communicate student progress knowledgeably and responsibly, based on the collected assessment data to students, parents, and other colleagues.

The artifact does show the teacher's ability to assess different types of learner objectives and to enhance students' learning by incorporating various assessment strategies (i.e., multiple-choice items, constructed response writing items, and a performance assessment into the unit). The use of these various item types allows students with different strengths an opportunity to successfully demonstrate having met learning instructional objectives in meaningful ways and to express their personal understanding and findings. While one might question the construction of several of the traditional items on the test, the teacher's use of specific questions in multiple-choice items supports all learners because it helps students with underdeveloped abilities focus their attention on specific issues and look for key words or topics in the source material. The collected data from these assessment methods could help the teacher monitor the progress and diagnose the weak areas of the unit to provide corrected instruction.

Despite its narrowness, the example does address at least one important area within the expectations set for Principle 8: the teacher's ability to employ a variety of formal assessment item types and techniques to evaluate student progress and performances.

However, a reviewer would need to see some attention to informal assessment methods (e.g., a quiz before the unit to diagnose prior knowledge of students, oral questions, observation checklists of student engagement and progress, and conferences with the students); some attention to collecting, maintaining, interpreting, and communicating assessment results; and some attention to incorporating self-assessment into his or her assessment strategies. In addition, the reviewer would likely want to see more detailed criteria for each of the open-ended assessment rubrics. Instead of giving one criterion and the maximum points (e.g., 4 points for a constructed response item), the teacher might include criteria for the different score points that would help students understand the teacher's expectations.

WRITING A REFLECTION FOR PRINCIPLE 8

Now let's look at the reflection that accompanies the artifact. How does it work as a reflection, and how well does it support the case for the teacher having met the expectations outlined in Principle 8? Maybe some of the Principle 8 requirements that were not evident in the artifact will be revealed in the candidate's reflection.

RATIONALE FOR PRINCIPLE 8: ASSESSMENT

Principle 8 states that teachers need to understand and use formal and informal assessment strategies to evaluate and ensure the continuous intellectual, social, and physical development of the learner. I have included a number of artifacts to provide evidence to prove that I can employ a variety of formal and informal assessment techniques. Moreover, I show that I can evaluate student progress and performances, use assessment strategies to involve learners in self-assessment activities, help them become aware of their learning behaviors, strengths, needs, and progress, and encourage them to set personal goals for learning through specific rubric criteria. Finally, I give evidence to show my ability to evaluate the effect of class activities on both individual students and the class as a whole, and to collect information through analysis of student work, maintain useful records of student work and performances, and communicate student progress knowledgeably and responsibly based on appropriate assessment data.

I try to use this knowledge to help me cope with students' intellectual, social, and physical development and to build assessment methods along with the lesson objectives and activities, which will both fit my students' capabilities and challenge them. In my professional course work, I had several classes that addressed the topics of assessment strategies. These courses are listed on my transcript (Artifact 1): Teaching Methods, Teaching Social Studies, Teaching Mathematics, and Teaching Science. I earned A's in all of these courses. Topics covered in these classes included formal (summative) and informal (formative) assessment, how to make objective and constructed-response tests, validity and reliability of standardized tests, how to maintain grade records using spreadsheets, how to interpret standardized scores and communicate data responsibly to students, parents, and district personnel. I also learned how to utilize assessment data to monitor student learning and to provide corrected instruction. In my content methods courses, I learned how to create scoring rubrics for writing assignments and performance-based projects. In addition, my assessment plan provides a self-assessment benchmark for me to see if my unit plan objectives are met and measured by each of the assessment strategies.

These courses helped me understand the connection among curriculum goals and content standards, my lesson objectives, instructional strategies, and assessment methods. This gave me a theoretical foundation on which to build my assessment plans. This knowledge was refined by content methods courses, which gave me more specific information related to teaching content by developing a backward instructional design as Wiggins and McTighe suggested in their book on performance assessment. In this backward design, I learned to create assessment plans before planning activities and details. Though I do not view these theories and models of effective teaching as complete pictures of how to teach, I do believe there is much of value that can be applied from them.

For my second-grade science unit on ecosystems (Artifact 7), I created an assessment that included multiple-choice and constructed-response questions, as well as a performance assessment. I addressed learner diversity by varying my assessment methods through the presentation of the material to accommodate students of all abilities. Students worked in cooperative learning groups, with partners and individually. Considering their developmental levels and learning styles, students had opportunities during instruction to engage in hands-on, kinesthetic learning activities as well as to read, write, and draw about what they had learned. The range of instructional activities led me to develop various assessment methods including multiple-choice items, constructed-response items, and performance items. The scoring rubrics and correct answers provided the assessment benchmarks necessary to determine if students had achieved the objectives of the lesson. My cooperating teacher confirms in his evaluation reports that my assessment methods are the appropriate tools to measure if students have achieved the unit goals and objectives (Artifact 8). One will note his specific interest in and approval of my use of multiple-choice items, constructed-response writing items, and a performance project, along with scoring rubrics for each of them. He was impressed that I was able to use the assessment data when we discussed the effectiveness of the unit.

The mean of the multiple choice items (94 out of 100) demonstrated that most of the students had correct answers (Artifact 9). These data indicate student learning. The constructed response items, however, did not provide strong evidence of student learning—quite a few students were struggling with the logic of writing and how to explain the roles. Some students wrote the definition of the role rather than explaining it. The criteria should have been more specific. I should have provided an example of explaining the roles rather than giving only a one-sentence direction. It was also hard to decide how to differentiate between the responses that received 4 points and those that received 3 points because I did not specify the criteria for each point. I need to learn how to develop more effective scoring rubrics.

The performance items were not very successful, even though they were better than the constructed responses. Some students wrote three to five paragraphs, and some wrote only a couple of sentences. Again, I should have given more specific directions about the length of writing for each of the items. I should also have included grammatical and spelling accuracy as part of the criteria. Since I did not include the language accuracy, I was puzzled as to how many points I needed to deduct due to spelling or grammatical errors. All in all, my assessment on this unit was only moderately successful.

Developing effective assessment methods is not an easy task. I need to put myself into my students' shoes to see if the assessment rubrics provide easy-enough explanations for them to follow before they plan to create the projects or outline their writing assignments. My scoring rubrics were rather superficial and may work for me, but not for the second graders.

If my assessment methods were developed based on the students' intellectual, social, and physical development, were aligned with learning objectives, and were engaging activities for the unit, they could provide another instructional strategy that might motivate students to become more engaged in learning. When I revisited my unit objectives and the assessment strategies, I was surprised to see how these two were connected. I also found out that my objectives were not all included in my assessment plan. I need to go back to the objectives whenever I plan any assessment strategy, and I need to plan the assessment even before I choose activities. The results of the assessment demonstrated that the students responded very well when the assessment items were well explained in terms of their expected outcomes, but not very well when the criteria were not clearly explained.

Identification of context. The writer begins the reflection by restating the principle, offering some explication of the principle, references to formal and informal assessment strategies, and some sense that the teacher understands the basic elements of assessment. The teacher asserts the importance of connecting assessment strategies to students' intellectual, social, and physical development. While this discourse on assessment gives some excellent background, one would like to see more connections between the theories of effective assessment and his or her choice of assessment methods. As a result a reviewer might lean toward rating this as a "good reflection" because of its discussion of assessment but with some inclination toward the "weak reflection" because of the lack of an overt theoretical basis to support his or her thinking.

Observation and description of artifact (experience or document). The candidate gives considerable information about the assessment for the ecosystem unit (and related artifacts) although the descriptions are somewhat superficial, leaving the reviewer having to look for the assessment in order to fully understand what each portion of the assessment involves. The teacher offers interesting and telling discussion of the weaknesses of the rubrics for the constructed response items and of the instructions for the performance project. These critiques are based on the students' performance and so reveal an inclination and ability to analyze assessment data. For the most part, it is easy to understand what is going on in most of the reflection despite sometimes superficial description and limited information. One might again come down on the low side of the "good reflection" category for this portion of the rubric, suggesting that the teacher discuss his or her artifacts consistently in more explicit detail.

Application of theories or principles of effective practice. One would like to see greater evidence of the theoretical background the teacher is using to make his or her assessment decisions, including some identification of the candidate's knowledge of basic psychometrics. The references seem more like window-dressing than a serious expression of theoretical thinking. Here a reviewer might favor the "weak reflection" category of the rubric (i.e., "a reviewer might question depth of understanding"). However, the minimal reference made to theorists (Wiggins and McTighe) is neither incorrect nor inappropriate, so the reflection does not fall neatly into the category. On the positive side, the teacher presents ample evidence for making good decisions relative to instruction and keeping his or her students' prior knowledge, experiences, and development in mind when choosing assessment strategies. The impression left with a reviewer is generally positive though somewhat shallow. Evaluating this reflection is a tough call, then, but in keeping with the rubric, a reviewer would probably have to place this reflection into the "good reflection" slot.

Identification, analysis, interpretation of causes, and effects. Here the reviewer finds quite a bit of analysis and interpretation. One good example is the teacher's use of assessment data to explain why the multiple choice items were successful. A little later, additional analysis and interpretation occurs around the failure of the rubrics for the constructed response items and the performance project. Interestingly, the teacher shared the failure of the rubrics after analyzing the assessment data and explored what should be done to improve student performance on the assessments. This is a powerful and frank reflection on the candidate's learning based on concrete assessment data. People tend to want to focus on the positive within portfolios, but a thoughtful, research-informed recognition and analysis of failures is an essential and useful part of reflection and supports the belief that the teacher is indeed reflective. Failures and mistakes are our greatest sources of learning and professional growth. They should not be ignored. Based on this analysis, one is compelled to place this in the "good reflection" category.

Projection from observations toward problem solving and lifelong learning. The teacher offers at least some evidence of having thought about professional growth in the area of various assessment methods with scoring guides. The candidate "predicted and justified what he/she would do the next time based on the evidence, and acknowledged professional development needs without necessarily identifying the means for addressing those needs." Moreover, the candidate provided evidence of refinement of practice based on past experience within the classroom (i.e., what the teacher would do differently next time based on weaknesses discovered in the assessment data). Thus, we can easily place the reflection in the "good reflection" category with some room for improvement.

Based on this analysis, and applying the rubric holistically, we can say that although the reflection has some weaknesses, it is a generally good reflection, giving the reviewer enough evidence to get a clear impression that the candidate has some knowledge of and ability to use assessments to inform professional practice.

But what about the expectations of Principle 8? Are they sufficiently met by the evidence? We cannot be absolutely sure because we have not seen all the evidence. However, based on the one assessment presented and the reflection, where would you tend to place this teacher on the following summative evaluation rubric for INTASC Principle 8?

Meets the Standard	*Not Yet Meeting the Standard*
• The preservice teacher understands and uses formal and informal traditional and performance-based assessment strategies to evaluate and ensure the continuous intellectual, social, and physical development of the learner, including but not limited to understanding state knowledge/performance standards and their assessment.	• The preservice teacher demonstrates a basic knowledge of formal assessment strategies for a variety of purposes (i.e., intellectual, social, and physical assessment); alternatively, the candidate may reveal only a narrow range of even formal assessment strategies, tending to focus on whole-class knowledge testing.
• The candidate's evidence demonstrates knowledge of state or national knowledge/performance standards and their assessment.	• The candidate provides little or no evidence of knowledge of state or national knowledge/performance standards or their assessment.
• This teacher maintains and uses data from his or her assessment activities to inform instruction and to provide constructive and specific feedback to students, parents, and colleagues.	• The candidate offers little or no evidence of his or her ability to maintain useful records of student performance or to communicate constructive and specific feedback to students, parents, or colleagues.
• The candidate consciously encourages and supports students' self-assessment as a means of enhancing their own learning and achievement.	• There is little or no evidence that the candidate uses information generated from assessment to inform instruction or to foster student self-assessment or growth.
• Student work samples verify the candidate's assessment knowledge and skills.	• Knowledge and skills tend not to be supported by student work samples.

After reviewing the reflection and recalling the assessment artifact, a reviewer might come to the following conclusions about what the evidence reveals:

- The candidate demonstrates a basic knowledge of formal assessment strategies for a single purpose (i.e., intellectual assessment); the candidate does not reveal the ability to assess for any other domain identified by Principle 8; in addition, the candidate reveals the ability to use only formal assessment strategies, with a tendency to employ only whole-class knowledge testing.
- The candidate provides little evidence of knowledge of state or national knowledge/performance standards or their assessment; that is, while some standards are identified, they are not clearly assessed by the items on the example test.
- There is little evidence, though the candidate makes assertions to this effect, that the candidate uses information generated from assessment to inform instruction or to foster student self-assessment or growth. Any use of assessment data resulted from the need to write a reflection for the candidate's portfolio.
- There is little evidence of the candidate's ability to communicate constructive and specific feedback to students, parents, or colleagues.
- Assertions about knowledge and skills are not supported by student work samples.

So, although the reflection is well written, it does not ultimately reveal a candidate possessing the full breadth of assessment knowledge and skills required by Principle 8.

SUMMARY

Assessment is a key element in the instructional process. Teachers have to know if students have achieved the learning objectives. Moreover, they need to use this information for a variety of purposes, including providing feedback to students and their parents. They must also use the information to evaluate their own instructional practice. To gain this knowledge, teachers must use a variety of assessment techniques, formal and informal, before, during, and after instruction. Your portfolio must, then, show your ability to effectively develop, use, and evaluate a variety of informal and formal assessment types in the service of meeting your students' learning needs.

To give you a little push in that direction, think about the following guiding questions:

1. What do I take into account when I am developing an assessment method?
   - How do I balance formal and informal assessment methods?
   - How do I connect my assessment methods to the social, cognitive, and physical development of my students?
   - How do I maintain assessment data?
   - How do I effectively share the assessment data with students, parents, colleagues, and community members?
   - What external issues do I consider when planning assessment methods?
   - What resources can I tap to enrich the experience?

2. How do I make sure my assessment methods are relevant, meaningful, and coherent?
3. What range of assessment strategies do I have in my toolbox to help me determine how well my students understand the content?
4. What is the theoretical basis for the choices I make in developing the assessment methods?

5. How do I use assessment data to improve my teaching and my students' learning?
6. How do I bring parents and the community into the assessment process?

DISCUSSION QUESTIONS

1. For what purposes do teachers assess their students' learning and achievement?
2. What is the difference between formal and informal assessment strategies? What examples can you give of each of these two categories of assessment?
3. What is authentic assessment?
4. Why do teachers need to maintain useful records of student work and performances?
5. To what audiences and for what purposes do teachers communicate student progress?
6. What sorts of ethical considerations are involved in reporting student progress and achievement?

Implementing INTASC Principle 9 in Your Portfolio

12

The teacher is capable of reflection leading to self-knowledge, the metacognitive awareness that distinguishes craftsman from architect, bookkeeper from auditor. A professional is capable not only of practicing and understanding his or her craft, but of communicating the reasons for professional decisions and actions to others.

L. S. Shulman

Suzanne contemplated Principle 9, wondering what she could use to document her achievement relative to the expectations set by the principle. "I know I am a professional, but I haven't had a chance to engage in much of what this principle is looking for. Perhaps a combination of artifacts would work. What do I have that shows I am reflective, ethical, and involved in professional development?" As she explored her files, a pattern of behavior began to emerge, revealing a teacher who thought deeply about how best to meet her students' needs and sought out various resources to help her in that task. She also paged proudly through her teaching journal, sampling the various reflections on her classroom decisions and their impact on student learning and behavior. "I sure hated all this writing and thinking while it was going on, but it is fun to look back at what I have done and how I have grown." She discovered the action research project from her internship and the professional development log and certificates from throughout her program at the university. "I guess I have a lot more to work with than I thought. And I didn't even realize that I was becoming a professional."

QUESTIONS FOR CONSIDERATION

- How do professional educators behave? What standards guide their thinking and actions?
- How does my thinking and approach to my teaching define me as a professional educator?

- Where have I used *inquiry* to become a better teacher?
- What resources are available to me as I work to help all my students achieve to their potential?
- What is reflection? Why is it a professional behavior?
- How should professional development relate to student achievement?
- What ethical standards do I regularly apply in my interaction with students, parents, my colleagues and the community?

Teachers are professionals, like attorneys and medical doctors. As such they receive extensive professional training and are guided in their work and behaviors by professional standards and behavioral expectations. Your portfolio is documentation that you have reached a certain level of professional maturity and are, therefore, ready to become an accepted member of the profession. How do you prove this? It takes more than just showing that you can create and teach a lesson or that you know how to construct a test. Rather, your portfolio must demonstrate that you think and act like a professional and that you are committed to the profession, its principles of practice, and its ongoing progress toward improving the practice and achievement of its members.

UNDERSTANDING PRINCIPLE 9

Principle 9: The teacher is a reflective practitioner who continually evaluates the effects of his/her choices and actions on others (students, parents, and other professionals in the learning community) and who actively seeks out opportunities to grow professionally.

Principle 9 expresses two expectations:

1. You are *a reflective practitioner*, defined specifically as one "who continually assesses the effects of choices and actions on others."
2. You use the results of self-assessment to seek out professional development opportunities to improve instructional practice and your students' learning.

Reflective practitioners will do exactly that: Reflect on how they can teach better lessons, better communicate to the students, and prepare themselves more fully to educate others. This is what Principle 9 is all about.

Professional reflection is what distinguishes a professional from a technician. Reflection is based on professional knowledge, experience, and a standard for professional behavior. The first part of Principle 9 demands evidence of your ability and inclination to engage in the ongoing reflective process of assessing and evaluating your personal and professional actions. Such self-assessment should help you determine the effectiveness and appropriateness of your behavior both inside and outside the classroom. Moreover, it should inform future decision making and actions. In chapter 3, we discussed reflection, especially as it relates to the thought processes involved in thinking about your instructional actions and decisions. Principle 9 broadens the definition, expecting you to demonstrate how you are continuously thinking about your professional life and using that information to improve your own behaviors and practices—in particular, to improve student learning.

Professional development is the second expectation of Principle 9, and this is a taller order for most preservice teachers, given their limited perspective (in terms of time) and limited access to professional development opportunities outside of college. However, it clearly suggests minimally that you, based on self-reflection, should give evidence of consciously identifying professional development needs and seeking ways of fulfilling those needs (e.g., accessing professional literature, interacting with colleagues, participating in professional associations, engaging in professional development activities). Whether it is

By being around other professionals in my discipline, I can better determine if I am on the right track with my course content. The music education journals enable me to stay current with subject matter and the music literature I choose. Belonging to professional organizations also enables me to glean wisdom and knowledge from other educators. I can better reflect upon my teaching abilities because the only image coming back at me *is not* me.

talking to your cooperating teacher or attending professional development activities on campus, you must somehow demonstrate your active engagement in professional development, preferably tied to specific, identified needs related to the improvement of student learning.

Ethical behavior and decision making are implied within the standard in the form of an expectation that the preservice teacher has a set of professional ethical standards on which to base decisions and actions. Do you have a sense of what is appropriate behavior or by what moral standard you should weigh the professional decisions you make? Much of what defines a profession are the standards by which its members govern their decisions and actions, especially when it comes to how they interact with the people they serve—in an educator's case, the students.

The various national teacher organizations (NEA, AFT, NAEYC, NCTM, etc.) as well as many local and regional professional organizations have sets of standards to govern behavior. These may take the form of stated behaviors, values, and belief statements or statements of student rights. You should demonstrate awareness of one or more of these sets of standards, understand them, and apply them to your professional decision making (see appendix E: National Education Association: Code of Ethics of the Education Profession for one example of a teacher code of ethics).

WHAT ARE THE IMPLICATIONS OF THIS KNOWLEDGE BASE FOR MY PORTFOLIO?

Your portfolio reflections and artifacts should reveal that you possess these standards of professional behavior and apply them to all aspects of your work. A reviewer will expect to see evidence—via journal entries, reflections, action research, reviews of professional literature, proof of attendance at professional meetings, and professional development plans—that you are thinking and acting as a professional. Principle 9 establishes a significant set of expectations for the beginning professional.

You should use the knowledge, dispositions, and performances for the principle to further refine your choices of artifacts and to guide you in composing your reflection on the principle. Let's take some time to review the knowledge, skills, and dispositions presented within Principle 9:

Knowledge

- The teacher understands methods of inquiry that provide him or her with a variety of self-assessment and problem-solving strategies for reflecting on his or her practice, its influences on students' growth and learning, and the complex interactions between them.
- The teacher is aware of major areas of research on teaching and of resources available for professional learning (e.g., professional literature, colleagues, professional associations, and professional development activities).

Dispositions

- The teacher values critical thinking and self-directed learning as habits of mind.
- The teacher is committed to reflection, assessment, and learning as an ongoing process.
- The teacher is willing to give and receive help.

- The teacher is committed to seeking out, developing, and continually refining practices that address the individual needs of students.
- The teacher recognizes his or her professional responsibility for engaging in and supporting appropriate professional practices for her or himself and for colleagues.

Performances

- The teacher uses classroom observation, information about students, and research as sources for evaluating the outcomes of teaching and learning and as a basis for experimenting with, reflecting on, and revising practice.
- The teacher seeks out professional literature, colleagues, and other resources to support his or her own development as a learner and a teacher.
- The teacher draws on professional colleagues within the school and other professional arenas as supports for reflection, problem solving and new ideas, actively sharing experiences, and seeking and giving feedback.

ARTIFACT SELECTION

From these statements, we can distill at least the following three issues that need to be addressed in your reflection statement and the artifacts you choose:

- Valuing and applying self-assessment and critical inquiry to evaluate and improve professional practice.
- Knowing and accessing professional literature and other resources to improve professional practice to better meet the needs of students.
- Engaging in professional behavior in the form of giving and receiving professional assistance to colleagues.

TYPES OF ARTIFACTS

When deciding which artifacts to include in your portfolio, ask yourself at least the following questions:

1. Which artifacts will reveal my ability to critically reflect on my professional practice using a variety of self-assessment and problem-solving strategies and with an eye toward improving my teaching skills and my students' learning?
2. Which artifacts will show my willingness to pursue professional development activities, both formally (e.g., via professional development meetings) and informally (e.g., seeking the advice and input of other professionals)?
3. Which artifacts will reveal my commitment to the profession and willingness to give and receive professional advice?
4. Which artifacts will show my ability to make ethical decisions in and out of the classroom, but especially as they relate to my professional decision making and behaviors?

As sources for documenting your abilities as a reflective professional educator, the following categories of artifacts will be particularly fruitful:

1. *Communications* within the classroom; notes on conferences with students, parents, colleagues; newsletters to parents
2. *Reflections* on professional practice and decisions inside and outside the classroom, as well as reflections on student performance and instructional practice
3. *Projects or assignments* from professional course work dealing with issues of ethics and ethical behavior
4. *Case studies* on students or classroom issues illustrating the reflective or problem-solving processes you engage in to deal with these students/issues

5. *Evidence of involvement* in professional development activities, memberships in professional organizations, and reflection on what you gained from these experiences
6. *Research and literature* you have accessed to gain more insight into specific issues of professional practice
7. *Evaluations* from your cooperating teacher(s) and student teaching supervisor specifically focused on professional behavior, reflection, and decision making
8. (potentially) *Transcripts and test scores,* though less valuable, may help document your basic grasp of knowledge bases important to professional behavior

EXAMPLE ARTIFACT

Look at the following artifact and reflect on what it reveals about the teacher's ability relative to the professional behaviors demanded by Principle 9. This artifact contains several pieces of evidence to support the teacher's case for having met the expectations expressed in Principle 9.

ACTION RESEARCH PROJECT

The idea for my action research project came to me during my first student teaching experience in the Seventh Grade at Erehwon Middle School. I arrived in the class while the teacher was finishing up a unit on Islam, and I was present for the unit test. My first job was to grade the tests, and to my dismay, the level of mastery was not satisfactory.

Islam Test

105 students took the test

Test grade	A	B	C	D	F
Number of students with grade	27	30	20	15	13
Percentage of students with grade	26%	29%	19%	14%	12%

PROBLEM

The students did not have a high level of mastery as shown by their test scores. The test *should* have been a good indicator of how much the students actually learned because there were a variety of question types such as multiple choice, fill in the blank, matching, short answer, and constructed response. My goal was to help the students achieve a greater level of mastery on the next test: 100% of the students would get a C or above.

POSSIBLE SOLUTIONS

Several factors contributed to the students low test scores: inadequate test review, test anxiety, rushing through the test, not reading directions, and simply not studying. My goal was to address each of these problems during my unit.

MY PLAN IN ACTION

As the test on Africa approached, I began encouraging the students to study a little each night with a study guide I had given them. I also tried to encourage them and motivate them by letting them know that "I knew they could be successful." When the day of the test came, I didn't treat it like a day of reckoning. Instead I greeted them with a smile and I assured them of my confidence in their abilities. I then allowed 3 minutes before I passed out the test for them to get their brains focused on social studies, which to some meant reviewing notes and to others meant sitting quietly and praying that God would help them remember everything! I reminded them to read all directions very carefully, and I told them they must keep the test at their desk until I collected them, thus hoping they would not try to rush to be the first one finished.

The environment in the classroom was comfortable and relaxed. Though the environment was a bit more relaxed than their former Islam test environment, I don't believe I did that much differently than their teacher. She was also encouraging and motivating. There is one variable, though, that was vastly different from the environment surrounding their Islam test, and I strongly believe this variable was the most important element in improving the students' test scores.

VARIABLE IMPLEMENTATION

The main difference between the preparations for the Africa test and the Islam test was the review game the students participated in the day before the test. By the time the test came along, I had really gotten to know the students quite well. I was aware from observing them, and from just understanding adolescent development in general, that the students needed a unique test review environment, as opposed to the typical "sit there and fill out the 10-page review packet." From my experience and the knowledge I had in education classes, I took several facts into consideration:

- Researchers know that young adolescents are growing rapidly and have a high basal metabolic rate. This said, I understand that middle school students are kinesthetic learners who like to be active and moving whenever possible. I knew there had to be some productive way to get the students active during test review.
- I am also aware that middle school students are very social. They enjoy interacting with their peers, and at times this seems to get them into trouble. I, however, wanted to use this love of communicating and sharing ideas and suggestions among peers to aid them in their test review.
- I was also aware that the students loved competition! At this age especially, boys and girls are becoming distinctively different, thus the students love competing boys against girls. They also love the rush of trying to outdo the other team. (I personally believe at this age competition *does not* create disunity in the classroom—at least not in my class. My students know they are all in this thing together, and in the end, they all are pulling for each other to succeed. The element of competition is just something that gets them fired up to learn.)
- At the middle school age, students are also extrinsically motivated rather than intrinsically motivated, for the most part. Thus, I knew candy would serve as a great prize for the winning team in each class. With all of these developmental characteristics in mind, I sought to mesh them together to form a great test review environment. When the students entered the classroom the day before the test, I told them to divide into two groups, one with boys and the other with girls. At this point there were already many cheers. As they got situated in their teams (they could sit in desks in a circle or on the floor), they grew curious as to why there were nine empty desks in the middle of the

room: three rows of three desks. I explained that the nine chairs were set up like a tic-tac-toe board. I then explained that I was going to ask each team a question dealing with the unit on Africa and the group would get 25 seconds to answer the question. They were instructed to huddle together and decide as a team what the answer was. I also made it a rule that the first answer I heard would be the team answer, which helped to eliminate students just shouting out answers without conferring with team members. If the team answered the question correctly, they got one point and they were able to move one team member over to the tic-tac-toe board. I also told the students, if the previous team did not respond correctly then the other team would get a chance to answer. However, I would not repeat the question again, which motivated the students to listen closely. Whatever team got tic-tac-toe first received an additional 2 points. Then we cleared the board and started again. The questions I asked were not directly from the test, but the questions did review many of the concepts and ideas that would be on the test in some way or another.

Overall, the students loved the game and asked if they could play it every time before a test. The environment it created was intense because of the competition and time limits, but it was also fun and active. The students left the class full of energy and much more confident about the test the next day.

TEST RESULTS

The test results speak for themselves. The student's test grades improved dramatically! My goal of 100% scoring at a C or above was almost met, with 94% scoring at a high C or above.

Africa Test

105 students took the test					
Test grade	*A*	*B*	*C*	*D*	*F*
Number of students with grade	46	27	25	4	3
Percentage of students with grade	44%	26%	24%	3%	3%

Overall, I believe that being knowledgeable of adolescent development and molding instruction to be "developmentally appropriate" were the keys to the students' success. I believe that the students who still did poorly were in need of additional motivation. If I would have had more time with the students, I would have privately called out the students who needed improvement and had them get together and set goals as a group, under my supervision, concerning the next test. The students need to know they are not alone, that other students are struggling and need additional help. They are not bad students because of a test grade. I believe that this would help keep these students accountable to each other, and I hope they would work hard to achieve their goals as a group.

First, the artifact is an example of *reflection on action*. It is evidence that the teacher can undertake personal inquiry based on observed student performance to improve instructional practice and student achievement. The action research plan is an example of applied inquiry. It arises out of a need, offers a hypothesis in the form of an altered instructional strategy, and applies both observed and theoretical information to support the choice of strategy.

Second, the teacher draws on professional knowledge and literature to support his or her decisions. We have clear evidence of theory-based thinking in the design process the teacher undertakes. Finally, the teacher displays other important professional dispositions:

- Being supportive of student confidence and self-esteem: "I also tried to encourage them and motivate them by letting them know that I knew they could be successful."
- Being nonjudgmental: "The students need to know they are not alone, that other students are struggling and need additional help. They are not bad students because of a test grade."
- Continuously reflecting on practice: "If I would have had more time with the students, I would have privately called out the students who needed improvement and had them get together and set goals as a group, under my supervision, concerning the next test."

This is an excellent choice of artifact to demonstrate, in part, having met the expectations set by Principle 9.

WRITING A REFLECTION FOR PRINCIPLE 9

Now let's look at a reflection for Principle 9. How does it work as a reflection, and how well does it support the case for the teacher having met the expectations a professional must demonstrate as outlined in the principle?

TEACHING COMPETENCY: TEACHER AS A REFLECTIVE PRACTITIONER

Artifact:

F: Rationale attached to lesson plans

H: Music notation lesson plan

K: Revised music notation lesson plan

L: Videotaped lesson reflection

M: Fine arts unit and assessment

There was a group of teachers in a school where I worked. Each noon hour they ate together and enlightened the rest of us to the utter stupidity and idiocy of each student and the student's parents. According to them, these students did not learn because they or their parents "——" (fill in the blank). I found it amazing that they perpetually found a way to put any learning deficits occurring in their classes on the parents, the home environment, the class interruptions, or the "dumb students." Not once did they see these classroom failures as reflecting upon themselves. A reflective practitioner will do exactly that: reflect on how she or he can teach better lessons, better communicate to the students, and prepare more fully to educate others. This is what Principle 9 is all about.

When I first began student teaching, I lived in the principal's office during my prep time or after school. I also had a mentor teacher I conferred with constantly, particularly during the first semester. I had no training in classroom management, knew nothing about what was expected as far as team efforts in the school, and was so insecure about myself it was pathetic. This was a new experience for me. Because of my previous work experience, I speak frequently, I entertain people in my home, and I often present programs and have taught children of every age in the church. I know my former role intimately. However, the school environment was as strange to me as Mars.

My principal and my mentor had the patience of Job. For every deficiency I found with myself, they helped me find the solution or they helped me to figure out that the problem wasn't mine at all. Teachers who approach their classes with a "God complex" are heading for an enormous fall. We are not perfect. We will fail. We all need guidance to find solutions to difficult questions.

Rather than playing the blame game when things don't go as we have hoped or planned in our classes, we need to look to ourselves. How could we have planned that lesson differently? What tools could we have used or what different instructional method could we have employed? There are so many places to go for help and new ideas. The Internet alone has hundreds of sites for teachers, to say nothing of listservs and chat rooms. Before we decide where to go for help, we have to admit we need it.

This was borne home to me in startling clarity during my first segment of student teaching. I was presenting rhythmic notation to the fifth-grade class (Artifact H). I knew my material, I understood how to count music, I understood how the note values broke down like fractions. *I understood*—they did not. And when the assessments came in, I was stunned by the utter failure of my instructional plan. I spent a great deal of time thinking about how I approached those lessons once I realized the problem wasn't them, it was me. I totally revamped my approach and instructional strategy (Artifact K), using manipulatives and movement to help the students understand and experience the music concepts. As a result, the students had a much easier time—the second time around—understanding and applying the new concepts.

Reflection served me well during my field experience in Rock River/East Erehwon. I taught the fine arts class there for several weeks (Artifacts M). The students did poorly on their assessment. As my cooperating teacher and I reflected at great length, we came to several conclusions: (a) They blew me off because I was a "temp." (b) They were used to open-book tests exclusively and not the type of test I gave with a mixture of objective questions and short essay. (c) This was a problem across the board in this school—the school was going on a watch list. (d) I was going to review the material with them in a different manner, and they were going to take the test again. I felt I had to take some of the responsibility. Their teacher, Mrs. S, disagreed vigorously. She felt I didn't know the students well enough to realize what they were doing. However, I believe when a class fails miserably, some of the responsibility has to rest with the teacher. The failure may be in one's teaching strategy or method of communication, but the problem cannot lie only with the students. The students may indeed have been fulfilling their own agenda, but what transpires in the classroom ultimately rests with the teacher. And in the end, whatever the students may be trying, isn't it the teacher's responsibility to figure that out and then to do something about it? I was somewhat distressed by Mrs. S's willingness to accept the poor performance and just go on. I could not in good conscience do that.

As I continued to reflect on my own, I was baffled by the fact that the students had responded so well to the instructional activities but not on the assessment (Artifact M). They prepared their group presentations and appeared to enjoy and benefit from the cooperative learning methods I employed. I should not have relied on this *impression* of the activity's success. I should have been using continuous assessment of some type to get a sense along the way of where the students were succeeding and where they were not. By waiting until the final assessment, I had lost a lot of valuable opportunities to reteach or correct student misconceptions. If I had implemented a reflection journal within the class, I would have been able to assess student understanding and get a handle on the problem earlier.

I have learned so much since beginning my training in the College of Education. The flip side is that the more I learn, the more I realize I don't know! I have already begun thinking about pursuing another degree. My students deserve a teacher who pursues excellence personally before ever demanding it of them. There is a code for teachers. Among other things it requires that I reflect on my abilities and see if I have deficits and then find a way to remedy the situation. That code requires that I present myself not as one who has all the answers, but rather one who will seek the correct information.

As the adage goes "A man who measures himself by himself is a fool." This is one reason why professional organizations and collegial in-service opportunities are so valuable. They enable me to hear what others are doing in their programs and to determine if my programs measure up. Another proverb that certainly applies to the reflective teacher is "Iron sharpens iron." By being around other professionals in my discipline, I can better determine if I am on the right track with my course content. The music education journals enable me to stay current with subject matter and the musical literature I choose. Belonging to professional organizations also enables me to glean wisdom and knowledge from other educators. I can better reflect on my teaching abilities because the only image coming back *at* me *is not* me.

First, let's compare this reflection with the elements of a good reflection:

Identification of context. In the first paragraph the teacher takes a different, more creative approach to establishing context. First, the teacher opens the reflection with an anecdote that provides a context for the discussion of reflective practice and professionalism. This opening provides a view into a professional ethical dilemma: Who is responsible for a student's performance in a teacher's classroom? And how should professionals talk about their students and parents? The writer of this reflection at least explicitly states a position on the issue of responsibility and clearly implies a position on the ethics of how professionals should talk about students and parents. In a sense, the teacher begins with an object lesson that encourages the reader to consider the kinds of issues facing professionals. In the succeeding paragraphs, the teacher explores more fully who is responsible for student learning and refines his or her stance on the issue. She or he also begins to explore the kinds of questions a reflective practitioner ought to be asking about the classroom and the potential sources for professional development and assistance. Finally, in the last sentence, the teacher paraphrases the major elements of the standard.

Observation and description of artifact (experience or document). To illustrate the points made in the introductory discussion, the teacher gives a series of useful examples of how reflection on ineffective instruction can lead to more effective teaching and learning. Moreover, the teacher also confronts the issue of who is responsible for student achievement. This series of examples is given in enough detail to effectively illustrate the teacher's point and is tied to specific artifacts.

Application of theories or principles of effective practice. The evidence of reflection supported and informed by theory and professional literature is slim in this reflection; however, we do have much evidence of principles of effective practice and good reflection on action: for example, "I should have been using continuous assessment of some type to get a sense along the way of where the students were succeeding and where they were not. By waiting until the final assessment, I had lost a lot of valuable opportunities to reteach or correct student misconceptions. If I had implemented a reflection journal within the class, I would have been able to assess student understanding and get a handle on the problem earlier."

Identification, analysis, and interpretation of causes and effects. This reflection offers ample evidence of cause-and-effect thinking. Each artifact and discussion exhibits this thinking.

Identification, analysis, and interpretations of interconnections among practices. The teacher offers several examples of how understanding, achievement, and performance are integrally entwined. For example, he or she discovers how instructional and assessment strategies impact the level of student understanding (". . . when the assessments came in, I was stunned by the utter failure of my instructional plan. . . . I totally revamped my approach and instructional strategy (Artifact K), using manipulatives and movement to help the students understand and experience the music concepts." And "They were used to open-book tests exclusively and not the type of test I gave with a mixture of objective questions and short essay." And "I should not have relied on this *impression* of the activity's success. I should have been using continuous assessment of some type to get a sense along the way of where the students were succeeding and where they were not"). In another vein, the teacher talks about the interconnection of professional behavior and relationships with professional growth and improved classroom practice.

Projection from observations toward problem solving and lifelong learning. The teacher explicitly refers to a code of behavior for teachers with regard to seeking professional development to better serve their students. Also, she or he highlights the need for ongoing, lifelong learning for professionals. Here the teacher talks about professional journals and other professionals as resources for professional growth and problem solving.

Based on this analysis and applying the rubric holistically, we can conclude that this reflection is indeed strong. It gives the reviewer ample evidence to judge that the candidate is performing appropriately well when measured against the rubric for reflection.

What about the expectations of Principle 9? Are they sufficiently met by the evidence? We cannot be absolutely sure because we have not seen all the evidence. However, based on the reflection alone, where would you tend to place this teacher on the following rubric?

Meets the Standard	*Not Yet Meeting the Standard*
• The preservice teacher is a reflective practitioner who demonstrates the capacity and the inclination to examine and assess the effects of his or her choices and actions on him or herself and others; the candidate's reflections analyze the impact of actions on student learning (versus merely describing what transpired).	• The preservice teacher does not consistently exhibit the ability to think about and articulate the quality of his or her own learning, choices, and actions on student learning.
• The candidate offers evidence that he or she consciously applies professional ethical standards within this reflective process.	• There may be evidence that this teacher can articulate and apply professional ethical standards to situations posed to him or her; alternatively, there may be no evidence that the individual has considered ethical standards.
• This candidate uses reflection to analyze actions and decisions, and based on his or her findings the candidate refines practice or seeks out opportunities to grow professionally.	• This candidate's reflections are primarily descriptive of what occurred; if reflection is used at all, it yields at most only minor refinements in learning and practice, seeking no opportunities for professional growth.

Clearly, the teacher fits into the "Meets the Standard" column of the rubric. The reflection and the artifacts referred to in the reflection seem to reveal a reflective practitioner with a clearly defined set of ethical dispositions, which he or she applies routinely to classroom practice, interactions with students and colleagues, and other professional behaviors. Moreover, she or he is focused on student achievement and sees it as a specific professional responsibility. There is ample evidence that "The teacher is committed to reflection, assessment, and learning as an ongoing process." Additionally, she or he "is committed to seeking out, developing, and continually refining practices that address the individual needs of students" and "recognizes his or her professional responsibility for engaging in and supporting appropriate professional practices for him or herself and colleagues."

SUMMARY

Being a professional educator is not just "knowing how to teach." Important dispositions toward students, parents, colleagues, the broader community, and toward one's own professional self take us from being merely knowledgeable technicians to becoming professionals who deserve respect and responsibility. It is incumbent on all of us to know what it means to be a professional and to behave professionally. Your portfolio must reveal a picture of the practicing professional, supported by theory, who thinks critically and reflectively and who exhibits behavior clearly based on a solid set of professional standards.

Here are some questions to help you gather your evidence and prepare your reflection:

1. Where have I used self-assessment and problem-solving strategies to reflect on my professional practice or to improve my students' learning and achievement?

   • In what situations have I used classroom observation or information about my students to modify my practice?
   • When have I consciously used research, my own and that of others, as sources for evaluating my teaching and my students' learning?
   • When have I experimented with, reflected on, and revised practice?

2. When have I actively sought out and become involved in professional development activities?

   • When have I accessed professional literature, colleagues, and other resources to support my own development as a learner and a teacher?
   • When have I approached professional colleagues within the school and other professional arenas as supports for reflection, problem solving, and new ideas?
   • In what venues have I actively shared experiences by seeking and giving feedback?

3. When have I made ethical decisions in and out of the classroom based on a code of professional behavior?

   • When have I had to employ my professional decision making?
   • Where have I been required to think about and exhibit professional behaviors?

DISCUSSION QUESTIONS

1. How might teachers apply self-assessment and critical inquiry to evaluate and improve their professional practice?

2. What is professional literature? How might it and other resources help a teacher improve her or his professional practice to better meet the needs of students?

3. How may interactions (e.g., giving and receiving professional assistance) with other professionals and colleagues be considered professional behavior?

4. What ethical rules govern (or should govern) the behavior of professional educators?

13

Implementing INTASC Principle 10 in Your Portfolio

It takes a village to raise a child.

African Proverb

As he left the eighth-grade counselor's office, Daniel felt he finally had a plan and some allies to help him make it work. Patty, one of his eighth grade students, just wasn't doing well, and her troubles were creating problems for the entire class. While he suspected Patty had typical teenage social issues, clearly she had some kind of undiagnosed learning disability that was preventing her from connecting with the content and with others in her class. He had taken a course in exceptionalities in his teacher preparation program, but that knowledge merely helped him note that there was likely a problem that needed addressing.

His meeting with the counselor, his cooperating teacher, and the curriculum coordinator had led to a plan for some testing and parent conferences, perhaps leading to an IEP for Patty. In the meantime, though, the two seasoned professionals had helped him develop several strategies for assisting Patty immediately and ensuring the opportunity for her classmates to learn. "I guess that is what professional relationships are all about," he said to himself. "I need to write this one up for my student teaching journal and for my portfolio."

QUESTIONS FOR CONSIDERATION

■ What relationships actually impact student learning and well-being on a daily basis?

■ What relationships have the potential to impact student learning and well-being?

■ What do "school colleagues, parents, and agencies in the larger community" have to offer teachers and students in the learning process?

■ What positive and not-so-positive interactions did you have with "school colleagues, parents, and agencies in the larger community" that had impacts on student learning and well-being?

- What constitutes a student's well-being?
- How have you personally supported your students' learning and well-being?
- What is a "learning community"? How does being a member of one affect the student, the teacher, and the family?

Teachers do not act alone when educating children. While a host of others actually impact the learning and well-being of students, even more have the potential to affect their learning and well-being. Your portfolio needs to show that you recognize both actual and potential influences on student learning and well-being and that you can engage these forces to support your students. That said, this is not an easy task since preservice teachers may have fairly narrow opportunities to significantly alter or develop supports for individuals or groups of students. Most candidates have some possible evidences, however, including having worked with local agencies or organizations to arrange field trips, interviews with school professionals outside the actual classroom, parent conferences, IEP meetings, or simulated interactions, such as case studies. Whatever the form, you must demonstrate via several pieces of evidence that you interact with, understand, and can draw on the various resources, decision makers, and consultants who may help a teacher in the complex task called teaching.

UNDERSTANDING PRINCIPLE 10

Principle 10: The teacher fosters relationships with school colleagues, parents, and agencies in the larger community to support students' learning and well-being.

This principle asks for evidence that the preservice teacher, in his or her professional capacity, has built positive professional relationships with a variety of stakeholders in the learning process: students, parents, school colleagues, and the larger community.

"... a lesson designed to connect my students with some of the cultural and artistic resources in the community and to explore the meaning and value of the arts and their own understanding of the 'culture.'"

Fostering relationships with school colleagues, parents, and agencies in the larger community is a complex task because of the varying nature of these constituencies and the limited time one has to connect with them. Moreover, their makeup and availability tend to shift and change over time. Like a filing cabinet where you know to look for just the right file, these relationships are repositories of information, assistance, materials, influence, support, and much more, all potentially available to aid the professional educator in his or her endeavors to support student learning and well-being.

School colleagues include principals, other teachers, resource teachers, support staff, library-media professionals, district staff and administrators. This represents a large community of knowledge, experience, and influence that you can marshal to aid you in supporting your students' success.

Parents (and other caregivers) are integral to your students' learning and well-being. They can be motivators or obstacles; they can be interested and involved or they can be hands-off and disengaged. Whatever the case, family members are the ultimate authority to which teachers are accountable. As a result, it is important to know family members and the home they create for their children, but more important, it is essential to maintain open communication with them.

"Agencies in the larger community" sounds perhaps more sterile than it really ought to sound. Art museums and zoos are *agencies*. So are the Division of Family Services and Parents as Teachers. The community is an amazing resource for teachers and students. It represents a wealth of information, opportunities, assistance, and material resources.

WHAT ARE THE IMPLICATIONS OF THIS KNOWLEDGE BASE FOR MY PORTFOLIO?

In your portfolio, a reviewer will expect to see evidence that you are actively involved in school and district activities to enhance the lives and learning of your students. This may take the form of participation in collegial activities designed to make the entire school a productive learning environment (e.g., staff meetings, professional development meetings, and parent-teacher conferences). Journals and reflective artifacts ought to yield evidence of your ability to identify problems, identify appropriate resources and services, and then connect with those resources to solve the problem. Case studies might reveal the same sorts of thinking and acting, as might projects and presentations. Certainly, one would like to see the whole process of intervention from problem identification to evaluation of the results of actions taken.

Additionally, though not specifically identified within the principle itself, preservice teachers must understand how schools are organized and the variety of local, state, and federal laws, rules, and regulations that govern their operation. Whether involving recognition of a state law requiring the classroom teacher observing self-destructive behavior in a child's drawing to report it to others or understanding the professional way to seek change in the school organization, your portfolio must reveal you as a professional who carefully observes his or her students and then, when need arises, seeks professional assistance from others in the school or elsewhere with more sophisticated or specialized knowledge.

Principle 10, then, seeks ample evidence of your ability to work collaboratively with your colleagues, parents, students, and the broader community to meet the educational needs of your students. Let's review the knowledge, skills, and dispositions presented with Principle 10:

Knowledge

- The teacher understands schools as organizations within the larger community context and understands the operations of the relevant aspects of the system(s) within which she or he works.
- The teacher understands how factors in a student's environment outside of school (e.g., family circumstances, community environments, health and economic conditions) may influence the student's life and learning.
- The teacher understands and implements laws related to students' rights and teacher responsibilities (e.g., for equal education, appropriate education for students with disabilities, confidentiality, privacy, appropriate treatment of students, and the requirement to report possible child abuse).

Dispositions

- The teacher values and appreciates the importance of all aspects of a child's experience.
- The teacher is concerned about all aspects of a child's well-being (cognitive, emotional, social, and physical) and is alert to signs of difficulties.
- The teacher is willing to consult with other adults regarding the education and well-being of his or her students.
- The teacher respects the privacy of students and the confidentiality of information.
- The teacher is willing to work with other professionals to improve the overall learning environment for students.

Performances

- The teacher participates in collegial activities designed to make the entire school a productive learning environment.
- The teacher makes links with the learners' other environments on behalf of students, by consulting with parents, counselors, teachers of other classes and activities within the schools, and professionals in other community agencies.
- The teacher can identify and use community resources to foster student learning.
- The teacher establishes respectful and productive relationships with parents and guardians from diverse home and community situations and seeks to develop cooperative partnerships in support of student learning and well-being.
- The teacher talks with and listens to the student, is sensitive and responsive to clues of distress, investigates situations, and seeks outside help as needed and appropriate to remedy problems.
- The teacher acts as an advocate for students.

Principle 10, then, prescribes a set of knowledge, skills, and performances, which may be distilled into the following strands:

- Appreciates the influence of all aspects of a child's experience and environment (e.g., family circumstances, community environments, health and economic conditions) and factors these into his or her educational strategies
- Connects with learners' other environments on behalf of students by consulting with parents, counselors, teachers of other classes and activities within the schools, and professionals in other community agencies
- Implements laws related to students' rights and teacher responsibilities
- Talks with and listens to the students, is sensitive and responsive to clues of distress, investigates situations, and seeks outside help as needed and appropriate to remedy problems
- Identifies and uses community resources to foster student learning
- Acts as an advocate for students
- Demonstrates an understanding of school cultures and their relationships with the larger community context and the ability to work within these cultures to support student success
- Participates in collegial activities designed to make the entire school a productive learning environment

Your reflection and artifacts, at a minimum, ought to address some combination of these strands (though it is not likely you will deal with all of them).

ARTIFACT SELECTION

When deciding which artifacts to include in your portfolio, you must ask yourself at least the following questions:

- What examples do I have of my considering my student's experience and environment when making decisions about how and what I teach?
- What documents or other artifacts illustrate my ability and willingness to consult with parents, school colleagues, and the community to enhance my students' learning opportunities?

■ What examples do I have of my consideration of laws related to students' rights and teacher responsibilities in my educational decision-making process?

■ What artifacts show me talking and listening to the students and responding to students' needs or seeking community resources to foster their learning?

■ What examples show me acting as an advocate for students?

■ What documents can demonstrate my understanding of how schools work? What evidence do I have for working within the system and with the community to support student success?

■ What professional and school activities have I been involved in that were intended to make the school a productive learning environment?

TYPES OF ARTIFACTS

Consider using the following portfolio artifacts:

■ *Communications* with students, parents, school/district professional staff, and community resources

■ *Notes* from student-teacher conferences and parent-teacher conferences

■ *Reflections or journal entries* on issues involving professional relationships and their impact on student learning and well-being

■ *Certificates or verification* of involvement in school/district activities and reflection of those activities as they relate to student learning and well-being

■ *Notes from meetings* with appropriate school personnel (nurse, counselor, social worker, etc.) and community resources (field-trip sites, guest speakers, etc.) to enhance student learning and well-being

■ *Evaluations* from your cooperating teacher and your student teaching supervisor

EXAMPLE ARTIFACT

Now let's review an artifact and reflect on what it reveals about the teacher's knowledge, dispositions, and performance skills relevant to Principle 10. The lesson plan on the following pages was one of several artifacts offered to document one teacher's having met the expectations of the principle.

The artifact shown in Figure 13.1 is a good example of the candidate's attempt (proposed, if not actually implemented) to connect with family members. The initiative indicates that the candidate understands the need to help the families of middle school students understand their children and the changes they are going through. Moreover, it serves as an attempt to inform families about the structure of the school environment and other school resources available to them and their children. The program itself is a way of drawing families into the school setting and into the continuing process of their children's education.

By virtue of these features, this artifact addresses the following themes present in Principle 10:

■ Appreciates the influence of all aspects of a child's experience and environment (e.g., family circumstances, community environments, health and economic conditions) and factors these into his or her educational strategies

■ Acts as an advocate for students

■ Connects with learners' other environments on behalf of students by consulting with parents, counselors, teachers of other classes and activities within the schools, and professionals in other community agencies

So this artifact, in conjunction with other relevant artifacts, will be useful in making the case that the candidate meets the standard set by Principle 10. In addition, this

FIGURE 13.1

Collaboration Artifact

Proposed Parent Education Program

The goals of the parent education program resulted from a discussion among the teachers and guidance counselors in the middle school in response to the following question: What do you believe parents need to know about middle school learners and learning in order for them to understand and become actively involved in supporting your efforts in the classroom? A survey was also distributed to each family concerning what they would be interested in hearing about.

The sessions will meet at the school just prior to the end of the school day or in the evening, depending on the time constraints for parents. Each session will be offered more than once to accommodate parents' different schedules. Each meeting will consist of a brief overview of the night's topic, role-playing, question-and-answer sessions, and cooperative group work among the parents.

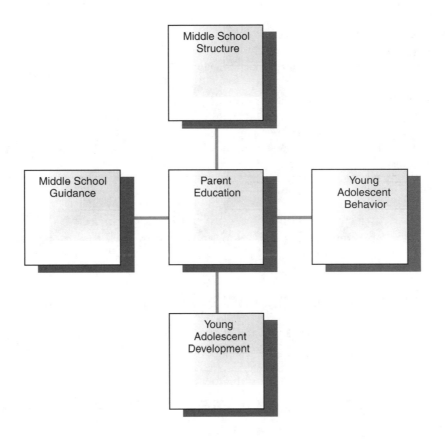

Session 1: What is happening to my young adolescent?

Topic for discussion:

1. Developmental Issues of Young Adolescents
   - Cognitive
   - Physical
   - Psychosocial
   - How these developmental characteristics affect students' lives.

Session 2: What is unique about young adolescent behavior?

Topics for discussion:

1. Autonomy
2. At-risk behaviors
   - Drugs
   - Alcohol
   - Teen pregnancy statistics and prevention; abstinence

(Continued)

FIGURE 13.1

Continued

- Eating disorders
- Delinquent behavior

Session 3: What is unique about the middle school structure?

Topics for discussion:

1. Interdisciplinary teams
2. Interdisciplinary units
3. Block scheduling
4. Looping
5. Exploratory programs
6. Advisor-advisee program

(There are so many new concepts introduced in middle school. The students' parents probably did not experience any of the developmentally responsive middle school programs offered today.)

Session 4: What is unique about the middle school approach to guidance?

Topics for discussion:

1. Principles of middle-school guidance and counseling
2. Guidance staff
3. Job descriptions and contact information for counseling staff

(Often parents don't know who to go to with their problems. It will encourage parents to voice their concerns and support if they knew who held what position and how to contact the various school staff member.)

---

artifact may reinforce documentation for Principle 2 ("The teacher understands how children learn and develop, and can provide learning opportunities that support their intellectual, social and personal development.").

WRITING A REFLECTION FOR PRINCIPLE 10

Now let's look at the reflection to see how well it presents the case for the candidate having met the expectations of Principle 10.

INTASC TEACHING COMPETENCY REFLECTION: PRINCIPLE 10

LEARNING COMMUNITIES

In my mind, Principle 10 is talking about educators creating and being a part of a learning community, people working together to build and support an environment that is welcoming, safe, and comfortable so that learning takes place naturally. Such a community must involve me and my students, but also my school colleagues, parents, and agencies in the larger community.

I am excited to be able to foster a sense of community among the students in my classroom. We will become a working community by developing a sense of admiration and respect for each other. As I have learned in Harry Wong's book, *The First Days of School*, developing a learning community must be my focus from day one! This is not an easy task, but it is a necessary task if I am to be successful in helping my students learn and develop.

In my field experience for Teaching Language Arts 5-12 I saw an ideal classroom that, to me, was the epitome of a learning community. It's hard to put into words what I observed. The students in this middle school classroom truly cared for each other. Each student was free to be himself or herself. They were not afraid to ask questions, offer responses, and take risks. Even if they were wrong, the students supported each other and cheered each other on. The teacher obviously set the tone of mutual respect and acceptance, and she did not let them get away with anything less.

The school as a whole is a learning community. I see this exemplified in school assemblies where students are brought together and encouraged and challenged. The research I have read is conclusive in that extracurricular activities such as sports, music, theater, and clubs are great learning communities that I will encourage my students to be involved in.

Today's middle school concept is focused on learning communities. In middle schools especially, advisement programs are a great benefit. In my middle school Web class, I learned that the definition of an advisory program is "a planned effort in which each student has the opportunity to participate in a small interactive group with peers and school staff to discuss school, personal, and societal concerns." The advisory programs help students develop a meaningful relationship with at least one significant adult in the school. I believe that I have a clear understanding of the benefits and am confident that I can create a positive advisement program. Interdisciplinary teams are also a great way for middle school students to form friendships with other students and have a sense of group identity in the school.

As part of my student teaching, I had to develop and present a series of advisement lesson plans. The example included among my artifacts (Artifacts: Tab 7—Advisement Lesson Plan) is a lesson designed to connect my students with some of the cultural and artistic resources in the community and to explore the meaning and value of the arts and their own understanding of the culture. This effort took two parts: the first was a field trip to the art museum for a tour of the galleries and to engage in art activities. This is part of a program available for free to schools within the metropolitan area. Many of the students had never been to the museum, so we talked in class about what to expect, and the students generated a list of guidelines for behavior and how to make the most of the visit. At the end of the visit, the students got to display and discuss their own works. The second part of the plan happened the day after we returned to school when we debriefed on the experience and talked about why art (in all its forms) is important to them and their community.

The students were excited about the experience and behaved beautifully throughout their time at the museum, keeping to the rules they had developed themselves. The museum officials even commented on the class's behavior and the insightfulness of their questions and comments. This was reinforced by the discussions on the bus back to school and in the next day's conversations. It proved to me that if students have a hand in defining their own rules and have a chance to take responsibility for their own learning, they (most often) rise to the challenge and succeed.

Another vital learning community is the home. I must seek opportunities as a teacher to develop relationships with parents and guardians. The positive relationships will, I hope, develop into a partnership in support of student learning. In my dealings with parents thus far, I have learned that I must listen to their concerns first and then support and encourage them when they are struggling with their child. Parents must be involved in schooling from day one all the way through high school as room parents, volunteer book readers, PTA members, and the list continues. Students will reap the benefits of their involvement, and so will they. If a student knows his or her parents value education, the student will value the education. My desire is to bring the "parents on the fringe" into the action, so my students can reap the benefits as well. I hope to achieve this through parent volunteering in the classroom, parent-student-teacher conferences, educational and informational programs for parents, and letters, e-mails, and phone calls to parents.

In my middle school curriculum and instruction course, I had to develop a parent education program introducing parents to middle school (Artifacts: Tab 7—Proposed Parent Education Program). I had to base the program on the school in which I was interning (and would be student teaching). While I never got to enact my program, I see the importance of these kinds of programs and plan to propose it to the school in which

I eventually get a job if the school does not already have such an event in its parent information efforts.

Many other resources exist outside the classroom, school, and home that will help students learn. The local community has a plethora of volunteers just waiting to be used. From my own experience, I have volunteered to come in and read a book to middle school students to show them that I, along with other adults, value reading. There are also various opportunities to incorporate knowledgeable guest speakers. I will not be an expert on all areas of the content I teach; however, I do know guest speakers with specific knowledge and life experiences that can teach students from an insider's perspective are available. Local museums, parks, historic landmarks, community agencies, and government buildings are great field trip opportunities for active learning that will expand the classroom walls. The community in which the school exists, and for that matter in the school as well, suggests many opportunities for service learning projects. Service learning projects allow students to learn responsibility, respect, and generosity in their dealings with others, along with other positive character traits.

During my internship/student teaching experience, I helped my cooperating teacher develop the year's service learning project (Artifacts: Tab 3—Service Learning Project). I had to do some research into available community agencies we could cooperate with and contact these agencies to gather information and discuss possible projects with each. We gave the students the list and gave them a chance to add to it and to decide which project we would as a home room take on. The students amazed me with the thoughtfulness of their suggestions and discussions. In the end they decided to help one of the agencies I had researched (a local homeless shelter) because they felt it would be one they could be most successful helping and for which there was enough work for everyone. Before we began, we visited the shelter, talked to the head of the shelter, and discussed the shelter's needs and our capabilities. The students decided to make sandwiches every Friday for delivery to the shelter. This involved raising money, exploring health codes and good health practices, determining jobs, shopping, organizing the work, and delivery. The students did the bulk of the work with some supervision.

The project was a success. While there were moments of difficulty, overall the students worked well together and carried their responsibility. It is not easy to engage in long-term projects. It is easy to get bored with the routine and want to give up. I learned a lot about how to set up such projects and some of the pitfalls facing teachers and students. My College of Education has a graduate certificate in experiential learning, which I have already begun to explore. Students really benefit from such learning opportunities, and I would like to be prepared to provide more of these experiences to my students.

Other important communities of learning for a teacher's growth in particular are professional organizations. Professional organizations such as NEA, ASCD, NMSA, and NCSS will allow me as a teacher to continue to grow. From experience, I have already gained great insight by attending the educational conferences at Erehwon University and national conferences, such as the Association of Supervision and Curriculum Development (Artifacts: Tab 7—ASCD Conference Reflections).

The learning community for teachers within the school is another tremendous resource. The opportunity to share ideas and learn with other colleagues is a valuable resource I will certainly not neglect. As a young teacher I am mindful that I have a lot to learn, and I have learned in student teaching that it is to my benefit to ask as many questions as possible. I understand that I do not have to conquer my first years of teaching alone. The mentor relationship is certainly valuable for my development in my younger years. I have, thus far, asked numerous questions, borrowed many resources, discussed ideas with other teachers, and at times felt inferior for not grasping the material without their explanation and guidance. I have learned, though, that I must not let my pride get in the way of becoming the best teacher I can be! I am well aware that I will be given the opportunity to return the favor to other young teachers as I progress on my journey.

Identification of context. The candidate spends a little time at the beginning of the reflection discussing the expectations of the principle and her or his conception of a learning community. This acts as a good introduction to the reflective essay and gives a beginning impression of the candidate's understanding of the principle and the themes it raises.

Observation and description of artifact (experience or document). Except for the final set of artifacts (Conference Reflections), the candidate gives at least some background for each artifact: where and why it was developed, who was involved, what happened, and how it turned out. Sometimes the descriptions leave the reviewer wanting more details, but overall enough information is available to introduce the artifact and to see how it fits within the scope of Principle 10 expectations.

Application of theories or principles of effective practice. Only one theorist (Harry Wong) is mentioned in the reflection. While there is a lot of recent research about learning communities, parent and community involvement in student achievement, character education, sociomoral development, and so on, the reflection does fairly well without it. One can glean from the actions, plans, statements, and dispositions displayed in this reflection that the candidate has a fairly good notion of who and what is involved in learning communities and how to access the resources available there.

Identification, analysis, and interpretation of causes and effects: For most artifacts, the candidate talks about effects but not much about causes. One finds some analysis of the impact of students taking responsibility for developing their own rules and self-management guidelines. It would be better to see a few more sentences for each artifact talking about the causes for successes and weaknesses arising in the chosen experiences.

Projection from observations toward problem solving and lifelong learning. We find few different instances of projection going on in this reflection. The candidate, for instance, wants to actually propose his or her parent education program. While this is not an issue of lifelong learning, it is reflective of forward thinking and application in the future. In the area of experiential learning, the candidate expresses an interest in and a need for more preparation, even identifying a program and asserting an effort to begin the process of seeking further professional training. In the final paragraph, the candidate expresses the need for mentoring and the further assistance of seasoned professionals. She or he expresses also the expectation of taking on the role of mentor after gaining more experience. This is enough to give the reviewer a solid impression that the candidate is thinking about a future of professional development in a number of forms.

All in all, this reflection would fit neatly into the "good reflection" category and will work well for the candidate who submits it.

Now, based on this artifact and the reflection (with its described artifacts), where would you place the candidate on the following rubric for Principle 10?

Meets the Standard	*Not Yet Meeting the Standard*
The preservice teacher seeks opportunities to develop caring, professional, and productive relationships with the school colleagues, parents, and educational partners in the school and larger community to support student learning and well-being. The candidate demonstrates knowledge of when and how to access specialized services.	The preservice teacher confines his or her activities to the classroom and to interactions with the cooperating teacher. The candidate shows no evidence of going beyond the classroom to connect with others to support student learning, including but not limited to knowledge of when and how to access specialized services.

Based on what we have seen, it is clear this candidate demonstrates most of the knowledge, skills, and dispositions of Principle 10. Ample evidence, within the reflection and among the artifacts, is cited to demonstrate competence in understanding and creating learning communities, as well as the ability to interact with colleagues, the community, and family members to support student learning. We do not, however, see much evidence for the final element of the rubric: Accessing specialized services. This expectation is important and should be documented among the candidate's artifacts and reflection. A reviewer will want to see that a candidate at least knows what specialized services are available in the school, the district, and the community. Better yet, evidence of actually connecting with these resources will better document the candidate's ability to go outside the classroom to meet the social, physical and educational needs of students.

Still, we see evidence of the teacher connecting with the community for field trips and community service opportunities, so one might infer the ability to also access other more specialized services. With this inference, enough evidence exists to help us conclude that this candidate does meet most of the expectations set by Principle 10.

SUMMARY

Educating a child is not a solo effort involving only the one teacher and one child. Rather, education is a collaborative process, involving many people both in the school and outside its walls. Your school colleagues, including the teacher in the next room and the various other professionals within the building, are all resources who can help in your endeavors to meet each child's needs. Family members also have a stake and role to play in the education of their children. Beyond these two interested partners, there exists an entire community of interested citizens, agencies, and community resources eager to support education in a broad range of ways. These resources rarely come looking for the teacher; rather, they are available when the teacher seeks them out. A little creativity, some good sense, and the willingness to collaborate with others will serve you well as you begin to develop the web of resources needed to create a rich, meaningful, and supportive learning environment for all your students.

Here are some questions to help you gather your evidence and prepare your reflection:

1. How do I document my knowledge of the many resources available to a teacher in her or his efforts to create a supportive learning environment for all students?
2. What kinds of collegial activities have I engaged in to make school a productive learning environment for all students?
3. When, how, and to what end have I connected with my students' other environments on behalf of students, by consulting with families, counselors, teachers of other classes and activities within the schools, and professionals in other community agencies?
4. What community resources have I accessed to foster student learning? How have I used these community resources to support my students' learning?
5. When and how have I built and used relationships with parents and guardians to support student learning and well-being?
6. What are the clues of distress among students? When have I noticed these, investigated the causes, and sought outside help to remedy problems?
7. When and how have I acted as an advocate for students?

DISCUSSION QUESTIONS

1. How may family circumstances, community environments, health and economic conditions, and other aspects of a child's experience and environment influence the instructional choices a teacher makes and the strategies he or she might use?

2. What resources (human and nonhuman) might an educator draw on to meet the personal and educational needs of his or her students and to promote their learning and achievement?

3. What laws govern students' rights and teacher responsibilities?

4. How may a teacher act as an advocate for students? Why should a teacher do so?

5. What roles do schools play in the larger community context?

6. What does it mean for a school to exhibit a culture? Why is it important for an educator to understand and be able to work within a school culture? Why and how is it important to student success?

7. How can an educator have a positive impact on her or his school community?

Implementing the ISTE Technology Standards in Your Portfolio

14

Our Age of Anxiety is, in great part, the result of trying to do today's jobs with yesterday's tools.

Marshall McLuhan

Geeta gazed across the classroom, amazed at how intently the students were working in their design groups. Each team was huddled around a table with a laptop, pieces of poster paper, markers, books, and other source materials, much of it from the Internet. The lesson had to do with biomes and adaptations. Each team was responsible for developing a Hyperstudio presentation, an interactive teaching/learning module to help other students in the class understand the characteristics of specific biomes and how animals had adapted to those characteristics. In the past few classes, the students had done their research, both text based and via the Internet; now they were designing and creating the Hyperstudio module to present and teach the information. They were even creating an assessment portion for the module to allow classmates to self-assess their learning. Geeta was almost embarrassed by how little she had to do, just some circulating around the class, a little help with minor technical problems, some questioning to challenge the students to be more rigorous. That was what her instructors at the university meant by "teacher as facilitator." She had thought long and hard about how to make this happen; now it seemed a breeze. "I've got to put this into my portfolio, if nothing else to show that I know how to teach using technology."

QUESTIONS FOR CONSIDERATION

- With what teaching and learning technologies are you familiar?
- How comfortable are you with using them?
- What does *technology enhanced* mean for teachers and classrooms?
- What does *facilitating learning* mean in the classroom?
- What roles do teachers and students play in such a classroom?

■ How can technological tools be a key feature of classroom management?

■ What does *the safe use of technology* mean in the context of computers and the Internet? What does it mean in the context of the science, math, physical education, or home economics classroom?

■ What ethical issues may play a role in using technology as a tool for teaching and learning?

Knowing how to use e-mail or find lesson plans on the Internet is far from sufficient to prove you know technology and how to use it to increase the effectiveness of your teaching and the achievement of your students. Merely printing prepackaged lessons from the Internet or showing lists of Web sites used as resources for teaching shows nothing of your ability to harness the power of technology to actively engage students in learning and to challenge them to extend their understanding of the content beyond the basics. What's more, technology is not limited to the computer, especially in the areas of math and science, where calculators and tools for scientific analysis are becoming more and more complex. Therefore, across the range of artifacts included in your portfolio and within your reflective statement, you must show that you understand technology of many types, are competent with a range of software, and possess the ability to use these tools to help all students achieve in various content areas (as appropriate to your certification area).

Understanding the ISTE National Educational Technology Standards for Teachers (NETS•T)

NETS•T Standards Synopsis (Technology in Teaching and Learning): The preservice teacher understands the theory and practice of technological operations, concepts, tools, and software and can use these to create meaningful learning opportunities for all students. (See also appendix D: International Society of Technology Education {ISTE} Standards.)

The NETS•T standards ask for evidence of a number of achievements:

1. Sound understanding of technology operations and concepts
2. Ability to plan and design effective learning environments and experiences supported by technology
3. Ability to implement curriculum plans that include methods and strategies for applying technology to maximize student learning
4. Ability to apply technology to facilitate a variety of effective assessment and evaluation strategies
5. Use of technology to enhance productivity and professional practice
6. Understanding of the social, ethical, legal, and human issues surrounding the use of technology in K–12 schools and the ability to apply that understanding in practice.

"The educational gains are just as great for the teacher as for the students. As a teacher I can greatly benefit from the variety of software available to teachers for grading purposes. I have used MicroGrade first hand during student teaching and it makes life so easy! At the touch of a button a student's grade report is printed out and ready for a parent conference."

The term *technology operations and concepts* refers to a general understanding of how technology works, its intended uses, and how it may be applied to teaching and learning. While most of us are not aware of the nuts and bolts of building a computer or constructing a program, we need to know how to connect a printer, use a scanner, install a mathematical modeling program, or connect to the Internet. Also, we need to know what such things are good for in the classroom and how they can interact with the curriculum to increase student learning.

Planning and designing effective learning environments and experiences supported by technology and *implementing curriculum plans that include methods and strategies for applying technology to*

"My student's success in my classroom and in the world in which they are living is dependent on my technology understanding. I must teach them to responsibly use the gift of technology to enhance their lives and the lives of those around them."

"We cannot ignore the fact that our children are technologically advanced and they expect us to be as well. With movies, video games, Game Boys, and many more stimulating electronic devices competing for attention, we must make sure education keeps pace, or students will tune us out."

maximize student learning are self-explanatory. How does one plan learning opportunities with technology in the tool chest? How can technology, in its varied forms, enrich the learning experience to increase engagement, improve motivation, and challenge students?

Applying technology to facilitate a variety of effective assessment and evaluation strategies asks the teacher to move out of the traditional assessment forms and to use technology as a means of creating and supporting more performance-based assessments, assessments that get students to apply what they have learned in meaningful, real-world situations. This can also include forms of electronic self-assessment, allowing students to gain feedback while gauging their progress toward curriculum goals.

Using technology to enhance productivity and professional practice gets into the area of the teacher's world. Here we find word processing, e-mail, presentation software, and Internet research, as well as tools like electronic grade books. These tools allow the busy professional to create and transmit professional communications, shorten grade calculation times, and draw on a world of information without having to spend hours in the library.

Understanding the social, ethical, legal, and human issues surrounding the use of technology in K–12 schools and applying that understanding in practice asks the teacher to consider the implications of technology from a range of philosophical and human perspectives. The Internet contains a great deal of information, not all of it suitable for student uses and not all of it accurate. What are the reasonable limits necessary to assure student safety? What about plagiarism, for both the students and the teacher? What software will truly challenge students and what software will not? How do we balance the enticements of technology with the value of student interaction with each other? What about issues of equity of access and the halo effect that technology can have on perceptions of student performance? All these issues must be considered when determining the appropriate, most effective uses of technology in your classroom.

What Are the Implications of This Knowledge Base for My Portfolio?

In your portfolio you must be able to document both a working knowledge of relevant hardware and software, your consideration of the implications of its uses, and how you consciously use that knowledge to build lessons, instructional activities, and assessments. Your reflections, journal entries, and commentaries must make explicit reference to the technological tools you use. The reviewer must see you using technology as both a source for instructional designs and actions, including assessment and grading, and for communicating with a variety of audiences about instruction and student performance. Your lesson designs and classroom management choices must also clearly exhibit your consideration of these tools and their practical application to address student needs—sometimes, perhaps, even revealing your willingness to reject a computer-based solution in favor of a more traditional one simply because the latter is more appropriate to your students' needs. Additionally, your artifacts should show you evaluating the appropriateness of different technologies and applications, as well as your evaluation of the effectiveness of activities and strategies using technology. Furthermore, you must exhibit your ability to encourage students to make responsible decisions regarding technology use.

The NETS•T standards, then, prescribe a significant breadth of knowledge, skills, and performances. The full set of NETS•T standards may be found at www.prenhall/foster. However, we can distill the following strands:

■ Demonstrates continual growth in the uses and troubleshooting of current and emerging computer technologies to run software; to access, generate, and manipulate data; and to publish results

- Applies current research on teaching and learning with technology to plan and deliver developmentally appropriate learning opportunities that integrate a variety of software, applications, and learning tools (graphing calculators, language translators, scientific probe-ware, musical composition software, electronic maps, etc.) to support the diverse needs of learners
- Identifies, locates, explores, and evaluates for accuracy and suitability computer/technology resources including applications, tools, educational software, and associated documentation
- Designs and utilizes technology-enhanced, learner-centered classroom strategies and activities (including teaming or small-group collaboration) to address the diverse needs of students
- Facilitates technology-enhanced learning experiences that develop students' higher order thinking skills, creativity, and problem-solving skills; content standards; and student technology standards
- Uses technology resources in assessing student learning of subject matter using a variety of assessment techniques to collect and analyze data, to interpret results, and to communicate findings to improve instructional practice and maximize student learning (including the use of technology resources for learning, communication, and productivity)
- Uses technology resources to engage in ongoing professional development and lifelong learning
- Evaluates and reflects continually on professional practice to make informed decisions regarding the use of technology in support of student learning
- Uses technology to communicate and collaborate with peers, parents, and the larger community in order to nurture student learning, conduct research, and solve problems
- Models and teaches legal and ethical practice related to technology, information, and software resources, as well as the safe and healthy use of technology resources
- Applies technology resources to enable and empower learners with diverse backgrounds, characteristics, and abilities, including facilitating equitable access to technology resources for all students

Your reflection and artifacts, at a minimum, ought to address some combination of these strands (though it is not likely you will deal with all of them).

ARTIFACT SELECTION

When deciding which artifacts to include in your portfolio, you must ask yourself at least the following questions:

1. Which documents and other artifacts (videos, URLs, PowerPoint presentations) reveal my understanding of the whats, hows, and whys of technology in teaching and learning?
2. Which documents reveal my ability to develop rigorous and challenging lessons and activities using a variety of technological tools?
3. Which artifacts show me using technology to teach and assess my students?
4. Which pieces of my work show my use of technology to increase my own productivity in and out of the classroom?
5. Which artifacts show the kinds of things I take into consideration when choosing to use technology to support my students' learning and achievement?
6. Which documents show my ethical use of technology and my consideration of other social and legal issues when bringing technology and its resources into my classroom and practice?

TYPES OF ARTIFACTS

As sources for documenting your knowledge and skills relevant to diverse student populations, the following categories of artifacts will be particularly fruitful:

- *Lesson plans and unit plans* clearly revealing your use of technology to enhance student experience/knowledge levels, meaning construction, and engagement
- *Electronic/technological artifacts* (PowerPoint presentations, WebQuests, self-constructed Web sites, etc.) demonstrating your understanding and application of electronic tools and technology of various sorts
- *Assessments* (both formal and informal) revealing your ability to gather and analyze meaningful and useful information about student learning through the use of technology
- *Reflections and journal entries* showing your reflection on the value and effectiveness of technology before and after its use in your classroom
- *Essays or projects* from professional courses exhibiting your understanding and use of technology
- *Case studies and action research* revealing your application of critical analysis and evaluation of technology and its appropriate use for enhancing student achievement
- *Evaluations* from your cooperating teacher and your clinical experience supervisor revealing others' recognition of your ability to use technological tools to enhance classroom practice
- *Transcripts* (optional) showing you have taken courses in the what and how of technology

EXAMPLE ARTIFACT

Now let's review an artifact and reflect on what it reveals about the teacher's knowledge, dispositions, and performance skills relevant to the NETS•T standards.

Figure 14.1 shows a selection of slides from a PowerPoint presentation developed by a student teacher for a fifth-grade science lesson. The entire presentation includes 16

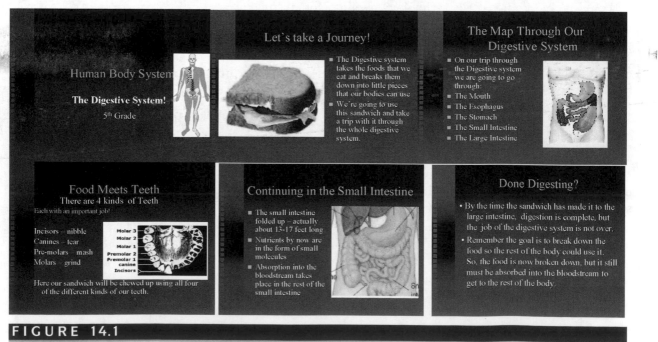

FIGURE 14.1

Technology Artifact

slides describing the different stages of the digestive system, including vocabulary, explanation, and graphic illustrations. This artifact offers some evidence for several issues from the NETS•T standards:

- Demonstrates continual growth in the uses and troubleshooting of current and emerging computer technologies to run software; to access, generate, and manipulate data; and to publish results.
- Applies current research on teaching and learning with technology to plan and deliver developmentally appropriate learning opportunities that integrate a variety of software, applications, and learning tools (graphing calculators, languages translators, scientific probe-ware, musical composition software, electronic maps, etc.) to support the diverse needs of learners.

First, the presentation reveals this teacher's ability to use presentation software and hardware, including PowerPoint, the computer, and LCD projectors. Moreover, we can infer from the slides that the teacher also knows how to use word processing software and the Internet for capturing and inserting graphic objects into a presentation. Therefore it reveals some technological expertise.

That said, the artifact does not show the teacher's having met several other issues from the standards:

- Designs and utilizes *technology-enhanced, learner-centered classroom strategies and activities* (including teaming or small-group collaboration) to address the diverse needs of students.
- Facilitates technology-enhanced *learning experiences that develop students' higher order thinking skills, creativity, and problem-solving skills; content standards; and student technology standards.*
- Uses technology resources to assess *student learning of subject matter* using a variety of assessment techniques to collect and analyze data, to interpret results, and to communicate findings to improve instructional practice and maximize student learning (including the use of technology resources for learning, communication, and productivity).

On its face, this artifact seems to imply a traditional, direct-instruction model for teaching, and it only reveals the teacher having access to or control of the technology. The NETS•T standards expect teachers to be technology proficient (i.e., to know technology), but the standards also expect teachers to use that knowledge to provide opportunities for their students to use the technology to advance their own thinking and learning. It would be good to see evidence, via lesson plans and student work, of students using technology in the context of rich learning opportunities facilitated by the teacher. This is not to say that this presentation is not a good artifact, nor does it imply that direct instruction is necessarily bad; rather it is meant to suggest that a range of artifacts will likely be necessary to reveal both understanding of technology and how to use it effectively in the classroom to facilitate learning.

WRITING A REFLECTION FOR THE NETS•T STANDARDS

Now let's look at the reflection addressing the NETS•T standards. How does it work as a reflection, and how well does it support the case for the teacher having met the expectations outlined earlier?

TECHNOLOGY IN TEACHING AND LEARNING

In today's digital world, we are surrounded by the benefits and challenges of advanced technology. The benefits far outweigh the negative side effects, and education is one of the arena's reaping the greatest benefits. Technology is beneficial to today's teacher because it can significantly enhance student learning experiences and opportunities. However, I must *not* simply use technology, such as the Internet, PowerPoint, and movies, to teach my students for me; rather, I must use it to *enhance* my students' learning.

As a teacher I know there are a variety of uses for technology that will enhance my student's education. We cannot ignore the fact that our children are technologically advanced and they expect us to be as well. With movies, video games, Game Boys, and many more stimulating electronic devices competing for attention, we must make sure education keeps pace, or students will tune us out.

The main technological device for educational growth is the computer. Today's student learns very early how to navigate the computer, from the Internet to word processing and creative software. In the classroom, the computer can be a valuable tool for producing fluent writers through word processing software. I employ the writing process within my classes, expecting students to brainstorm, draft, revise, and edit their writing before turning it in for a grade. The software gives the student the opportunity to write freely with unlimited revision and editing possibilities at the click of a button. And by printing out their work for critical reviews by me and their classmates, students gain valuable perspectives on their work and make better choices when revising and editing. In my own learning, I enjoyed writing more when my teachers said the process would be done on the computer. I felt free to express myself and get my thoughts out because I knew I could easily rearrange, regroup, and delete at any time. My students demonstrate the same preference for the word processing tools.

The Internet is also an extremely valuable tool for today's students. Virtual field trips bring the world to life and online museums bring historical artifacts into the classroom. It's amazing! During my student teaching, I used the Internet to create a number of "treasure hunts," asking students to explore various topics using an Internet "map" and "clues" to guide their searches (Artifacts: Tab 5—Internet Treasure Hunts). The lesson was a hit every time because the students learned a great deal about the given subject through the Web site I had created in advance. The Internet sites I wanted them to search were chosen for them, and they enjoyed learning the information because it was hands-on and technological. I actually heard a few of the seventh-grade students say they didn't know you could find "educational stuff" on the Internet! These students were opened to a whole new world of possibilities.

Students are fascinated by the power of the Internet, and as a teacher I can channel that fascination and get them to enjoy learning new information. Web quests and virtual scrapbooks have also proven very exciting to students. I have learned how to use these tools by reading about them over the Internet, exploring their possibilities and value for student learning, and putting them into practice. It's as simple as that!

The Internet also provides a link to other cultures. Through Web sites and e-mail, students can exchange ideas with students from around the world. This is truly revolutionary, especially as I think about teaching social studies. Geography can be greatly enhanced, as can understanding of international issues. I have used the Internet to research many major (and not so major) historical documents at the touch of a button. Students are then able to study history from primary sources, reading historical documents and memoirs firsthand. I have spent hours upon hours exploring thousands of sites, and I never ceased to be amazed by all I learn. I want my students to have that kind of hunger for learning and for using technology to further their educational goals.

The educational gains are just as great for the teacher as for the students. I can benefit from the variety of software available to teachers for grading purposes. I have used

MicroGrade firsthand during student teaching, and it makes life so easy. At the touch of a button a student's grade report is printed out and ready for a parent conference. E-mail is also a wonderful communication tool for teachers to use throughout the day to communicate with others in the school and with parents.

The Internet is also a great tool for teachers to get ideas. Search engines make it easy to find interesting lesson plans and educational enhancement tools. In my Teaching Social Studies class, we had to create a database of social studies lesson plans, map-making Web sites, and other Web sites that enhance social studies whether it be a virtual field trip or a simulation. The Web is full of endless possibilities and can at times be overwhelming. I also use the Internet as a great refresher tool. I did a lesson on AIDS in South Africa, and the Internet came in handy when I was looking for the most up-to-date statistics and interventions.

PowerPoint is wonderful software that can enhance a teacher's presentation with video clips, neatly organized notes, and clip art. After creating a unit on Franklin Delano Roosevelt with PowerPoint, I understand the immense advantage of having the notes, pictures, graphs, and videos so neatly organized for my students. The class is able to flow much smoother, and students are visually stimulated (Artifacts: Tab 5—FDR PowerPoint).

The ability for me as a teacher to have my own Web page is another perk of technology. In my Technology Applications class, I learned how to create a Web page, and I know the benefits are many (Artifacts: Tab 5—Sample Web Page). A Web page allows the teacher to post information for students and parents such as homework, upcoming assignments, class notes, and interesting information or links that will enhance the classroom experience, plus it provides a way for students to contact the teacher via e-mail while he or she is at home.

I must also be aware of the risks associated with technology, because they are many. I must protect my students' minds and make sure they are not exposed to Internet sites they should not see. I must also make sure that the Internet is not abused and that people's ideas are not plagiarized. My students' success in my classroom and in the world in which they are living is dependent in part on my understanding of technology. I must teach students to responsibly use the gift of technology to enhance their lives and the lives of those around them.

Technology truly is exciting! Today's educators have such an edge if they will only take advantage of the opportunities. I know that computers will continue to advance, Web sites will continue to be updated, and bigger and better software will continue to be produced. I must take the responsibility to stay up to date and informed so as not to be left behind.

Identification of context. In the first few paragraphs, the candidate establishes a context for talking about technology in teaching and learning. She or he talks about the prevalence and influence of technology on students and the value it has for increasing student engagement and access to information and content-specific documents. Within the discussion, the candidate narrows the focus to the computer and the Internet. The bulk of the reflection describes aspects of these tools and how they serve the work of the teacher and the learning of the students.

Observation and description of artifact (experience or document). One would like to see more detailed descriptions of the contexts surrounding each artifact described, how lessons were designed, what technology tools were used, and the kinds of students involved in the teacher's experiences. We do, however, gain some insight into how the teacher used technology to enhance student learning and the results of that effort.

Application of theories or principles of effective practice. Rarely in the reflection does the teacher refer to theories or principles of effective practice. One example is the reference to the writing process: "I employ the writing process within my classes, expecting students to brainstorm, draft, revise, and edit their writing before turning it in for a grade. The software gives the student the opportunity to write freely with unlimited revision and editing possibilities at the click of a button. And by printing out their work for critical reviews by me and their classmates, students gain valuable perspectives on their work and make better choices when revising and editing." This gives us a sense that the teacher is applying some theory to his or her use of technology. The closest other example we get is by inference from the many references to student engagement (excitement and interest) resulting from the technology. Motivation is an important element of classroom management and learning. A reviewer would like to have the candidate overtly make this connection.

Identification, analysis, and interpretation of causes and effects. As with the criterion noted earlier, one may infer cause and effect, if only from the teacher's references to the students' excitement and the lessons being "a big hit." Still one would like to see overt recognition of the underlying psychology of that excitement and the educational value resulting from the technology-rich lesson. Did the students learn the material? Are they exhibiting more critical abilities? Is their writing showing measurable improvement? Are the students achieving more?

Projection from observations toward problem solving and lifelong learning. The teacher seems to be aware of the constant evolution of technology and its potential impact on teaching and learning. At the very end of the reflection, she or he states, "I must take the responsibility to stay up to date and informed so as not to be left behind." The implication is that the teacher will continue to seek more knowledge and expertise in technology as his or her career advances.

Are the expectations of the NETS•T standards sufficiently met by the reflection and the referenced evidence? We cannot be absolutely sure because we have not seen all the evidence. However, based on the one lesson and the reflection, where would you tend to place this teacher on the following rubric that the teacher has.

Meets the Standard	*Not Yet Meeting the Standard*
• Demonstrates continual growth in the uses and troubleshooting of current and emerging computer technologies to run software; to access, generate, and manipulate data; and to publish results.	• Demonstrates at most a basic (or very limited) knowledge of computer technologies with little recognition of the need to stay abreast of evolving technologies.
• Applies current research on teaching and learning with technology to plan and deliver developmentally appropriate learning opportunities that integrate a variety of software, applications, and learning tools (graphing calculators, languages translators, scientific probe-ware, musical composition software, electronic maps, etc.) to support the diverse needs of learners.	• Plans and delivers learning opportunities that integrate computers into the classroom, but these opportunities employ only a limited range of learning software and little beyond games, word-processing, presentation software, and computerized work sheets.
• Identifies, locates, explores, and evaluates, for accuracy and suitability, computer/technology resources including applications, tools, educational software, and associated documentation.	• Identifies computer/technology resources including applications, tools, and educational software, but does not evaluate these critically with regard to such issues as developmental appropriateness, accuracy, or suitability to support local, state, or national standards.
	• Designs and utilizes technology-based, teacher-centered classroom strategies and activities, with no differentiation of instruction.

Meets the Standard

- Designs and utilizes technology-enhanced, learner-centered classroom strategies and activities (including teaming or small-group collaboration) to address the diverse needs of students.

- Facilitates technology-enhanced learning experiences that develop students' higher order thinking skills, creativity, and problem-solving skills; content standards; and student technology standards.

- Uses technology resources to assess student learning of the subject matter using a variety of assessment techniques to collect and analyze data, to interpret results, and to communicate findings to improve instructional practice and maximize student learning

- Uses technology resources for learning, communication, and productivity.

- Uses technology resources to engage in ongoing professional development and lifelong learning.

- Continually evaluates and reflects on professional practice to make informed decisions regarding the use of technology to support student learning.

- Uses technology to communicate and collaborate with peers, parents, and the larger community in order to nurture student learning, conduct research, and solve problems.

- Models and teaches legal and ethical practice related to technology, information, and software resources, as well as the safe and healthy use of technology resources.

- Applies technology resources to enable and empower learners with diverse backgrounds, characteristics, and abilities, including facilitating equitable access to technology resources for all students.

Not Yet Meeting the Standard

- Teaches using technology but limits the use to knowledge or basic-skills acquisition and communication.

- Exhibits little or no use of technology resources in assessing and managing data on student learning of the subject matter; alternatively, uses technology to assess only the recall/recognition of knowledge and basic skills.

- Uses a limited range of technology for personal and professional learning, productivity and communication.

- Reveals little or no evidence of the inclination or ability to use technology resources to enhance professional development learning.

- Rarely reflects on professional practice regarding the use of technology in support of student learning.

- May use technology to communicate with peers but not with parents and the larger community or to collaborate or conduct research.

- Models legal and ethical practice related to technology, information, and software resources but does not demonstrate the inclination to teach this to students; alternatively, may disregard matters of copyright or fair acknowledgment of resources and materials taken from print or electronic sources; expresses some concern for the safe and healthy use of technology resources.

- Does not use technology resources as a means to empower learners with diverse backgrounds, characteristics, and abilities; does not overtly consider the issue of equitable access to technology resources for all students.

The reflection and the artifacts referenced give plenty of evidence about the candidate's knowledge of technology and to some extent how it might be used in the classroom. There are a couple of gaps that need to be addressed, including determining the developmental appropriateness of technology-centered instructional activities, reviewing software for appropriateness, using technology to address the needs of diverse students, using technology for assessment, and applying current research to teaching with technology. The NETS • T sets detailed expectations for teachers' use of technology in the classroom, so it will be hard to address every area of the standards in your portfolio. Still, issues of diversity, theory-based instruction, assessment, and appropriateness of technology choices are all worth addressing in some way within your artifacts and reflection. Even with these gaps, one would likely give this candidate a passing score for this section of the portfolio based on the combination of the discussion given in the reflection and the referenced artifacts (assuming they, in fact, exhibit the qualities the teacher has asserted).

SUMMARY

We are truly in an age driven by technology and information. Technological tools touch all aspects of our lives and, by extension, every content area we teach. Technology can compete with learning or it can enhance the process and engage the learner. The educator's job is to make the electronic world work for enhancing student learning rather than detracting from it. The NETS • T standards set a high bar for what teachers need to know about technology and how they should use it. They also provide a set of valuable criteria for assessing the ways we use technology in our classrooms. Your portfolio, then, must show that you understand the expectations for technology knowledge and practices in the classroom and that you are working to meet those expectations. The following questions will help you gather your evidence and prepare your reflection.

1. How can I demonstrate my knowledge of the uses and troubleshooting of current and emerging computer technologies?
   - What range of software applications can I employ in my teaching?
   - How do I use technology to access, generate, and manipulate data and to publish the results of my work?

2. When and how have I combined current research on teaching and learning with technology to plan and deliver developmentally appropriate learning to support the diverse needs of learners?

3. How do I ensure the quality of the technology tools and applications I use with my students? In what situations have I done this?

4. What examples exist of my ability to design and use technology-enhanced, learner-centered classroom strategies and activities (including teaming or small-group collaboration) to address the diverse needs of students?

5. What examples do I have of my ability to facilitate technology-enhanced learning experiences that develop students' higher-order thinking skills, creativity, and problem-solving skills, as well as the content knowledge specified by local, state, and national content standards?

6. How have I used technology resources to assess student learning?

7. How have I used technology tools and resources to enhance my productivity and communication?

8. How have I used technology resources to engage in ongoing professional development and lifelong learning, and how do I plan to continue to use them?

9. How have I used technology to communicate and collaborate with peers, parents, and the larger community in order to nurture student learning?

10. In what overt ways do I consider, model, and teach legal and ethical practice related to technology, information, and software resources, as well as the safe and healthy use of technology resources?

11. How do I advocate for and facilitate equitable access to technology resources for all students?

DISCUSSION QUESTIONS

1. What technologies (hardware and software; high tech and low tech) should teachers be able to use to support students learning?

2. Why are student developmental and learning theories important when it comes to using technology in teaching?

3. Why is it worthwhile to consider and use a variety of software, applications, and learning tools to support the diverse needs of learners?

4. Why should teachers preview and evaluate the suitability of different software packages and hardware before introducing them to the classroom?

5. What are "technology-enhanced, learner-centered classroom strategies and activities"? How might they be used to support the diverse needs of students?

6. How might technology-enhanced learning experiences help develop students' higher-order thinking skills, creativity, and problem-solving skills?

7. How may technology be used to assess student learning of subject matter?

8. How can a teacher use technology to engage in ongoing professional development and lifelong learning?

9. Why should teachers continually evaluate and reflect on their professional practice relative to the use of technology in support of student learning?

10. What legal and ethical practices related to technology, information, and software resources should a teacher be aware of and follow?

11. What issues of safety and health are involved in the use of technology resources?

12. How can technology be used to enable and empower learners with diverse backgrounds, characteristics, and abilities?

13. What classroom, school, and district practices facilitate equitable access to technology resources for all students?

15

Converting Your Certification Portfolio Into a Job-Search Portfolio, Professional Development Portfolio, or National Board Portfolio

I'm not about to throw this thing [portfolio] away. I've put too much time into it, and I'm proud of what it says about me.

Li Ming, new teacher

Tim held his completed, graded, and passing portfolio in his hands. The bulk of it amazed him. How had he been able to finally pull it all together? He had griped every step of the way, but now that it was complete, he was pretty proud of what he had created. It was an impressive record of what he had done and what he could do. Too bad he could not use it for some other purpose—that is, other than cannibalizing it to use when he began teaching. His professors had said it could be used for his job search, but his friends already out in the workforce had told him principals and human resources people would not look at such a huge document. They just didn't have enough time. Still there was a lot of good work in there; surely there would be some way of using it again.

QUESTIONS FOR CONSIDERATION

- How does a job-search portfolio differ from a college certification portfolio?
- What might be added to or removed from your portfolio to make it more interesting to and useful for someone looking to hire a good teacher?
- How can your portfolio be used to guide your further professional development?
- How can your portfolio be maintained and modified to serve your district's ongoing teacher evaluation process?
- How can your portfolio be the seed for a National Board for Professional Teaching Standards (NBPTS) board certification portfolio?

It is a common complaint: "Why must I work so hard creating this portfolio when I can never use it again?" It is a shame to let your portfolio sit on a shelf collecting dust or be cannibalized to pull out lessons to use when you get a job. Why can't it be useful for finding a job or for other professional purposes? It can, and it should be.

MODIFYING YOUR PORTFOLIO TO HELP YOU FIND A JOB

To revise your portfolio to find a job, you need to begin thinking about what an employer in a school district is looking for. Then you need to use this knowledge to begin refining your artifacts and reflections to match those expectations or desired qualities. Moreover, you will want to include some artifacts you may not have in your original certification portfolio.

Most employers have a picture in mind of the kind of employee needed to fill the job available. They go through each application, résumé, and interview trying to find a person who matches that picture. The one who most closely matches the picture is the one who gets the job offer. Your task, then, is to create a picture of yourself that most closely matches the one in the employer's mind. Simple, right? But where do you find out what that picture looks like? And how do you mold your portfolio into an approximation of that picture?

Actually, you have some tools already at hand. Appendix B presents a chart that compares the INTASC Principles with Charlotte Danielson's Four Domains of Effective Teaching and the National Board for Professional Teaching Standards' Core Propositions and Criteria. Notice how well aligned they are? That alignment shows how universal are the conceptions of what a good teacher knows, is like, and can do. You have based your portfolio on one of these lists. INTASC Principles are developed with beginning teachers in mind, Danielson's Domains and the NBPTS Core Propositions were developed with practicing teachers in mind, but they reference and emphasize the same essential knowledge, skills, and dispositions. Danielson's work is the more detailed description of teacher characteristics and behaviors, however. Any one of these will give you a picture of what a principal or human resources professional is looking for when trying to hire a new teacher. The portfolio you put together, then, ought to highlight those characteristics.

We can capture some of these attributes of a hire-able young teacher in the following list:

1. Has a solid understanding of the content area(s) he or she will be teaching
2. Has a clear sense of the developmental issues inherent within the grade level or range he or she is likely to be teaching
3. Knows how to create lesson and unit plans that present this content in meaningful ways and that will prepare students to perform well on district, state, and national tests of student achievement
4. Knows how to adapt, adjust, or substitute classroom activities, assignments, and tests to meet the needs of all students, including students with disabilities, special language needs, cultural differences, and giftedness
5. Can maintain a safe and orderly classroom environment for all learners
6. Can communicate with parents personally, in writing, and via other media to keep them involved in their children's learning
7. Can assess student learning in a variety of ways and keeps accurate records of student performance to inform grading and conversations with parents and colleagues
8. Knows how to infuse technology into teaching and learning
9. Is a reflective practitioner who thinks about what he or she does and can talk about the "whys," "whats," "hows," "why nots," and "what nexts" of his or her practice
10. Can connect with the community in positive ways to support students' achievement

District administrators are also interested in the following more mundane issues:

1. Can the applicant fill multiple roles in the school?
2. Has she or he had relevant training for and experience in the classroom?
3. Is he or she licensed to teach in the areas and at the grade levels required by the position?

Finally, principals and human resources persons are looking for people with a number of personal characteristics that make for a good employee:

- Enthusiasm
- Punctuality
- Personal grooming
- Communication skills
- Cheerfulness
- Good work ethic
- Willingness to work as part of a team
- Loyalty to the district

You must exhibit some of these traits during the interview, but you can exhibit others via the artifacts you may have gathered for your portfolio (letters of recommendation, supervisor evaluations, notes from parents, etc.).

Much of the documentation for these attributes is already in your certification portfolio. Some you will need to draw from other sources.

CONSTRUCTING YOUR JOB SEARCH PORTFOLIO

Begin by getting a much smaller binder, not more than $1\frac{1}{2}$ inches thick. In it you will include four (4) tabs:

I. Personal and Professional Experience and Qualifications
II. Evidence of Professional Ability
III. Evidence of Professional Dispositions
IV. Recommendations

In *Tab I: Personal and Professional Experience and Qualifications,* you will include background information about your experience and qualifications:

- A *cover letter* introducing yourself, highlighting your relevant skills and experience, and asking for a job
- A *résumé* describing your relevant education, training, certification, work experience, and references (also relevant hobbies or sports expertise if these might be useful for district purposes)
- A copy of your college *transcript* showing that you have graduated from an accredited institution of higher learning with appropriate course work, degree(s), and GPA
- A copy of your teaching *license* or *certificate*
- (optional) A copy of your state-required exit test score(s)

These artifacts satisfy a number of elements of the picture the person hiring you has in his or her mind.

In *Tab II: Evidence of Professional Ability,* you will have a number of subtabs for the various artifacts relevant to your teaching ability:

- A classroom management plan (including a behavior management component)
- A yearly curriculum planner

- A unit plan aligned to state standards, curriculum goals, and assessments
- A sampling of a range of assessment types
- Samples of student work
- Excerpts from your student-teaching grade book (be sure to black out student names)
- Sample communications to parents and other constituents
- A list of technologies (hardware and software) with which you are proficient
- A list of other roles and responsibilities you performed in your student teaching experience or other school-based experiences

This highly selective gathering of documents (not too bulky) will give the person reviewing your application a sampling of what you can produce as a practicing teacher.

In *Tab III: Evidence of Professional Dispositions,* you will include evidence of your professional commitment:

- Professional memberships you hold
- Professional development activities in which you have engaged
- Professional, academic, or community awards and honors you have received

Finally, in *Tab IV: Recommendations,* you will include *detailed* letters of recommendation from your cooperating teacher(s), the supervising principal of the school in which you completed your clinical experience, other education professionals who are aware of your abilities and preparation, and college faculty. These give outsiders validation of your qualifications and abilities. Note the emphasis on *detailed* letters. Vague and general praise does little to prove your professional value. Rather, ask those who would write letters of recommendation to speak clearly and in detail about the qualities and qualifications you possess and the quality of your performance in the classroom.

CREATING A PROFESSIONAL PERFORMANCE PORTFOLIO

All districts perform ongoing evaluation of their teachers. Some districts use ongoing observations of their teachers' performance, while other districts require their teachers to compile yearly review documents. Your job search portfolio can be a good beginning to creating these review documents. Again, you will benefit from looking at Danielson's domains and the rubrics she has included in her *Framework for Professional Development of Teachers* (1996). But more important, just as you have been using standards to derive the structure and contents of your portfolio for other purposes, for the professional performance portfolio, use your district's rubric or expectations to guide your evidence gathering.

Here you might use Danielson's four domains as organizing elements:

- Domain 1: Planning and Preparation
- Domain 2: The Classroom Environment
- Domain 3: Instruction
- Domain 4: Professional Responsibilities

For each domain, then, you would provide documentation showing your activities and accomplishments during the period being evaluated.

If you are using the evaluation criteria your district has adopted, you would organize your portfolio by those criteria, gathering evidence to demonstrate your work and accomplishments relevant to these criteria. Here are a few areas for which districts frequently seek evidence:

- Planning, instruction, and assessment
- Student performance on internal and external assessments

■ Professional development and continued learning
■ Evidence of active engagement and leadership within the district
■ Evidence of active engagement and leadership within the community
■ Extracurricular activities within and outside of the school/district
■ Awards and honors received
■ Letters of support from district personnel and others within the community
■ Professional behavior and responsibilities

Each of these areas, then, would require documentation similar to that used in your teacher certification portfolio and your job-search portfolio. In fact, if you were to continually update your job-search portfolio, maybe reorganizing it to fit the district's evaluation criteria, you would be well on your way to having a set of documents ready for evaluation.

CREATING A NATIONAL BOARD FOR PROFESSIONAL TEACHING STANDARDS (NBPTS) PORTFOLIO

If you have kept your district professional performance portfolio up to date, you will be well on your way to compiling the much more complex National Board certification portfolio. Here is a place where having an electronic portfolio (devised on your own or created with commercial software) will serve you well. National Board portfolios are literally boxes of documentation (reflective essays, lesson plans, professional development documentation, letters of support, videotapes of teaching, etc.) designed to do much the same thing your certification portfolio was intended to do—that is, gain access to another level of the profession.

The NBPTS Core Propositions and Their Indicators are listed next. You may wish to use these as a way to organize the artifacts and reflections you save over time.

NBPTS CORE PROPOSITION 1. TEACHERS ARE COMMITTED TO STUDENTS AND THEIR LEARNING

1. Teachers recognize individual differences in their students and adjust their practice accordingly.
2. Teachers have an understanding of how students develop and learn.
3. Teachers treat students equitably.
4. A teacher's mission extends beyond developing the cognitive capacity of students.

NBPTS CORE PROPOSITION 2. TEACHERS KNOW THE SUBJECTS THEY TEACH AND HOW TO TEACH THOSE SUBJECTS TO STUDENTS

1. Teachers appreciate how knowledge in their subjects is created and linked to other disciplines.
2. Teachers command specialized knowledge of how to convey a subject to students.
3. Teachers generate multiple paths to knowledge.

NBPTS CORE PROPOSITION 3. TEACHERS ARE RESPONSIBLE FOR MANAGING AND MONITORING STUDENT LEARNING

1. Teachers call on multiple methods to meet their goals.
2. Teachers orchestrate learning in group settings.

3. Teachers place a premium on student engagement.
4. Teachers regularly assess student progress.
5. Teachers are mindful of their principal objectives.

NBPTS CORE PROPOSITION 4. TEACHERS THINK SYSTEMATICALLY ABOUT THEIR PRACTICE AND LEARN FROM EXPERIENCE

1. Teachers are continually making difficult choices that test their judgment.
2. Teachers seek the advice of others and draw on education, research, and scholarship to improve their practice.

NBPTS CORE PROPOSITION 5. TEACHERS ARE MEMBERS OF LEARNING COMMUNITIES

1. Teachers contribute to school effectiveness by collaborating with other professionals.
2. Teachers work collaboratively with parents.
3. Teachers take advantage of community resources.

Teachers may seek National Board certification after they have been teaching a minimum of three years, although one would have to be a truly exceptional teacher to be ready after only three years. The process takes more than a year to complete and includes interviews, assessments, and the professional teaching portfolio—one based on the detailed standards for specific teaching assignments versus the considerably more general NBPTS core propositions quoted earlier. Teachers who are organized, save their best work, continually reflect in writing, and document their development are the ones most likely to complete the process.

If you think you will be seeking NBPTS certification, it would behoove you to maintain your certification portfolio (combined with your job-search portfolio), keeping it updated and adding exhibits and reflections along the way. If you can digitize much of your work via scanning, digital audio/video/photographs, or computer-generated documents, then you will have an easier time manipulating and organizing your pieces. Get in the habit of regular written reflection on your professional practice and experiences. This will be invaluable later as you begin to think again about what each artifact reveals about your professional growth and proficiency. Starting early is always the better plan when it comes to seeking ongoing certification.

SUMMARY

You will put a great deal of time and effort into developing your certification portfolio. Only you will determine whether it is a waste of time or not. If you take a little time, you can turn that portfolio into several other products that will serve you in the near and long terms. What's more, if you recognize the value of the habits you have developed while creating your portfolio (i.e., collecting important artifacts, organizing documentation by standards of professional practice, and maintaining ongoing personal and professional reflections) and continue these habits while assuming your professional roles and responsibilities in the classroom and district, you will grow that beginning portfolio into a powerful tool for documenting and promoting your professional stature. It is truly up to you.

Here are some questions to guide your thinking about the next steps you will take with your portfolio:

1. What are district personnel looking for in a new teacher?
2. What do I have to offer a district that matches what the district is looking for in a new teacher? How can I document those qualifications?
3. What are the strands that run through all of the various portfolios I am likely to produce over the course of my professional life?
4. What criteria do districts in my region/state use to evaluate the performance of their professional teaching staff?
5. What are the benefits in my state of becoming a National Board certified teacher?

DISCUSSION QUESTIONS

1. How might your college portfolio serve you in your job search? How might it serve you once you enter the teaching profession?
2. In what ways will a job search portfolio differ from a certification portfolio?
3. Why will a potential employer want to see a different set of artifacts than would be found in a certification portfolio?
4. How is a professional performance (teacher evaluation) portfolio different from both the job search and the certification portfolio? How is it similar to the certification portfolio?
5. How are the NBPTS standards similar to and different from the INTASC principles?
6. Why is National Board certification a good thing for teachers to seek?

16

Preparing a Digital Portfolio

Media is now more easily created, manipulated, processed, and managed than ever before. And different media can coexist in compound multimedia documents. . . . Digital convergence, affordability, and ease-of-use are creating portfolio opportunities for more disciplines while enhancing the opportunities for fields with long portfolio traditions.

Gary Greenberg

"First they want me to make a portfolio. Now they want me to create an e-portfolio? What the heck is that? Sounds like a virus—like Ebola or something! It's just another thing, busywork!" Marissa harrumphed.

"I don't know," chided Carla. "I kinda like the idea. Most of my work is saved on my computer anyway. We use technology all the time: digital cameras, different software, the Internet. Why not have the portfolio use some of those things? Besides, I want to be able to put some video clips of my teaching and interaction with students in my portfolio. It's sure to be easier for the readers to simply click on a link and start the video than it would be for them to find a VCR to play a tape. From what I hear, they never view the videos anyway. And did you see the size of those binders last semester's student teachers were carrying around? A CD or Web site is much easier to carry around and to show. I think they are doing us a favor!"

QUESTIONS FOR CONSIDERATION

- How is a digital portfolio like a paper portfolio? How are they different?
- What specialized software might I need to develop an electronic portfolio?
- How can a digital portfolio help me better demonstrate my professional competence?
- What challenges does a digital portfolio pose?

Given the increased emphasis on technology and the Internet, it is no wonder many educator preparation institutions are looking at digital portfolios as a way of harnessing the power of these new tools in the service of candidate assessment. If only because paper portfolios cause a huge storage problem, these digital versions of the three-ring binder are worth looking into if you have the interest, the tools, and the support.

WHAT IS A DIGITAL/ELECTRONIC PORTFOLIO?

On one hand, just like a paper portfolio, an electronic portfolio is a purposeful collection of candidate work (i.e., artifacts) that exhibits the candidate's efforts, progress, and achievements—but in digital formats. On the other hand, electronic portfolios differ from paper portfolios in that they allow candidates to collect, digitize, save, manage, and store information electronically using a combination of multimedia technologies, including audio recording, digital pictures, hypermedia programs, databases, spreadsheets, videos, and word processing software. So digital portfolios can be a more flexible and potentially more creative way of organizing, summarizing, and sharing artifacts, information, and ideas about teaching, learning, and personal and professional growth.

Digital portfolios are not miracle workers, however. Just like paper portfolios, digital portfolios have their advantages and challenges. In fact, because they are more sophisticated and require more complex media to create and store them, digital portfolios have a few more of each that you need to consider.

WHAT ADVANTAGES AND CHALLENGES DOES THE DIGITAL PORTFOLIO OFFER?

ADVANTAGES

Accessibility

Electronic portfolios can be a solution to the problem of creating, managing, and storing a teaching portfolio. Whereas paper portfolios are bulky and static, making them hard to manage, store, and share, digital portfolios are comparatively small, infinitely and easily changeable, compact and yet capable of storing huge amounts of data/images, and easy to share with multiple audiences at the same time. Paper portfolios do not easily allow dynamic illustrations of candidate performance (through the use of PowerPoint, WebQuests, videos of classroom teaching, etc.), because multimedia artifacts are not easily incorporated into paper portfolios and are often overlooked by reviewers. This situation limits the candidate's use of technology-oriented artifacts in the paper portfolio. Digitally created portfolios, however, are composed of more than static words on a page and can include graphic images, photographs, large documents (e.g., a 50-page unit plan), active links to the Internet as teaching resources, and audio and video recordings. This enhanced medium offers a dynamic means to showcase progress, achievement, and performance.

Creativity

Once you have the tools to create, store, and share multimedia files and documents, you are open to be more creative with the kinds of documentation you can include in your portfolio. Electronic portfolios can be used to (a) prepare and showcase lesson plans and class newsletters (via word processing and publishing programs); (b) record student scores, run statistics, and calculate grades (via spreadsheet and database software); (c) link to lesson-specific instructional resources or materials (via Internet sites and pre-edited video clips on lesson content); and (d) record, store, and link to videos that showcase you and your students' performance (via digital imaging programs). As you become more comfortable with multimedia presentations while creating the electronic portfolio, you may find more creative ways to integrate your technology skills to develop more effective instructional activities. These, then, can become other artifacts for your portfolio.

Portability

Unlike the bulky three-ring binder, digital portfolios may be slipped into an envelope or a jacket pocket. They may be as easy to access as any Web site on the Internet. Yet these electronic presentation tools allow far more space for your evidence than the largest three-ring binder. After a portfolio's template has been created, candidates can (a) copy narratives from a data file into the template, (b) copy journal articles from a electronic source on the Internet into the template page, (c) drag pictures from an Internet source or digital camera to the template page, (d) insert a hyperlink to Web sites or to files stored elsewhere, and (e) insert audio and video recordings. Electronic portfolios are easily edited, cross-referenced, and inexpensively duplicated for faculty or employers, and you can copy and share lightweight CDs or Web site resource locators (URLs) with anyone you choose.

"Share-Ability"

Portfolios in electronic format can be easily and inexpensively reproduced and shared on CDs and the World Wide Web. Candidates can easily tailor and streamline their portfolios to showcase their work for their teacher education officer and for certification, as well as for potential employers. When candidates view each other's portfolios, they can gain access to useful ideas and resources and form a professional community through sharing.

Confidence in Technology

Preparing materials in digital formats for the portfolio requires candidates to develop and reinforce technology knowledge and skills. Learning new techniques, although most of them are not difficult, often results in greater technology confidence in the classroom. As an added benefit, prospective employers are likely to be more confident in your technology skills because of the technology they see in the digital portfolio.

CHALLENGES

Despite the advantages, electronic portfolios also present challenges. They may include a candidate's lack of technology skills, a lack of useful technological support, limited or no access to equipment or an Internet server, the cost of commercial software, a reviewer's lack of technology skills and equipment, and a presentation that may possibly detract from the portfolio's content and purpose.

Candidates' Technology Skills

To put together a working digital portfolio, candidates need to know how electronic portfolios work, as well as have skill in using various hardware tools (e.g., digital cameras and scanners) and software packages (e.g., Adobe Photoshop, Hyperstudio, FrontPage, and PowerPoint). Gathering and organizing materials for digital portfolios requires that the candidate understand how to create, store, and organize multimedia materials to meet the criteria of each of the INTASC standards. The candidate needs to know how to convert the formats of various artifacts into digital formats (e.g., scanning student work and converting it to a PDF file, or taking digital pictures and downloading them into folders). Without benefit of these skills, the candidate will need professional technical support.

Technological Support

Even for candidates well versed in technology, problems still arise with software and hardware that are beyond a candidate's knowledge or capability. In these instances, a qualified technical support staff is useful. Not all colleges and universities have available technical support staff to assist candidates with their digital portfolios and the numerous technical glitches that may arise. If your institution requires a digital portfolio and you are not well acquainted with the technology necessary to prepare the portfolio, you may want to identify a fellow classmate, faculty member, or technical support person whom you can approach for assistance. Many software and hardware makers also provide technical support for their products. While some will only provide support for the actual owners of the software and hardware they manufacture, their Web sites often contain useful information, plug-ins, patches, and troubleshooting ideas. Make use of these when you can. Beyond these resources is the Internet with its many listservs and bulletin boards, many devoted to sharing problems and solutions for software and hardware difficulties.

Realistically, though, your institution, if it is requiring a digital portfolio, will likely provide technical assistance to its candidates and professional development for its faculty to help them support candidate success. Commercially available online portfolio services will also likely offer online tutorials to help you.

Access to Software, Equipment, and Internet Servers

It is hard to find a college or university that has not invested heavily in computer and Internet technology, so you will probably find much of the software and hardware you need to create and maintain your digital portfolio. Assuming, however, that you are determined to create an online, Web-based portfolio, you must have access to space on a server connected to the Internet. If you are interested in including video, digital images, and audio files in your portfolio, you will need a server space large enough to house and allow quick access to your larger digital files. A single digital photo, depending on the resolution, may be nearly a megabyte in size; audio files of any length will be multiple megabytes in size, and videos will be multiple megabytes in length, as well. The space needed to store these files and your various other documents and allow them to be quickly retrieved will be equal to that of a medium-sized hard drive. Servers are expensive and information technology folks are very protective of their server space, so it may be difficult to find access—free or for a fee—to house your portfolio. Before you start building a complex, Web-based portfolio, be sure you have a place to store it that offers easy access to whomever you will be allowing to review it.

One answer to the problem is to use server space offered by one of the Web-access groups (e.g., Yahoo!, AOL, MSN); most offer free server space to subscribers. Of course, a reviewer will have to go through much commercial "noise" to get to your Web site, but at least you will have a space. Another solution is to put your "Web site" on a CD-ROM or flash drive, including the software needed to run it. The possible hangup may be that the reviewer does not have a CD drive or USB port to access your files.

Note: Be sure to save your text documents as Rich Text Format (.rtf) or as PDF files, so MAC users and PC users can both open them.

Viewers' Technology Skills and Equipment

As we have mentioned, if your reviewer does not have the software or hardware to view your "slick" digital portfolio, then it will do you little good. Granted, most people in a position to review your portfolio will have access to at least a CD-ROM, or a USB port, and probably the Internet, too. Some people, especially those of a particular age group, however, are less comfortable with technology than others. Sometimes these people make up the audience for your portfolio. You need to ask yourself how easy your portfolio is to access and navigate. If it is too complex, your audience will be put off by the difficulty of finding the evidence you say is there but they cannot find.

In designing your portfolio and choosing your software and storage medium, you must think about who will be reading your document.

- Is it easy to open? Does it require specialized software or special skills to open?
- Are the links clear, logical, and easy to follow?
- Can the reviewer easily return to his or her starting point?
- Do files open quickly and run smoothly?
- Does the portfolio work on both MAC and PC platforms?

Early in your design process, think about who will be reviewing the portfolio and what the likely barriers are; then have many people try out your design before springing it on a more critical audience.

Presentation That May Detract From Content

Finally, glitzy technology can sometimes mask a candidate's real accomplishments and competence. When too much emphasis is placed on high-tech multimedia and too much or too little information is included to effectively document your competence, then the reviewer will have a good sense of your ability to use technology but little idea of how good a teacher you are. You must always keep in mind the purpose of your portfolio: to document your ability to assume the role of a professional educator. You need also to see that technology is only a tool, a medium for conveying that impression to an outsider who may or may not know you.

When you choose to use technology, choose to use it sparingly. The more complex your portfolio, the more chances exist that it will not work. And the flashier your technology, the more chance there is for it to draw attention to itself and away from your accomplishments. The temptation is to spend lots of time with the technology (e.g., editing video clips, entering slick transitions, or including multiple digital images of the same event or object). The more time you spend with the technology, however, the less time you can spend on refining the impression the whole portfolio gives or the less time you have for refining your reflections to highlight the important aspects of your documentation.

Granted, a certain "haloing" can occur when you use sophisticated technology to present your portfolio, much like the haloing effect given by presenting a typed paper as opposed to a handwritten one. The quality may be the same, but the typed copy will likely get a better grade—unless the typed version is so full of grammatical errors and misspellings that it is difficult to read. The same holds true for hi-tech portfolios. If the content is not convincing, too complex to get into or understand, or flawed, no amount of technology can mask that fact. It is best, then, to make sure the documentation and reflections are strong and nearly flawless before putting them into a digital portfolio, and any technology should be used carefully and for a specific, intended effect. Less is often more when it comes to the use of technology as a medium for expression.

WHAT TOOLS ARE THERE?

Design tools for developing digital portfolios include (a) desktop software and program languages and (b) online portfolio vendors. Desktop software and program languages include Microsoft Word, HyperStudio, Kid Pix (www.learningco.com), Adobe Acrobat, Teacher's Portfolio by Aurbach & Associates (www.aurbach.com), Netscape Composer, and HTML editors (e.g., FrontPage and Dreamweaver). Online software or servers include LiveText, Open Source Portfolio, Blackboard Academy Suite, and FolioTek by Lanit. Storage media for electronic portfolios include flash drives, CDs, zip disks, and file servers through the World Wide Web (e.g., the Internet).

HOW DO YOU DEVELOP AN ELECTRONIC PORTFOLIO?

The electronic portfolio follows steps similar to those explained in chapter 2. The differences include template development, hyperlinking, and sharing. Whatever digital medium you use, you will adapt this same procedure to build your portfolio. The following list summarizes the six steps for developing electronic portfolios:

1. *Developing* a standards-based template
2. Producing, *collecting, categorizing, and annotating* artifacts
3. *Selecting* the best evidences
4. *Hyperlinking* your artifacts and reflections
5. *Reflecting* on your selections
6. *Sharing* and *presenting* your portfolio for external review

DEVELOPING A STANDARDS-BASED TEMPLATE

You need to create a template that includes two parts. The first part has a cover page linked to professional and personal information (e.g., philosophy of teaching, contact information, résumé, and autobiography). The second part (linked to the cover page) includes 11 pages (if you are creating an INTASC-based portfolio), one page for each of the ten INTASC principles and one for ISTE technology standards. Each page will illustrate (a) a standard (e.g., INTASC 1), (b) artifacts for the standard, and (c) reflective writing. On the cover page, you need to include a table of contents with hyperlinks from each category of content to the file containing that content (e.g., hyperlink the category of philosophy of teaching from the table of contents to the file containing the philosophy of education). See Figure 16.1 and 16.2 for an example of a cover page and a table of contents page.

PRODUCING, COLLECTING, CATEGORIZING, AND ANNOTATING ARTIFACTS (SEE CHAPTER 2)

Designate a working portfolio storage file (e.g., yellow folder in Microsoft Word) to collect and organize your artifacts. As you create documents, copy them immediately into the collection folder. Be sure that different drafts of the same piece are identified in a way that will allow you to find the one you want. Draft numbers or dating will help you do this. You may even put subfolders into your collection folder to allow you to begin sorting your evidence by INTASC principle or type of evidence. It is easy to save the same file in more than one folder or subfolder.

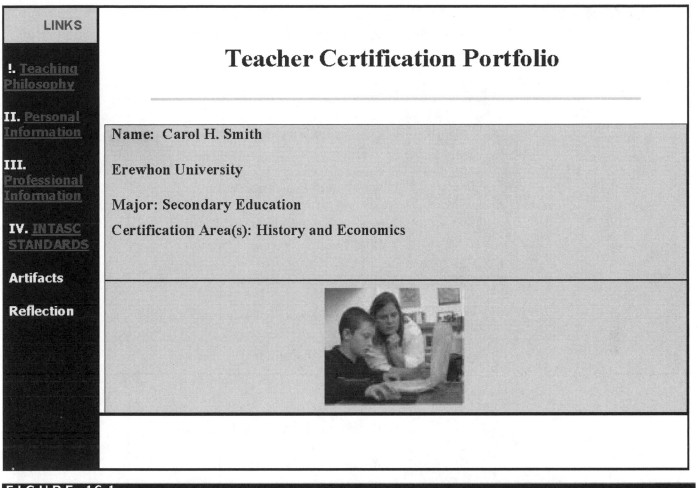

FIGURE 16.1

Digital Portfolio Cover Page

SELECTING THE BEST EVIDENCES

Make a final yellow folder with the best evidences/artifacts for the presentation portfolio. This will be the final working folder to which you will go to upload or link your documentation to your contents page or to links within your reflections. Use the guidelines in chapter 2 to help you select the best evidence. When selecting digital evidence (digital photos, videos, PowerPoint presentations, etc.), be sure you choose examples that are:

- Relatively short
- Clear and easy to see, read, and understand (audio)
- Directly appropriate to the point you are trying to prove/document
- Edited to protect the privacy of your students and other people visible or identifiable in the evidence

HYPERLINKING YOUR ARTIFACTS AND REFLECTIONS

For the second part of the template (i.e., INTASC principle pages), after you select the best evidences, you must hyperlink each of the artifacts from the final yellow folder to the standard page or to references within the reflective statement. The process differs slightly from one program to the next, but the basic idea is to highlight a reference from

FIGURE 16.2

Digital Portfolio Table
of Contents

	Cover
	Interstate New Teacher Assessment and Support Consortium (INTASC) Principles
__INTASC 1:__	Making Content Meaningful
__INTASC 2:__	Child Development and Learning Theory
__INTASC 3:__	Diversity and Learning Styles
__INTASC 4:__	Instructional Strategies and Problem Solving
__INTASC 5:__	Motivation and Behavior
__INTASC 6:__	Communication
__INTASC 7:__	Planning for Instruction
__INTASC 8:__	Assessment
__INTASC 9:__	Professional Growth and Reflection
__INTASC 10:__	Professional and Collaborative Relationships
__NETS•T:__	Technology in Teaching and Learning

the contents page or within the reflection, go to the menu for creating or "inserting" a hyperlink, and type or copy the file location for the digital artifact as the destination for the hyperlink.

For example, you may want to hyperlink a reference in your reflection ("Artifact G: Fractions Lesson Plan") to the lesson plan itself (C://MyDocuments/foster/portfolio chapters/chapter 3 reflections—final/Artifact G: Fractions Lesson Plan). In Microsoft Word, you would highlight the reference (Artifact G: Fractions Lesson Plan), go to the "Insert" drop-down menu in the toolbar, and click on *Hyperlink.* In the dialog box that appears, you can give the link a name and find the file to which it refers. Once you have selected the file to which you want the link to direct the reader, you click OK and the link is created for you.

For online portfolios, you do not have to worry about hyperlinking artifacts. Program templates often offer you prelinked slots for artifacts and reflections, so all you have to do is copy files into the already existing framework of linked slots.

REFLECTING

Each of the INTASC principle pages should list (as hyperlinks) the artifacts for that principle and have a link to the reflection for that principle. Follow the guidelines in chapter 3.

INTASC 7: PLANNING FOR INSTRUCTION

"The beginning teacher recognizes the importance of long-range planning and curriculum development and develops, implements, and evaluates curriculum based upon student, district, and state performance standards."

Artifacts:

1. Unit Plan on Ecosystems (This artifact can be found in chapter 10)

      Grade: Second grade

      Duration: 5-6 weeks

2. Concept Map of the Unit

3. Video Taped Presentation on the Unit Plan

Reflection:

Sample reflection on Ecosystem (This reflection can be found in chapter 10)

Principle 7 states that teachers need to understand how to plan instruction based on knowledge of subject matter, students, the community, and curriculum goals. It is important for teachers to provide evidence to prove their ability to plan instruction based on four important issues: (a) subject matter, (b) students, (c) the community, and (d) curriculum goals. When I introduced the ecosystem project *(Artifact 1)*, I gave the sentence for them to use on the mirror to make the project as concrete as possible. I next gave the students my basic expectations by sharing an assessment rubric with specific criteria or expectations. The only new skill the students would have to learn would be doing the science and reporting the result with the ecosystem they created, and I assured them that these tasks would not be difficult and that I would help them out.

FIGURE 16.3

Sample Digital Portfolio Reflection Page With Hyperlinks

Reflective Analysis and Your Portfolio to reflect on your artifacts and the quality of your professional practice. Be sure to insert hyperlinks when you refer to an artifact you want the reviewer to look at or access while reading. (See Figure 16.3 for an example reflection containing hyperlinks to artifacts.)

SHARING AND PRESENTING

When you are ready to share or present your portfolio for review, the process can be as simple as handing the reviewer a CD-ROM that contains your electronic portfolio, especially if you choose to use desktop software. Or you can load the portfolio into a computer that is attached to a projector and present your portfolio in person. Make sure you have checked with the reviewer to ensure she or he has access to the necessary hardware and software.

If you have chosen to create an online portfolio, you can simply give the reviewer the URL (i.e., the Web address) for your portfolio. Sometimes if it is membership-based software (e.g., LiveText), you will need to give the reviewer a visitor's password to share your electronic portfolio.

SUMMARY

Technology is changing the face of portfolios, allowing beginning teachers to include much more varied supporting evidence in a broader range of forms. However, the purpose of the portfolio remains the same, and thoughtful collection, selection, reflection, and presentation must still guide your portfolio development. Just like paper portfolios, digital portfolios have their advantages and challenges, which you will need to understand and address. However, the digital portfolio can make the task much easier to complete and allows the portfolio to take on many faces to meet its many purposes and audiences.

DISCUSSION QUESTIONS

1. What is a digital/electronic portfolio, and how is it alike and different from a paper portfolio?
2. What are some of the benefits of using a digital portfolio? What are some of the challenges?
3. What tools are available to help you develop and share a digital portfolio?
4. What is hyperlinking, and how can it make a digital portfolio easier to navigate?
5. How can the technology get in the way of a portfolio's success?
6. How can a digital portfolio affect or enhance the sharing/presentation stage of portfolio development?

APPENDIX A

Interstate New Teacher Assessment and Support Consortium (INTASC) Principles

Principle #1: The teacher understands the central concepts, tools of inquiry, and structures of the discipline(s) he or she teaches and can create learning experiences that make these aspects of subject matter meaningful for students.

KNOWLEDGE

- The teacher understands major concepts, assumptions, debates, processes of inquiry, and ways of knowing that are central to the discipline(s) s/he teaches.
- The teacher understands how students' conceptual frameworks and their misconceptions for an area of knowledge can influence their learning.
- The teacher can relate his/her disciplinary knowledge to other subject areas.

DISPOSITIONS

- The teacher realizes that subject matter knowledge is not a fixed body of facts but is complex and ever-evolving. S/he seeks to keep abreast of new ideas and understandings in the field.
- The teacher appreciates multiple perspectives and conveys to learners how knowledge is developed from the vantage point of the knower.
- The teacher has enthusiasm for the discipline(s) s/he teaches and sees connections to everyday life.

- The teacher is committed to continuous learning and engages in professional discourse about subject matter knowledge and children's learning of the discipline.

PERFORMANCES

- The teacher effectively uses multiple representations and explanations of disciplinary concepts that capture key ideas and link them to students' prior understandings.
- The teacher can represent and use differing viewpoints, theories, "ways of knowing" and methods of inquiry in his/her teaching of subject matter concepts.
- The teacher can evaluate teaching resources and curriculum materials for their comprehensiveness, accuracy, and usefulness for representing particular ideas and concepts.
- The teacher engages students in generating knowledge and testing hypotheses according to the methods of inquiry and standards of evidence used in the discipline.
- The teacher develops and uses curricula that encourage students to see, question, and interpret ideas from diverse perspectives.
- The teacher can create interdisciplinary learning experiences that allow students to integrate knowledge, skills, and methods of inquiry from several subject areas.

Source: Council of Chief State School Officers. (1992). Model standards for beginning teacher licensing, assessment, and development: A resource for state dialogue. Washington, DC: Author. www.ccsso.org/content/pdfs/corestrd.pdf.

Principle #2: The teacher understands how children learn and develop, and can provide learning opportunities that support their intellectual, social and personal development.

KNOWLEDGE

- The teacher understands how learning occurs—how students construct knowledge, acquire skills, and develop habits of mind—and knows how to use instructional strategies that promote student learning.
- The teacher understands that students' physical, social, emotional, moral and cognitive development influence learning and knows how to address these factors when making instructional decisions.
- The teacher is aware of expected developmental progressions and ranges of individual variation within each domain (physical, social, emotional, moral and cognitive), can identify levels of readiness in learning, and understands how development in any one domain may affect performance in others.

DISPOSITIONS

- The teacher appreciates individual variation within each area of development, shows respect for the diverse talents of all learners, and is committed to help them develop self-confidence and competence.
- The teacher is disposed to use students' strengths as a basis for growth, and their errors as an opportunity for learning.

PERFORMANCES

- The teacher assesses individual and group performance in order to design instruction that meets learners' current needs in each domain (cognitive, social, emotional, moral, and physical) and that leads to the next level of development.
- The teacher stimulates student reflection on prior knowledge and links new ideas to already familiar ideas, making connections to students' experiences, providing opportunities for active engagement, manipulation, and testing of ideas and materials, and encouraging students to assume responsibility for shaping their learning tasks.
- The teacher accesses students' thinking and experiences as a basis for instructional activities by, for example, encouraging discussion, listening and responding to group interaction, and eliciting samples of student thinking orally and in writing.

Principle #3: The teacher understands how students differ in their approaches to learning and creates instructional opportunities that are adapted to diverse learners.

KNOWLEDGE

- The teacher understands and can identify differences in approaches to learning and performance, including different learning styles, multiple intelligences, and performance modes, and can design instruction that helps use students' strengths as the basis for growth.
- The teacher knows about areas of exceptionality in learning—including learning disabilities, visual and perceptual difficulties, and special physical or mental challenges.
- The teacher knows about the process of second language acquisition and about strategies to support the learning of students whose first language is not English.
- The teacher understands how students' learning is influenced by individual experiences, talents, and prior learning, as well as language, culture, family and community values.
- The teacher has a well-grounded framework for understanding cultural and community diversity and knows how to learn about and incorporate students' experiences, cultures, and community resources into instruction.

DISPOSITIONS

- The teacher believes that all children can learn at high levels and persists in helping all children achieve success.
- The teacher appreciates and values human diversity, shows respect for students' varied talents and perspectives, and is committed to the pursuit of "individually configured excellence."
- The teacher respects students as individuals with differing personal and family backgrounds and various skills, talents, and interests.

- The teacher is sensitive to community and cultural norms.
- The teacher makes students feel valued for their potential as people, and helps them learn to value each other.

PERFORMANCES

- The teacher identifies and designs instruction appropriate to students' stages of development, learning styles, strengths, and needs.
- The teacher uses teaching approaches that are sensitive to the multiple experiences of learners and that address different learning and performance modes.
- The teacher makes appropriate provisions (in terms of time and circumstances for work, tasks assigned, communication and response modes) for individual students who have particular learning differences or needs.
- The teacher can identify when and how to access appropriate services or resources to meet exceptional learning needs.
- The teacher seeks to understand students' families, cultures, and communities, and uses this information as a basis for connecting instruction to students' experiences (e.g. drawing explicit connections between subject matter and community matters, making assignments that can be related to students' experiences and cultures).
- The teacher brings multiple perspectives to the discussion of subject matter, including attention to students' personal, family, and community experiences and cultural norms.
- The teacher creates a learning community in which individual differences are respected.

Principle #4: The teacher understands and uses a variety of instructional strategies to encourage students' development of critical thinking, problem solving, and performance skills.

KNOWLEDGE

- The teacher understands the cognitive processes associated with various kinds of learning (e.g. critical and creative thinking, problem structuring and problem solving, invention, memorization and recall) and how these processes can be stimulated.

- The teacher understands principles and techniques, along with advantages and limitations, associated with various instructional strategies (e.g. cooperative learning, direct instruction, discovery learning, whole group discussion, independent study, interdisciplinary instruction).
- The teacher knows how to enhance learning through the use of a wide variety of materials as well as human and technological resources (e.g. computers, audio-visual technologies, videotapes and discs, local experts, primary documents and artifacts, texts, reference books, literature, and other print resources).

DISPOSITIONS

- The teacher values the development of students' critical thinking, independent problem solving, and performance capabilities.
- The teacher values flexibility and reciprocity in the teaching process as necessary for adapting instruction to student responses, ideas, and needs.

PERFORMANCES

- The teacher carefully evaluates how to achieve learning goals, choosing alternative teaching strategies and materials to achieve different instructional purposes and to meet student needs (e.g. developmental stages, prior knowledge, learning styles, and interests).
- The teacher uses multiple teaching and learning strategies to engage students in active learning opportunities that promote the development of critical thinking, problem solving, and performance capabilities and that help students assume responsibility for identifying and using learning resources.
- The teacher constantly monitors and adjusts strategies in response to learner feedback.
- The teacher varies his or her role in the instructional process (e.g. instructor, facilitator, coach, audience) in relation to the content and purposes of instruction and the needs of students.
- The teacher develops a variety of clear, accurate presentations and representations of concepts, using alternative explanations to assist students' understanding and presenting diverse perspectives to encourage critical thinking.

Principle #5: The teacher uses an understanding of individual and group motivation and behavior to create a learning environment that encourages positive social interaction, active engagement in learning, and self-motivation.

KNOWLEDGE

- The teacher can use knowledge about human motivation and behavior drawn from the foundational sciences of psychology, anthropology, and sociology to develop strategies for organizing and supporting individual and group work.
- The teacher understands how social groups function and influence people, and how people influence groups.
- The teacher knows how to help people work productively and cooperatively with each other in complex social settings.
- The teacher understands the principles of effective classroom management and can use a range of strategies to promote positive relationships, cooperation, and purposeful learning in the classroom.
- The teacher recognizes factors and situations that are likely to promote or diminish intrinsic motivation, and knows how to help students become self-motivated.

DISPOSITIONS

- The teacher takes responsibility for establishing a positive climate in the classroom and participates in maintaining such a climate in the school as whole.
- The teacher understands how participation supports commitment, and is committed to the expression and use of democratic values in the classroom.
- The teacher values the role of students in promoting each other's learning and recognizes the importance of peer relationships in establishing a climate of learning.
- The teacher recognizes the value of intrinsic motivation to students' life-long growth and learning.
- The teacher is committed to the continuous development of individual students' abilities and considers how different motivational strategies are likely to encourage this development for each student.

PERFORMANCES

- The teacher creates a smoothly functioning learning community in which students assume responsibility for themselves and one another, participate in decisionmaking, work collaboratively and independently, and engage in purposeful learning activities.
- The teacher engages students in individual and cooperative learning activities that help them develop the motivation to achieve, by, for example, relating lessons to students' personal interests, allowing students to have choices in their learning, and leading students to ask questions and pursue problems that are meaningful to them.
- The teacher organizes, allocates, and manages the resources of time, space, activities, and attention to provide active and equitable engagement of students in productive tasks.
- The teacher maximizes the amount of class time spent in learning by creating expectations and processes for communication and behavior along with a physical setting conducive to classroom goals.
- The teacher helps the group to develop shared values and expectations for student interactions, academic discussions, and individual and group responsibility that create a positive classroom climate of openness, mutual respect, support, and inquiry.
- The teacher analyzes the classroom environment and makes decisions and adjustments to enhance social relationships, student motivation and engagement, and productive work.
- The teacher organizes, prepares students for, and monitors independent and group work that allows for full and varied participation of all individuals.

Principle #6: The teacher uses knowledge of effective verbal, nonverbal, and media communication techniques to foster active inquiry, collaboration, and supportive interaction in the classroom.

KNOWLEDGE

- The teacher understands communication theory, language development, and the role of language in learning.
- The teacher understands how cultural and gender differences can affect communication in the classroom.

- The teacher recognizes the importance of nonverbal as well as verbal communication.
- The teacher knows about and can use effective verbal, nonverbal, and media communication techniques.

DISPOSITIONS

- The teacher recognizes the power of language for fostering self-expression, identity development, and learning.
- The teacher values many ways in which people seek to communicate and encourages many modes of communication in the classroom.
- The teacher is a thoughtful and responsive listener.
- The teacher appreciates the cultural dimensions of communication, responds appropriately, and seeks to foster culturally sensitive communication by and among all students in the class.

PERFORMANCES

- The teacher models effective communication strategies in conveying ideas and information and in asking questions (e.g. monitoring the effects of messages, restating ideas and drawing connections, using visual, aural, and kinesthetic cues, being sensitive to nonverbal cues given and received).
- The teacher supports and expands learner expression in speaking, writing, and other media.
- The teacher knows how to ask questions and stimulate discussion in different ways for particular purposes, for example, probing for learner understanding, helping students articulate their ideas and thinking processes, promoting risk-taking and problem-solving, facilitating factual recall, encouraging convergent and divergent thinking, stimulating curiosity, helping students to question.
- The teacher communicates in ways that demonstrate a sensitivity to cultural and gender differences (e.g. appropriate use of eye contact, interpretation of body language and verbal statements, acknowledgment of and responsiveness to different modes of communication and participation).
- The teacher knows how to use a variety of media communication tools, including audiovisual aids and computers, to enrich learning opportunities.

Principle #7: The teacher plans instruction based upon knowledge of subject matter, students, the community, and curriculum goals.

KNOWLEDGE

- The teacher understands learning theory, subject matter, curriculum development, and student development and knows how to use this knowledge in planning instruction to meet curriculum goals.
- The teacher knows how to take contextual considerations (instructional materials, individual student interests, needs, and aptitudes, and community resources) into account in planning instruction that creates an effective bridge between curriculum goals and students' experiences.
- The teacher knows when and how to adjust plans based on student responses and other contingencies.

DISPOSITIONS

- The teacher values both long term and short term planning.
- The teacher believes that plans must always be open to adjustment and revision based on student needs and changing circumstances.
- The teacher values planning as a collegial activity.

PERFORMANCES

- As an individual and a member of a team, the teacher selects and creates learning experiences that are appropriate for curriculum goals, relevant to learners, and based upon principles of effective instruction (e.g. that activate students' prior knowledge, anticipate preconceptions, encourage exploration and problem-solving, and build new skills on those previously acquired).
- The teacher plans for learning opportunities that recognize and address variation in learning styles and performance modes.
- The teacher creates lessons and activities that operate at multiple levels to meet the developmental and individual needs of diverse learners and help each progress.
- The teacher creates short-range and long-term plans that are linked to student needs and performance, and adapts the plans to ensure and capitalize on student progress and motivation.

■ The teacher responds to unanticipated sources of input, evaluates plans in relation to short- and long-range goals, and systematically adjusts plans to meet student needs and enhance learning.

Principle #8: The teacher understands and uses formal and informal assessment strategies to evaluate and ensure the continuous intellectual, social, and physical development of the learner.

KNOWLEDGE

■ The teacher understands the characteristics, uses, advantages, and limitations of different types of assessments (e.g. criterion-referenced and norm-referenced instruments, traditional standardized and performance-based tests, observation systems, and assessments of student work) for evaluating how students learn, what they know and are able to do, and what kinds of experiences will support their further growth and development.

■ The teacher knows how to select, construct, and use assessment strategies and instruments appropriate to the learning outcomes being evaluated and to other diagnostic purposes.

■ The teacher understands measurement theory and assessment-related issues, such as validity, reliability, bias, and scoring concerns.

DISPOSITIONS

■ The teacher values ongoing assessment as essential to the instructional process and recognizes that many different assessment strategies, accurately and systematically used, are necessary for monitoring and promoting student learning.

■ The teacher is committed to using assessment to identify student strengths and promote student growth rather than to deny students access to learning opportunities.

PERFORMANCES

■ The teacher appropriately uses a variety of formal and informal assessment techniques (e.g. observation, portfolios of student work, teacher-made tests, performance tasks, projects, student self-assessments, peer assessment, and standardized tests) to enhance her or his knowledge of learners, evaluate students' progress and performances, and modify teaching and learning strategies.

■ The teacher solicits and uses information about students' experiences, learning behavior, needs, and progress from parents, other colleagues, and the students themselves.

■ The teacher uses assessment strategies to involve learners in self-assessment activities, to help them become aware of their strengths and needs, and to encourage them to set personal goals for learning.

■ The teacher evaluates the effect of class activities on both individuals and the class as a whole, collecting information through observation of classroom interactions, questioning, and analysis of student work.

■ The teacher monitors his or her own teaching strategies and behavior in relation to student success, modifying plans and instructional approaches accordingly.

■ The teacher maintains useful records of student work and performance and can communicate student progress knowledgeably and responsibly, based on appropriate indicators, to students, parents, and other colleagues.

Principle #9: The teacher is a reflective practitioner who continually evaluates the effects of his/her choices and actions on others (students, parents, and other professionals in the learning community) and who actively seeks out opportunities to grow professionally.

KNOWLEDGE

■ The teacher understands methods of inquiry that provide him/her with a variety of self-assessment and problem-solving strategies for reflecting on his/her practice, its influences on students' growth and learning, and the complex interactions between them.

■ The teacher is aware of major areas of research on teaching and of resources available for professional learning (e.g. professional literature, colleagues, professional associations, professional development activities).

DISPOSITIONS

■ The teacher values critical thinking and self-directed learning as habits of mind.

■ The teacher is committed to reflection, assessment, and learning as an ongoing process.

■ The teacher is willing to give and receive help.

- The teacher is committed to seeking out, developing, and continually refining practices that address the individual needs of students.
- The teacher recognizes his/her professional responsibility for engaging in and supporting appropriate professional practices for self and colleagues.

PERFORMANCES

- The teacher uses classroom observation, information about students, and research as sources for evaluating the outcomes of teaching and learning and as a basis for experimenting with, reflecting on, and revising practice.
- The teacher seeks out professional literature, colleagues, and other resources to support his/her own development as a learner and a teacher.
- The teacher draws upon professional colleagues within the school and other professional arenas as supports for reflection, problem-solving and new ideas, actively sharing experiences and seeking and giving feedback.

Principle #10: The teacher fosters relationships with school colleagues, parents, and agencies in the larger community to support students' learning and well-being.

KNOWLEDGE

- The teacher understands schools as organizations within the larger community context and understands the operations of the relevant aspects of the system(s) within which s/he works.
- The teacher understands how factors in the students' environment outside of school (e.g. family circumstances, community environments, health and economic conditions) may influence students' life and learning.
- The teacher understands and implements laws related to students' rights and teacher responsibilities (e.g. for equal education, appropriate education

for handicapped students, confidentiality, privacy, appropriate treatment of students, reporting in situations related to possible child abuse).

DISPOSITIONS

- The teacher values and appreciates the importance of all aspects of a child's experience.
- The teacher is concerned about all aspects of a child's well-being (cognitive, emotional, social, and physical), and is alert to signs of difficulties.
- The teacher is willing to consult with other adults regarding the education and well-being of his/her students.
- The teacher respects the privacy of students and confidentiality of information.
- The teacher is willing to work with other professionals to improve the overall learning environment for students.

PERFORMANCES

- The teacher participates in collegial activities designed to make the entire school a productive learning environment.
- The teacher makes links with the learners' other environments on behalf of students, by consulting with parents, counselors, teachers of other classes and activities within the schools, and professionals in other community agencies.
- The teacher can identify and use community resources to foster student learning.
- The teacher establishes respectful and productive relationships with parents and guardians from diverse home and community situations, and seeks to develop cooperative partnerships in support of student learning and well being.
- The teacher talks with and listens to the student, is sensitive and responsive to clues of distress, investigates situations, and seeks outside help as needed and appropriate to remedy problems.
- The teacher acts as an advocate for students.

Alignment of INTASC Principles, Charlotte Danielson's Domains, and the NBPTS Core Propositions and Criteria

INTASC Principles	*Danielson's Four Domains*	*NBPTS Core Propositions and Criteria*
Principle 1: The teacher understands the central concepts, tools of inquiry, and structures of the discipline(s) he or she teaches and can create learning experiences that make these aspects of subject matter meaningful for students.	**Domain 1: Planning and Preparation** 1a: Demonstrating knowledge of content pedagogy 1d: Demonstrating knowledge of resources	**NBPTS Core Proposition 2. Teachers know the subjects they teach and how to teach those subjects to students.** 1. Teachers appreciate how knowledge in their subjects is created and linked to other disciplines. 2. Teachers command specialized knowledge of how to convey a subject to students. 3. Teachers generate multiple paths to knowledge.
Principle 2: The teacher understands how children learn and develop, and can provide learning opportunities that support their intellectual, social, and personal development.	**Domain 1: Planning and Preparation** 1b: Demonstrating knowledge of students **Domain 3: Instruction** 3e: Demonstrating flexibility and responsiveness	**NBPTS Core Proposition 1. Teachers are committed to students and their learning.** 2. Teachers have an understanding of how students develop and learn. 4. Teachers' mission extends beyond developing the cognitive capacity of their students.

Source: Danielson, C. (1996). *Enhancing professional practice: A framework for teaching.* Alexandria, VA: Association for Supervision and Curriculum Development (ASCD).
Source: National Board for Professional Teaching Standards (NBPTS). (1989). *What teachers should know and be able to do: The five core propositions of the national board.* www.nbpts.org/about/coreprops.cfm

Principle 3: The teacher understands how students differ in their approaches to learning and creates instructional opportunities that are adapted to diverse learners.

Domain 1: Planning and Preparation
  1b: Demonstrating knowledge of students
  1c: Selecting instructional goals (suitability for diverse students, balance)

Domain 2: The Classroom Environment
  2b: Establishing a culture for learning

NBPTS Core Proposition 1. Teachers are committed to students and their learning.

1. Teachers recognize individual differences in their students and adjust their practice accordingly.

2. Teachers have an understanding of how students develop and learn.

3. Teachers treat students equitably.

Principle 4: The teacher understands and uses a variety of instructional strategies to encourage students' development of critical thinking, problem solving, and performance skills.

Domain 1: Planning and Preparation
  1d: Demonstrating knowledge of resources

Domain 3: Instruction
  3b: Using questioning and discussion techniques
  3c: Engaging students in learning
  3d: Providing feedback to students
  3e: Demonstrating flexibility and responsiveness

NBPTS Core Proposition 3. Teachers are responsible for managing and monitoring student learning.

1. Teachers call on multiple methods to meet their goals.

5. Teachers are mindful of their principal objectives.

Principle 5: The teacher uses an understanding of individual and group motivation and behavior to create a learning environment that encourages positive social interaction, active engagement in learning, and self-motivation.

Domain 2: the Classroom Environment
  2a: Creating an environment of respect and rapport
  2b: Establishing a culture for learning
  2c: Managing classroom procedures
  2d: Managing student behavior
  2e: Organizing physical space

NBPTS Core Proposition 3. Teachers are responsible for managing and monitoring student learning.

1. Teachers call on multiple methods to meet their goals.

2. Teachers orchestrate learning in group settings.

3. Teachers place a premium on student engagement.

Principle 6: The teacher uses knowledge of effective verbal, nonverbal, and media communication techniques to foster active inquiry, collaboration, and supportive interaction in the classroom.

Domain 3: Instruction
  3l: Communicating clearly and accurately
  3d: Providing feedback to students

Domain 4: Professional Responsibilities
  4c: Communicating with families

NBPTS Core Proposition 1. Teachers are committed to students and their learning.

3. Teachers treat students equitably.

4. Teachers' mission extends beyond developing the cognitive capacity of their students.

NBPTS Core Proposition 3. Teachers are responsible for managing and monitoring student learning.

(Continued)

1. Teachers call on multiple methods to meet their goals.

2. Teachers orchestrate learning in group settings.

3. Teachers place a premium on student engagement.

Principle 7: The teacher plans instruction based on knowledge of subject matter, students, the community, and curriculum goals.

Domain 1: Planning and Preparation
- 1a: Demonstrating knowledge of content
- 1b: Demonstrating knowledge of students
- 1c: Selecting instructional goals
- 1d: Demonstrating knowledge of resources
- 1e: Designing coherent instruction
- 1f: Assessing student learning

NBPTS Core Proposition 1. Teachers are committed to students and their learning.

1. Teachers recognize individual differences in their students and adjust their practice accordingly.

2. Teachers have an understanding of how students develop and learn.

NBPTS Core Proposition 2. Teachers know the subjects they teach and how to teach those subjects to students.

1. Teachers appreciate how knowledge in their subjects is created and linked to other disciplines.

2. Teachers command specialized knowledge of how to convey a subject to students.

3. Teachers generate multiple paths to knowledge.

NBPTS Core Proposition 3. Teachers are responsible for managing and monitoring student learning.

1. Teachers call on multiple methods to meet their goals.

5. Teachers are mindful of their principal objectives.

Principle 8: The teacher understands and uses formal and informal assessment strategies to evaluate and ensure the continuous intellectual, social, and physical development of the learner.

Domain 1: Planning and Preparation
- 1f: Assessing student learning

Domain 3: Instruction
- 3d: Providing feedback to students

NBPTS Core Proposition 3. Teachers are responsible for managing and monitoring student learning.

4. Teachers regularly assess student progress.

Principle 9: The teacher is a reflective practitioner who continually evaluates the effects of his or her choices and actions on others (students, parents, and other professionals in the learning community) and who actively seeks out opportunities to grow professionally.

Domain 4: Professional Responsibilities
  4b: Maintaining accurate records

Domain 4: Professional Responsibilities
  4a: Reflecting on teaching
  4e: Growing and developing professionally
  4f: Showing professionalism

NBPTS Core Proposition 4. Teachers think systematically about their practice and learn from experience.

1. Teachers are continually making difficult choices that test their judgment.

2. Teachers seek the advice of others and draw on education, research, and scholarship to improve their practice.

Principle 10: The teacher fosters relationships with school colleagues, parents, and agencies in the larger community to support students' learning and well-being.

Domain 4: Professional Responsibilities
  4c: Communicating with families
  4d: Contributing to the school and district

NBPTS Core Proposition 5. Teachers are members of learning communities.

1. Teachers contribute to school effectiveness by collaborating with other professionals.

2. Teachers work collaboratively with parents.

3. Teachers take advantage of community resources.

Web Sites for Learned Societies and pK–12 Standards

ART EDUCATION

Organization: INTASC (Interstate New Teacher Assessment and Support Consortium)

Standards for Teachers:

www.ccsso.org/projects/Interstate_New_Teacher_Assessment_and_Support_Consortium/Projects/Standards_Development/#arts

Organization: *NBPTS (National Board for Professional Teaching Standards)*

Standards for Teachers (Art, Ages 3–12; Art, Ages 11–18+):

www.nbpts.org/candidates/ckc.cfm

CAREER AND TECHNICAL EDUCATION

Organization: NBPTS (National Board for Professional Teaching Standards)

Standards for Teachers:

www.nbpts.org/candidates/ckc.cfm

EARLY CHILDHOOD EDUCATION

Organization: NAEYC (National Association for Education of Young Children)

Standards for Teachers of Students Ages 3–8:

www.naeyc.org/accreditation/next_era.asp

Organization: *NBPTS (National Board for Professional Teaching Standards)*

Standards for Teachers:

www.nbpts.org/candidates/ckc.cfm

ELEMENTARY EDUCATION

Organization: ACEI (Association for Childhood Education International)

Standards for Teachers:

www.acei.org/ncateindex.htm

Organization: *NBPTS (National Board for Professional Teaching Standards)*

Standards for Teachers of Students Ages 7–12:

www.nbpts.org/candidates/ckc.cfm

ENGLISH FOR SPEAKERS OF OTHER LANGUAGES

Organization: TESOL (Teachers of English to Speakers of Other Languages)

Standards for Teachers:

www.tesol.org

Organization: *NBPTS (National Board for Professional Teaching Standards)*

Standards for Teachers (English as New Language: Ages 3–12; Ages 11–18+):

www.nbpts.org/candidates/ckc.cfm

ENGLISH/LANGUAGE ARTS EDUCATION

Organization: NCTE (National Council for the Teaching of English)

Standards for Teachers of English Language Arts:

www.ncate.org/public/programStandards.asp?ch=4
K–12 Standards:
www.ncte.org/store/books/standards/105977.htm

Organization: *NBPTS (National Board for Professional Teaching Standards)*

Standards for Teachers (Ages 11–15; Ages 14–18+):

www.nbpts.org/candidates/ckc.cfm

FOREIGN LANGUAGE EDUCATION

Organization: ACTFL (American Council on the Teaching of Foreign Languages)

Standards for Teachers of Foreign Languages:
www.ncate.org/public/programStandards.asp?ch=4

Organization: *INTASC (Interstate New Teacher Assessment and Support Consortium)*

Standards for Teachers:
www.ccsso.org/projects/Interstate_New_Teacher_Assessment_and_Support_Consortium/Projects/Standards_Development/#arts

Organization: *NBPTS (National Board for Professional Teaching Standards)*

Standards for Teachers of World Languages Other Than English (to Students Ages 3–18+):

www.nbpts.org/candidates/ckc.cfm

HEALTH EDUCATION

Organization: AAHE (American Association for Health Education)

Standards for Teachers of Health Education:

www.aahperd.org/aahe/template.cfm?Template=ncate_elements.html

Standards for K–12 Students:

www.aahperd.org/aahe/template.cfm?template=natl_health_education_standards.html

MATHEMATICS EDUCATION

Organization: NCTM (National Council for the Teaching of Mathematics)

Standards for Teachers of Mathematics:

www.nctm.org/about/ncate

Standards for K–12 Students:

http://standards.nctm.org/document/appendix/numb.htm

Organization: *INTASC (Interstate New Teacher Assessment and Support Consortium)*

Standards for Teachers:

www.ccsso.org/projects/Interstate_New_Teacher_Assessment_and_Support_Consortium/Projects/Standards_Development/#arts

Organization: *NBPTS (National Board for Professional Teaching Standards)*

Standards for Teachers of Students Ages 11–15 and 14–18+:

www.nbpts.org/candidates/ckc.cfm

MIDDLE-LEVEL EDUCATION

Organization: NMSA (National Middle School Association)

Standards for Teachers:

www.nmsa.org/services/teacher_prep/index.htm

MUSIC EDUCATION

Organization: NBPTS (National Board for Professional Teaching Standards)

Standards for Teachers of Students Ages 3–12 and 11–18+:

www.nbpts.org/candidates/ckc.cfm

PHYSICAL EDUCATION

Organization: NASPE (National Association for Sports and Physical Education)

Standards for Teachers:

www.aahperd.org/naspe/template.cfm?template=
programs-ncate.html#standards

Standards for K–12 Students:

www.aahperd.org/naspe/template.cfm?template=
publications-nationalstandards.html

Organization: *NBPTS (National Board for Professional Teaching Standards)*

Standards for Teachers of Students Ages 3–12 and 11–18+:

www.nbpts.org/candidates/ckc.cfm

READING AND LITERACY EDUCATION

Organization: IRA (International Reading Association)
Note: IRA standards listed in the appendix represent only those intended for paraprofessionals and classroom teachers; the remaining standards are for specialists beyond the beginning-teacher level.

Standards for Teachers:

www.reading.org/resources/community/ncate_
standards.html

Organization: *NBPTS (National Board for Professional Teaching Standards)*

Standards for Teachers: Literacy: Reading Language Arts (Ages 3–12)

www.nbpts.org/candidates/ckc.cfm

SCIENCE EDUCATION

Organization: NSTA (National Science Teachers Association)

Standards for Teachers:

www.ncate.org/public/programStandards.asp?ch=4

Standards for K–12 Students:

www.nap.edu/readingroom/books/nses/html

Organization: *INTASC (Interstate New Teacher Assessment and Support Consortium)*

Standards for Teachers:

www.ccsso.org/projects/Interstate_New_Teacher_
Assessment_and_Support_Consortium/Projects/
Standards_Development/#arts

Organization: *NBPTS (National Board for Professional Teaching Standards)*

Standards for Teachers of Students Ages 7–15 and 14–18+:

www.nbpts.org/candidates/ckc.cfm

SOCIAL STUDIES EDUCATION

Organization: NCSS (National Council for the Social Studies)

Standards for Teachers:

www.socialstudies.org/standards/teachers

Standards for K–12 Students:

www.socialstudies.org/standards/introduction

Organization: *NBPTS (National Board for Professional Teaching Standards)*

Standards for Teachers of Students Ages 7–18+:

www.nbpts.org/candidates/ckc.cfm

SPECIAL EDUCATION

Organization: CEC (Council for Exceptional Children)

Standards for Teachers:

www.cec.sped.org/ps/perf_based_stds/
knowledge_standards.html

Organization: *INTASC (Interstate New Teacher Assessment and Support Consortium)*

Standards for Teachers:

www.ccsso.org/projects/Interstate_New_Teacher_
Assessment_and_Support_Consortium/Projects/
Standards_Development/#arts

Organization: *NBPTS (National Board for Professional Teaching Standards)*

Standards for Teachers (of Students Ages Birth–21+):
www.nbpts.org/candidates/ckc.cfm

TECHNOLOGY FOR ALL TEACHERS

Organization: ISTE (International Society for Technology in Education) Standards:

Foundational Knowledge for All Teachers:
http://cnets.iste.org/ncate/n_found.html

Organization: *International Technology Education Association/Council on Technology Teacher Education (ITEA/CTTE)*

Standards for Teachers:
www.ncate.org/public/programStandards.asp?ch=4

APPENDIX D

International Society of Technology Education (ISTE) National Educational Technology Standards for Teachers (NETS•T)

Foundational Knowledge for All Teachers

1. *Technology Operations and Concepts:* Teachers demonstrate a sound understanding of technology operations and concepts.

   Teachers

   1. Demonstrate introductory knowledge, skills, and understanding of concepts related to technology (as described in the ISTE National Education Technology Standards for Students).
   2. Demonstrate continual growth in technology knowledge and skills to stay abreast of current and emerging technologies.

2. *Planning and Designing Learning Environments and Experiences:* Teachers plan and design effective learning environments and experiences supported by technology.

   Teachers

   1. Design developmentally appropriate learning opportunities that apply technology-enhanced instructional strategies to support the diverse needs of learners.
   2. Apply current research on teaching and learning with technology when planning learning environments and experiences.
   3. Identify and locate technology resources and evaluate them for accuracy and suitability.

4. Plan for the management of technology resources within the context of learning activities.
5. Plan strategies to manage student learning in a technology-enhanced environment.

3. *Teaching, Learning, and the Curriculum:* Teachers implement curriculum plans that include methods and strategies for applying technology to maximize student learning.

   Teachers

   1. Facilitate technology-enhanced experiences that address content standards and student technology standards.
   2. Use technology to support learner-centered strategies that address the diverse needs of students.
   3. Apply technology to develop students' higher order skills and creativity.
   4. Manage student learning activities in a technology-enhanced environment.

4. *Assessment and Evaluation:* Teachers apply technology to facilitate a variety of effective assessment and evaluation strategies.

   Teachers

   1. Apply technology in assessing student learning of subject matter using a variety of assessment techniques.

Source: http://cnets.iste.org/ncate/n_found.html.

2. Use technology resources to collect and analyze data, interpret results, and communicate findings to improve instructional practice and maximize student learning.
3. Apply multiple methods of evaluation to determine students' appropriate use of technology resources for learning, communication, and productivity.

5. *Productivity and Professional Practice:* Teachers use technology to enhance their productivity and professional practice.

Teachers

1. Use technology resources to engage in ongoing professional development and lifelong learning.
2. Continually evaluate and reflect on professional practice to make informed decisions regarding the use of technology in support of student learning.
3. Apply technology to increase productivity.

4. Use technology to communicate and collaborate with peers, parents, and the larger community in order to nurture student learning.

6. *Social, Ethical, Legal, and Human Issues:* Teachers understand the social, ethical, legal, and human issues surrounding the use of technology in PK–12 schools and apply those principles in practice.

Teachers:

1. Model and teach legal and ethical practice related to technology use.
2. Apply technology resources to enable and empower learners with diverse backgrounds, characteristics, and abilities.
3. Identify and use technology resources that affirm diversity.
4. Promote safe and healthy use of technology resources.
5. Facilitate equitable access to technology resources for all students.

National Education Association: Code of Ethics of the Education Profession

PREAMBLE

The educator, believing in the worth and dignity of each human being, recognizes the supreme importance of the pursuit of truth, devotion to excellence, and the nurture of the democratic principles. Essential to these goals is the protection of freedom to learn and to teach and the guarantee of equal educational opportunity for all. The educator accepts the responsibility to adhere to the highest ethical standards.

The educator recognizes the magnitude of the responsibility inherent in the teaching process. The desire for the respect and confidence of one's colleagues, of students, of parents, and of the members of the community provides the incentive to attain and maintain the highest possible degree of ethical conduct. The Code of Ethics of the Education Profession indicates the aspiration of all educators and provides standards by which to judge conduct.

The remedies specified by the NEA and/or its affiliates for the violation of any provision of this Code shall be exclusive and no such provision shall be enforceable in any form other than the one specifically designated by the NEA or its affiliates.

PRINCIPLE I

COMMITMENT TO THE STUDENT

The educator strives to help each student realize his or her potential as a worthy and effective member of society. The educator therefore works to stimulate the spirit of inquiry, the acquisition of knowledge and understanding, and the thoughtful formulation of worthy goals.

In fulfillment of the obligation to the student, the educator—

1. Shall not unreasonably restrain the student from independent action in the pursuit of learning.
2. Shall not unreasonably deny the student's access to varying points of view.

Adopted by the NEA 1975 Representative Assembly
Source: www.nea.org/aboutnea/code.html.

3. Shall not deliberately suppress or distort subject matter relevant to the student's progress.
4. Shall make reasonable effort to protect the student from conditions harmful to learning or to health and safety.
5. Shall not intentionally expose the student to embarrassment or disparagement.
6. Shall not on the basis of race, color, creed, sex, national origin, marital status, political or religious beliefs, family, social or cultural background, or sexual orientation, unfairly—
   a. Exclude any student from participation in any program
   b. Deny benefits to any student
   c. Grant any advantage to any student

7. Shall not use professional relationships with students for private advantage.
8. Shall not disclose information about students obtained in the course of professional service unless disclosure serves a compelling professional purpose or is required by law.

PRINCIPLE II

COMMITMENT TO THE PROFESSION

The education profession is vested by the public with a trust and responsibility requiring the highest ideals of professional service.

In the belief that the quality of the services of the education profession directly influences the nation and its citizens, the educator shall exert every effort to raise professional standards, to promote a climate that encourages the exercise of professional judgment, to achieve conditions that attract persons worthy of the trust to careers in education, and to assist in preventing the practice of the profession by unqualified persons. In fulfillment of the obligation to the profession, the educator—

1. Shall not in an application for a professional position deliberately make a false statement or fail to disclose a material fact related to competency and qualifications.
2. Shall not misrepresent his/her professional qualifications.
3. Shall not assist any entry into the profession of a person known to be unqualified in respect to character, education, or other relevant attribute.
4. Shall not knowingly make a false statement concerning the qualifications of a candidate for a professional position.
5. Shall not assist a noneducator in the unauthorized practice of teaching.
6. Shall not disclose information about colleagues obtained in the course of professional service unless disclosure serves a compelling professional purpose or is required by law.
7. Shall not knowingly make false or malicious statements about a colleague.
8. Shall not accept any gratuity, gift, or favor that might impair or appear to influence professional decisions or action.

INDEX